W

S10
A S18
K S21
S23

BEST PRACTICE CREATIVITY

FOR MY FATHER, TOM, WHO WAS AN INVETERATE TINKERER AND WHO TAUGHT ME THE ART OF CURIOSITY. IN THE HOPE THAT MY TWO SONS, THOMAS AND JAMES, WILL FIND AS MUCH FORTUNE IN LEARNING.

BEST PRACTICE CREATIVITY

❖

Peter Cook

Gower

Published by
Gower Publishing Limited
Gower House
Croft Road
Aldershot
Hampshire GU11 3HR
England

Gower
Old Post Road
Brookfield
Vermont 05036
USA

Peter Cook has asserted his right under the Copyright, Designs and Patents Act 1988 to be identified as the author of this work.

British Library Cataloguing in Publication Data
    Cook, Peter
    Best practice creativity
    1. Creative ability in business 2. Creative ability
    I. Title
    658'.0019

ISBN 0 566 08027 3

Library of Congress Cataloguing-in-Publication Data
Cook, Peter, 1958–
    Best practice creativity / Peter Cook.
        p. cm.
    Includes bibliographical references and index.
    ISBN 0-566-08027-3
    1. Creative ability in business. 2. Creative thinking.
I. Title.
HD53.C66 1998
302.3'5—dc21   98-6783
                                                                                CIP

Typeset by Saxon Graphics Ltd, Derby and printed in Great Britain at the University Press, Cambridge.

CONTENTS

❖

LIST OF FIGURES

LIST OF TABLES

PREFACE

Creativity starts with a question, an itch to be scratched, some sand in your joints. This book started with 20 questions that I would like to share with you:

1. What is creativity made of?
2. Is creativity a personal thing or is it relevant to organizations?
3. How does creativity link with innovation?
4. Where are the opportunities in my organization for increased performance and how can a more creative approach help?
5. Can creativity be contrived or does one have to wait for it to pounce?
6. Is creativity of value to organizations or is it something that is best left at home?
7. What useful models can be employed to assess individual creativity?
8. From what principles do creative organizations operate?
9. Who are the creative organizations and what are they really doing?
10. Is creativity confined to private organizations or can it be encouraged within the constraints of public sector and educational environments?
11. How does culture, leadership style, and values support or limit creativity and innovation?
12. How do we welcome chaos into our organization? Where is it unwanted?
13. What is the role of organization structure and systems in supporting creativity and innovation? Is structure a 'red herring'?
14. Can creativity in organizations be leveraged by increasing employee skill levels and providing appropriate resources?
15. How is creativity involved in the process of organizational change and continuous learning?

16.   How can I get people in my organization to let go of the habits of a lifetime?

17.   What techniques and processes can help develop ideas so that they become successful innovations?

18.   How can I design bespoke techniques to inspire creativity and innovation that will fit the desired organizational culture?

19.   Are creative techniques sufficient in their own right or do other things need to be in place for a creative organization to emerge?

20.   If I could have 202 ideas about making my organization more creative, what would they be?

This book explores these and other questions. If it is working well it will leave you with further questions which, when answered, will provide you with an innovative mindset that will ultimately lead you to improved organizational performance.

The text is in four Parts, see Figure 0.0.

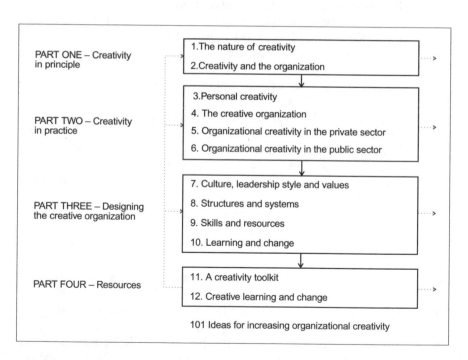

FIGURE 0.0   The structure of the book.

Although not a book on personal development some time is spent on personal creativity as it relates to organizations. The main theme of this volume is organizational creativity. I concentrate on creativity as the beginning of the process that leads to innovation and competitiveness, since there would be no innovation without creativity. Many of the later chapters describe organizational factors that lead to increased innovation and competitiveness.

The book is intended to be interactive, both with itself and with other resources. Thus, each Part and every chapter have links with the others. There are various exit pathways out of the text in the form of questions and exercises intended to provoke thought, action and change.

In each chapter you will find ideas, concepts and models supplemented by case studies and other examples that illustrate the realities of creative organizations. This oscillation between the 'big picture' and fine detail is intended to capture a range of reading styles. It is also likely that readers will select a route through the book that relates to the style they prefer. Key points are provided to summarize certain parts of the book. You are strongly encouraged to record your own learning points on the basis that my 'map' does not represent your 'territory', in terms of the meaning which you will take away with you.

Creativity at work is not confined to the world of organizations. As a musician I am acutely aware of the parallels between successful improvisation and creativity in organizations. We look beyond 'the box' into the worlds of art and science as part of a magical mystery tour for ideas that have practical relevance in even the most tightly controlled organizations.

As part of the preparation for this book, I researched a number of creative organizations. One of my key findings was that there are no instant recipes for creativity in organizations. In writing, the aim is to provide a broad range of strategies and tactics for developing creativity in your own organization. This should enable you to generate some recipes that will work in your organization, not by slavishly copying what others do, but by adapting and transforming their recipes into ones that fit your circumstances.

The book is necessarily incomplete – it represents a snapshot taken through research projects over the last five years. Like a piece of music, the instruments and interpretation of creativity in organizations vary – but the 'song' remains the same. As a lifelong learner I will be delighted to indulge in conversations with those who wish to add to (or subtract from) the ideas expressed in this volume. I can be contacted at:

91 Park Avenue
Gillingham
Kent ME7 4AG
UK
Tel +44 (0)1634 855267 – Fax +44 (0)1634 573788

Peter Cook

ACKNOWLEDGEMENTS

❖

In writing a book about the importance of intangible assets, such as creativity, it occurred to me that many of the people who contributed to my learning lie hidden from view. These people need to be brought to the surface lest they suffocate from lack of recognition.

To be truly creative, an idea needs to be converted into an innovation. In this context I wish to acknowledge the two people who have made significant contributions to the synthesis of ideas in this book, and their successful conversion to a finished product. Firstly, my wife, Alison, who ruthlessly critiqued the material with her cutting wit and earthy pragmatism. Secondly, my good friend, Stephen Fox, who willingly engaged in tireless dialogue on a range of subjects connected with the project.

I have learned a great deal from the writings of others and I would like to thank in particular those who have allowed me to quote and adapt their material. Others I have referenced have been instrumental in influencing and challenging my thinking on a continuing basis. My thanks also to the organizations which have contributed case studies and examples. These bring the subject to life in a way that could not otherwise be achieved.

My gratitude to Gower, in particular to Malcolm Stern, the creative champion of this book, who provided expert guidance in unfamiliar terrain, and to Solveig Gardner Servian, who cheerfully answered my many questions.

Looking back, several important people provided significant development opportunties. In particular, Paul Titley, my unofficial creative mentor. In many ways he provided the inspiration for things that led to my current career and writing this book. His no-nonsense brand of motivation and support was particularly welcome in my earlier years when I was faced with the loss of my parents.

Finally, I would like to thank all those not mentioned by name – the people I have been fortunate enough to work with in many organizations and rock bands. They have enabled me to practise the art of creative leadership. All have contributed in their own way to the ideas expressed here.

P.C.

PART ONE
CREATIVITY IN PRINCIPLE

❖

1

THE NATURE OF CREATIVITY

Microsoft's only factory asset is the human imagination.
(Bill Gates)

Success in product and service innovation depends on creativity. Without a healthy and continuing supply of ideas, organizations would cease to exist. A fundamental challenge facing the leaders of organizations is how to profit from individual potential and enhance it so that it produces organizational innovation and excellence.

The paradox is that people are inherently creative, yet people in many organizations keep their 'creative side' out of the workplace. This is at best a significant demotivator for the individuals concerned and, at worst, a massive opportunity loss for organizations. In an age of continuous change this is no longer an acceptable state of affairs and leading organizations are recognizing the contribution of creativity, both to internal processes and to external results.

This chapter defines creativity in the context of organizations and uses these definitions to review the multiplicity of perspectives on creativity. This will lead to the development of an integrated model of creativity as it applies to organizations. We look outside the world of organizations quite deliberately to widen the perspective.

DEFINING CREATIVITY

Creativity is something which many people believe is a vital ingredient in achieving excellence in a wide variety of fields, yet creativity is a 'loose' concept which is difficult to represent by words alone. To complicate the matter further, the definition of creativity varies – depending on the context in which it is used – for example, in painting, writing, crafts and business. Among the organizations in which I have been fortunate to work creativity has been associated with inspiration – something which is a gift – and a series of techniques and methods. It has also received a 'bad press' through a number of more negative associations, such as witchcraft and mental ill-ness. This is not surprising when one considers the connections that some people make between magic and creativity.

A starting definition for creativity is:

> The generation of novel ideas, without too much regard for
> their usefulness.

This definition emphasizes the **inputs** rather than the **outputs** of creativity and is rarely of interest to organizations.

Some further definitions take the output notion of creativity into account:

> The thinking of novel and appropriate ideas.
> (*Dr William E Coyne, Senior Vice President, Research and
> Development, 3M*)

> Doing something that hasn't been done before – involves
> conception + invention + exploitation.
> (*Charles Davis, Development Director, Psion Computers*)

These definitions illustrate the need for creative people to offer ideas which are both **different** and **appropriate**. Thus, ideas (creativity) must be capable of being transformed into successful action (innovation). In practice, it may take various individuals to bring these relevant qualities to an organization. 3M and Psion are unusual in that they see a strategic role for creativity. In particular, these organizations seek to design products that 'change the basis of competition', that is products that redefine what is expected by the customer and 'leapfrog' the competition. This produces **creative leverage**.

Doing something different raises the question, 'How different?' Most organizational innovations comprise incremental improvements or re-arrangements of existing products and services. Thus organizational creativity is mostly **adaptive** rather than **radical**. Personal creative style and organizational expectations of what is acceptable also affect the levels of creative input that are possible.

A third definition focuses on the issue of perception:

> Creativity consists of looking at the same thing as everyone else
> and thinking something different.
> (*Albert Szent Gyorgyi*)

This illustrates the capacity of the creative person to see problems as opportunities by perceiving the situation through a 'different set of lenses'. A classic example of this is the move by First Direct Bank in the UK to make telephone banking more customer friendly than its traditional face-to-face equivalent. The concept of **reframing** (whereby a different perspective is given to a problem by virtue of changing its frame of reference) captures the essence of Szent Gyorgyi's definition.

The issue of diversity is raised by a fourth definition:

> I'm looking for people who won't fit the system.
> *(Dr Gareth Jones, Senior Vice President Human*
> *Resources, Polygram International)*

Dr Jones refers to the need for diversity in the workforce; some creative groups operate under conditions of conflict which can appear unproductive to outside observers. The winning move is to separate the conflict that leads to a net gain in outcome from the conflict that cripples an organization. Crippling conflict may occur when individuals mistake differences over ideas with personality and culture clashes within an organization. This limited thinking, extrapolated to the organizational level (accountancy versus marketing versus human resources and so on) is very dangerous indeed.

Others see creativity as a **process** consisting of a passage through a number of stages for success, although the stages may be separated by long time intervals. Wallas (1926) described the basic creative process as comprising the following stages:

O   First insight – problem/opportunity finding and redefinition.
O   Preparation – the groundwork is often done here.
O   Incubation – in many cases, this is where unconscious processes play an important part.
O   Illumination – often described as the 'aha' experience.
O   Verification – where the idea is validated and accepted by others.

In the context of organizations, there is often little emphasis on problem-finding due to the desire for an 'answer'. In some cases this means that the illumination phase is likely to solve the wrong problem. Most effective creative problem-solving routines include an initial stage to define the problem/opportunity because of this tendency.

Thus, we see that the definitions of creativity are many and varied. Some of the above definitions are appropriate to organizations.

Points to ponder

O   Which of the above definitions appeals to your organization?
O   What is your definition of creativity as it applies to your organization?

WHERE DOES CREATIVITY COME FROM?

Creativity has many origins, yet none of them on their own provides a complete account of the creative process. Creativity may be seen as follows:

○   A divine quality.
○   Serendipitous activity.
○   'Planned luck'.
○   Endurance.
○   'Method'.

A DIVINE QUALITY

> The worst is that the very hardest thinking will not bring
> thoughts. They must come like children of God and cry
> 'here we are'.
> *(Goethe)*

> I must give up everything else to develop and to cultivate
> the germ that God has planted in me.
> *(Tchaikovsky)*

There are many accounts of individuals who seem to be inspired by a divine gift and there seems little doubt that certain people appear to be genuinely gifted. An insight into this perspective is given by the following example.

> Kekulé is said to have discovered the chemical structure of the benzene ring via a flash of inspiration which involved connecting an image of a snake biting its own tail in a dream:

> 'I turned my chair to the fire and dozed. Again the atoms were gambolling before my eyes. This time the smaller groups kept modestly in the background. My mental eye, rendered more acute by repeated visions of this kind, could now distinguish larger structures, of manifold conformation; long rows, sometimes more closely fitted together; all twining and twisting in snakelike motion. But look! What was that? One of the snakes had seized hold of its own tail, and the form whirled mockingly before my eyes. As if by a flash of lightning I awoke ... Let us learn to dream gentlemen'

> (Extract from Koestler A (1964) *The Act of Creation*. London: Hutchinson.)

For an organization, the problem with the divinity perspective is that there would appear to be little to be done if genius is supplied by a 'higher order'. As we learn more about the creative process it becomes apparent that this is merely a partial explanation of creativity. Nevertheless, the divine perspective has a certain appeal for organizations, if it is recognized as a need to employ gifted people and support them in the pursuit of their goals.

SERENDIPITOUS ACTIVITY

> It's a kind of magic.
> *(Queen)*

Much evidence supports the 'lucky break' concept of creativity. A frequently cited example is that of the sweetening effect of saccharin (discovered accidentally by a chemist who happened to eat his lunch in the laboratory without washing his hands after some experiments). As with the divine perspective, luck is a proposition unattractive to organizations that would rather have serendipity 'on tap' as a resource that can be managed and developed.

'PLANNED LUCK'

> To be an inventor is an eclectic sort of life.
> *(Sir Clive Sinclair)*

> If you have no choice, you're dead. If you have one choice,
> you are a robot. If you have two choices, you have a dilemma.
> Three or more choices and you have the makings of choice.

> Lucky opportunities abound in the environment – it is that
> some firms have built radar stations to detect them.

'Planned luck' involves a mindset that consciously looks for more options and scans for opportunities. In other words, serendipitous creativity is much more probable if opportunities are seen and seized. This is far more attractive to organizations since it implies that it is possible to arrange things so that creativity is more likely to occur and the frequency of those occurrences is greater. Companies such as 3M, Hewlett Packard and Glaxo-Wellcome have given a good deal of consideration to the need to design their cultures to ensure that 'luck' is a highly probable and frequent occurrence.

ENDURANCE

> Experience is the name that everyone gives to their
> mistakes.
> *(Oscar Wilde)*

> I have had my solutions for a long time, but I do not know
> yet how I am to arrive at them.
> *(Gauss)*

The endurance perspective suggests the need for hard work and persistence. This contradicts the view that creativity is the sole domain of inspired 'poet in the attic'.

A case in point was Thomas Edison, who recognized failure as an important step in learning. After failing for the 1000th time to invent a light bulb, he was reputed to congratulate himself for finding **yet another way not** to invent a light bulb. Many scientific discoveries are born of a consuming mania with a particular problem and a willingness to view failure as an opportunity to learn more about success. For organizations, 'maniacs' have other less desirable qualities associated with conflict and attachment to a single project. More will be said about the value of conflict in Chapter 7.

When researching this book, I visited a wide range of organizations and encountered a number of people who regarded assertiveness as essential to ensure ideas were recognized in their organizations. In other words, there was plenty of creativity but often insufficient willpower and drive to voice and push ideas through the 'corporate immune system'.

'METHOD'

There is a school of thought that maintains that creative people are born and not made. Whilst it seems likely that genius may have a biological component and may be distributed unevenly across personality types, this belief is very limiting and inconsistent with evidence of the variety of people who have demonstrated creative capacity. Aspects of creativity can be studied and developed just like any other human capacity. There are a number of processes that may well be a feature of naturally creative people, yet they may also be learned as a way to enhance creativity in more 'ordinary' people. Examples include:

Bisociation

There is a good deal of evidence to demonstrate the value of force-fitting apparently unrelated ideas together to produce novel concepts. Arthur Koestler coined the term 'bisociation' for such processes. The essential quality is the ability to perceive a situation in two self-consistent but habitually incompatible frames of reference. Examples include:

O   Before the development of the float process by a research team under the leadership of Sir Alastair Pilkington, glass making was labour-intensive and time-consuming, mainly because of the need for grinding and polishing surfaces to get a brilliant finish. Pilkington's proprietary process involved floating the glass, after it was cast from a melting furnace, over a bath of molten tin about the size of a tennis court. The idea for rinsing glass came to Sir Alastair when he stood at his kitchen sink washing dishes.

O   Darwin's theory of evolution by natural selection. This is a good example, illustrating that creativity does not have to be radical but involves the combination of well-established patterns of thought. Many business innovations are the result of incremental creativity, for example, the use of supermarket loyalty cards as an adaptation of the credit card concept.

O The invention of 'cats-eyes' arose from making a connection between the reflective properties of cats' eyes in car headlights and the possibility of having reflective materials embedded into the road to improve driving vision at night.

Bisociation relies on the ability to think in at least two fields of expertise. Consequently, specialists are likely to be at a disadvantage if they only have access to a single discipline. In such circumstances, the power of creative teams comprising individuals from unrelated disciplines becomes apparent. This explains the potential advantages of diversity in 'brainstorming' groups and 'think tanks' drawn from a cross-section of disciplines, including individuals who, at first sight, have little or no relevant contribution to make.

Mental mobility

> Every creative act involves ... a new innocence of
> perception liberated from the cataract of accepted belief.
> *(Arthur Koestler)*

> The greatest thing by far is to be a master of the metaphor.
> *(Aristotle)*

Flexibility of thinking requires the ability to view a situation from many perspectives, some of which are more distant from the situation. One useful model for ensuring that a problem or opportunity is viewed from many angles is shown in Figure 1.1.

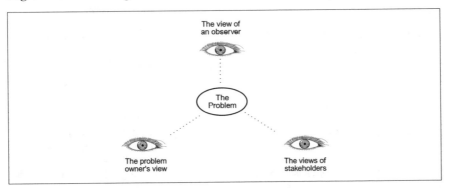

FIGURE 1.1 Changing viewpoints.

In this model, it is possible to adopt various positions in order to gain different perspectives:

O   The problem owner's view: often enmeshed in the details of the problem or opportunity; tends to have a fairly narrow perspective.

O   The stakeholder's view: likely to be more diverse; emphasis on the successful resolution of the problem or opportunity.

O   The detached observer: no interest in the problem/opportunity; can bring an objective analytical quality to the problem.

Point to ponder

O   You might like to try this routine out using a problem situation or an improvement opportunity that you are currently facing.

The ability to relate one experience to another through mental mobility is illustrated by the stories of Newton and the falling apple, and Archimedes in his bath. A more modern example of mental mobility as a 'method' is given by Edward de Bono's term 'lateral thinking' as a means of thinking in less obvious directions about problems or opportunities. 'Vertical' thinking proceeds directly from one state of information to another and is continuous in nature. A characteristic feature of lateral thinking is discontinuity. This may account for the negative reaction of some people to the process. The invention of the hovercraft is an example of lateral thinking in action (it succeeds because of the combination of the concepts of a fan and a skirt).

A comparison of the underlying processes for the two different thinking styles is shown in Table 1.1.

TABLE 1.1   Vertical and lateral thinking compared

Vertical thinking	Lateral thinking
Selects and judges according to conformity	Generates change for its own sake
Looks for solutions	Looks for questions
Uses yes/no decision criteria	Uses and/also decision criteria
Analytical and regressive	Provocative and future-oriented
Makes logical steps	Makes unjustified steps
Conclusion comes after the evidence	Conclusion may come before the evidence
Concentrates on what is relevant	Welcomes happy accidents

Source: de Bono E (1984) *Lateral Thinking for Management,* Harmondsworth: Penguin.

In practice, creative people will use both lateral and vertical thinking according to their needs. This is one aspect that distinguishes creative people from others, who tend to use the same thinking style for all issues.

Other ways of creating detachment from the problem include the use of metaphor and provocation.

Ambiguity tolerance

> Negative capability – that is when a man is capable of being
> in uncertainties, mysteries, doubts without any irritable
> reaching after fact and reason.
> *(John Keats)*

> If a man begin with certainties he shall end in doubts; but if
> he will be content to begin with doubts he will end with
> certainties.
> *(Francis Bacon)*

A further talent observable in creative people is the ability to tolerate (or even relish) ambiguity. They often do this by having an innate curiosity for the unfamiliar. This ability separates highly creative people from others who prefer to resolve a problem (often by accepting a sub-optimal solution). It is possible to cultivate the ability to perceive an ambiguous situation positively. If this perception can be held for a length of time, there is a higher probability that a novel idea will emerge from the resulting tension.

THE 'TOO DIFFICULT' IN-TRAY

I once worked for a Research and Development Director who had a strategy for ambiguity tolerance. He maintained a 'too difficult' in-tray for ideas which the organization could not implement in the current climate. Rather than forgetting these as is the norm for the average person, he systematically recycled these ideas on a frequent basis, to see when particular ideas or combinations of ideas were more likely to take root in the organization. This approach has been described as 'strategic opportunism'. An analogy is that of a frog on a lilypad waiting for a fly to come past. The 'too difficult' in-tray recognizes the importance of timing and the need for there to be sufficient tension in the organization concerning a particular issue for a radical idea to become acceptable. This lowers the risk associated with new initiatives and increases their chance of successful implementation.

Harnessing diversity of thinking

Research in the last 30 years or so offers new insights into the function of the two hemispheres of the brain and their relationship to creativity. The work done by Roger Sperry shows that the left and right hemisphere of the brain perform fundamentally different functions (Figure 1.2), although recent work suggests that they are perhaps not as separate as was first thought.

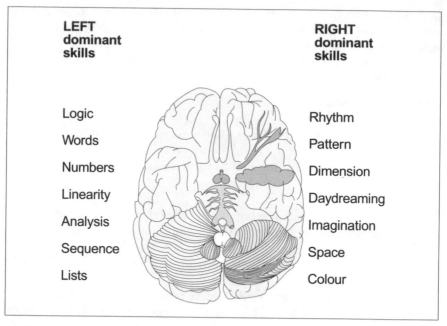

LEFT dominant skills	RIGHT dominant skills
Logic	Rhythm
Words	Pattern
Numbers	Dimension
Linearity	Daydreaming
Analysis	Imagination
Sequence	Space
Lists	Colour

FIGURE 1.2   The two brains.

Many traditional organizations are dominated by left-brain processes. Some sectors of business and commerce are more 'left-brained' than others. Frequently, such organizations respond to the desire to be creative by suggesting that they want to become 'right-brained'. This is a fundamental mistake, since it is the use of both functions in **harmony** that seems to distinguish true creative genius and truly creative organizations. Since everyone has the capacity to use both left and right brain functions, a more balanced approach can be developed through practice. In groups of people, it is not always necessary to rely on individuals to produce the entire creative output of the group since different people bring different talents to the situation.

AN INTEGRATED PERSPECTIVE

The perspectives of creativity outlined above broadly subdivide into a **passive** view (creativity is predetermined to some extent and cannot therefore be altered) and an **active** view (creativity can be developed in a variety of ways). My own research in this area and personal experience shows that **both** perspectives are important. High levels of creativity occur when a number of these qualities are combined within a single person or a group of people involved in new ideas. Figure 1.3 depicts the integrated perspective.

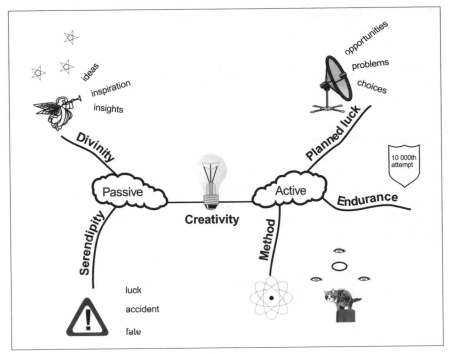

FIGURE 1.3   An integrated perspective.

Points to ponder

O   Do you hold a predominantly passive or active view of creativity?
O   What would happen to your organization if you decided to adopt the full range of possible views on creativity?

WHAT CAN ORGANIZATIONS LEARN FROM THE ARTS?

An artist friend of mine subscribes to the passive view of creativity. When asked about his lack of artistic output, he becomes defensive and says that he is waiting for the 'right sort of light', and that the 'muse' has left him. Thus, creativity is apparently out of his control. If I want him to paint a picture it is counter-productive to rationalize with him or to offer financial or other inducements. It is possible to motivate him into creative action through exciting him about a particular project that can use his individual flair.

We can learn some important principles from this example:

O   The importance of getting the climate right for creativity.

O   Attempts to induce creativity through organizational 'carrots and sticks', for example, bonuses or discipline, may also be counter-productive.

Furthermore it is surprising how many parallels there are between artists, computer technologists and research scientists. In general, there is much within the arts that can be applied to organizations.

CREATIVE ICONOGRAPHY

Since creativity is often apparently spontaneous, one way to study the processes involved is to look at creative individuals when they are in a state of creative 'flow', that is, totally involved in the creative process. Firstly, let us examine the world of music to look for processes that have useful parallels for organizations.

ROCK 'N' ROLL CREATIVITY – HOW DO CREATIVE MUSICIANS DO IT?

Creativity in music shares many of the same principles utilized by creative organizations. Consider these examples:

Lennon and McCartney

John Lennon and Paul McCartney produced a leap forward in pop music, yet the two individuals were very different in outlook and personality and their relationship was not without its creative conflicts. To convert their creativity into an innovation required the addition of a third element (George Martin). This illustrates the need to tolerate the conflict that ensues from collaborations between very different individuals and groups within organizations, and the use of 'boundary crossers'.

Wolfgang Amadeus Mozart – a letter

'When I am, as it were, completely myself, entirely alone, and of good cheer – say travelling in a carriage, or walking after a good meal or during the night when I cannot sleep: it is on such occasions that my ideas flow best and most abundantly. Whence and how they come, I know not; nor can I force them. Those ideas that please me I retain in memory, and am accustomed, as I am told, to hum them to myself. If I continue in this way, it soon occurs to me how I may turn this or that morsel to account, so as to make a good dish of it, that is to say, agreeable to the rules of counterpoint, to the peculiarities of the various instruments etc.

When I proceed to write down my ideas, I take them out of the bag of my memory; if I may use that phrase, what is previously collected into it in the way I have mentioned. For this reason the committing to paper is done quickly enough, for everything is, as I said before, already finished; and it rarely differs on paper from what it was in my imagination.'

This illustrates a kind of 'audiovisioning' process which involves thinking ends not means.

Davie Bowie

David Bowie wrote many of his lyrics by the random force-fitting of words and phrases which he cut up from larger pieces of writing. Many proprietary creative techniques rely on forced relationships between unrelated items, and the use of Post-it™ notes and clustering of ideas builds on this approach to song writing.

Jimi Hendrix

Jimi Hendrix was known to use almost any instrument and device to affect the way his guitar sounded. Amongst many of the innovative approaches he used Hendrix took the bold step of mixing the sound of a kazoo with the guitar (in the song 'Crosstown Traffic' from his *Electric Ladyland* album) in a desire to create a sound that had never been heard before. This illustrates the principle of breaking free of the boundaries imposed by technology.

Extending this approach, one can find recurrences of basic principles in most artistic and scientific disciplines, reflecting Koestler's notion that such distinctions are unhelpful, since art and science sit on a continuum. Ghiselin (1985) produced a vital compendium of letters and abstracts describing the process of creativity in his book, *The Creative Process*. The following abstracts are examples:

The role of this unconscious work in mathematical invention appears to me uncontestable, and traces of it would be found in other cases where it is less evident. Often when one works at a hard question, nothing good is accomplished at the first attack. Then one takes a rest, longer or shorter, and sits down anew to the work. During the first half hour, as before, nothing is found, and then all of a sudden the decisive idea presents itself to the mind ... it is probable that this rest has been filled out with unconscious work.
(*Henri Poincaré – Mathematical Creation*)

The painter passes through states of fullness and of emptying. That is the whole secret of art. I take a walk through the forest of Fontainebleau. There I get an indigestion of greenness. I must empty this sensation into a picture. Green dominates in it. The painter paints as if in need to discharge himself of his sensations and his visions.
(*Christian Zervos – Conversation with Picasso*)

These extracts illustrate the obsessive character of some creative people in organizations, and their somewhat random productivity schedules. The challenge facing the creative leader is to harness the energies of these 'maniacs with a mission' and guide them in a direction that is fruitful both to the individual and the organization.

> What I would say is that it (inspiration) relates to the
> exploitation of the chance meeting on a non-suitable
> plane of two mutually distant realities.
> *(Max Ernst – Inspiration to Order)*

This extract illustrates the passive view of creativity and the use of bisociation to produce something novel.

> It is a mistake for a sculptor or a painter to speak or write
> very often about his job. It releases tension required for his
> work. By trying to express his aims with rounded-off logical
> exactness, he can easily become a theorist whose actual work
> is only a caged-in exposition of conceptions evolved in terms
> of logic and words.
> *(Henry Moore – Notes on Sculpture)*

This piece warns against the excessive deconstruction of the creative process. A related idea in the world of organizations is the need to leave some 'looseness' in the organization thus avoiding over-systematizing creativity.

> Often the public forms an idea of inspiration that is quite
> false, almost a religious notion. Alas! I do not believe that
> inspiration falls from heaven. I think it rather the result of a
> profound indolence and of our incapacity to put to work
> certain forces in ourselves. These unknown forces work
> deep within us, with the aid of the elements of daily life, its
> scenes and passions, and, when they burden us and oblige
> us to conquer the kind of somnolence in which we indulge
> ourselves like invalids who try to prolong dream and dread
> resuming contact with reality, in short when the work that
> makes itself in us and in spite of us demands to be born, we
> can believe that this work comes to us from beyond and is
> offered us by the gods. The artist is more slumberous in
> order that he shall not work. By a thousand ruses, he
> prevents his nocturnal work from coming to the light of day.

> The play that I am producing at the Théâtre de l'Oeuvre,
> The Knights of the Round Table, is a visitation of this sort. I
> was sick and tired of waiting, when one morning, after
> having slept poorly, I woke with a start and witnessed, as
> from a seat in a theatre, three acts which brought to life an
> epoch and characters about which I had no documentary
> information and which I regarded moreover as forbidding.

> Long afterward, I succeeded in writing the play and I divined
> the circumstances that must have served to incite me.
> (*Jean Cocteau – The Process of Inspiration*)

Cocteau seems to bear out the 'process' view of creativity, with inspiration only coming after considerable preparation and incubation.

> Having drunk a pint of beer at luncheon – beer is a sedative
> to the brain, and my afternoons are the least intellectual
> portion of my life – I would go out for a walk of two or three
> hours. As I went along, thinking of nothing in particular, only
> looking at things around me and following the progress of
> the seasons, there would flow into my mind, with sudden
> and unaccountable emotion, sometimes a line or two of
> verse, sometimes a whole stanza at once, accompanied, not
> preceded by a vague notion of the poem which they were
> destined to form part of. Then there would usually be a lull
> of an hour or so, then perhaps the spring would bubble up
> again. I say bubble up, because, so far as I could make out,
> the source of the suggestions thus proffered to the brain was
> an abyss which I have already had occasion to mention, the
> pit of the stomach. When I got home I wrote them down,
> leaving gaps, and hoping that further inspiration might be
> forthcoming another day. Sometimes it was, if I took my
> walks in a receptive and expectant frame of mind; but
> sometimes the poem had to be taken in hand and
> completed by the brain, which was apt to be a matter of
> trouble and anxiety, involving trial and disappointment, and
> sometimes ending in failure.
> (*AE Housman – The Name and Nature of Poetry*)

Creative organizations deliberately set out to provide opportunities for people to daydream, using walking or other rituals to encourage the necessary distractions from conscious thought. Several organizations I know also pay for employees to have meetings in bars where they subsidize the drinks.

Point to ponder

O   What examples from the world of art do you have and how can their principles be adapted to your organization?

THE ART OF LEADERSHIP

As it is possible to learn about creativity in organizations through the study of creativity in the arts, it is also possible to enhance organizational creativity

through involvement with the arts. Art brings the following qualities to organizations:

O   Art has no regard for authority or qualification.
O   Art allows for both individual and group goals.
O   Art allows for pleasant surprises and encourages recovery from failure.
O   Art allows managers to begin to trust their intuition and creativity.
O   Art increases confidence in using new techniques or thinking in
         new directions.

Point to ponder

O   Consider the benefits of offering employees art workshops as a way
         of increasing confidence in being creative, instead of launching
         straight into seminars on creativity or problem-solving training
         courses.

SUMMARY

Here, creativity has been considered from a general perspective. In so
doing, no single concept of creativity has been advocated but an integrated
approach has been suggested, involving the combination of a number of
dimensions:

O   Creativity as a divine quality.
O   Serendipitous activity.
O   Creativity as 'planned luck'.
O   Creativity as endurance.
O   Creativity as 'method'.

Creativity can be developed like any other personal quality and there is a
contribution to be made by 'givens', such as luck and personality.

   We can learn a great deal about creativity and its management in organizations through the study of creativity in the arts.

   It is possible to enhance creativity through the arts rather than through the
use of more 'logical' methods such as creativity seminars.

   You will find it useful to consolidate your reading by reviewing the following questions:

About what you have learned

O   What has reading this chapter confirmed in your mind?
O   What new curiosities has it raised?

About putting the ideas to work

O   Does your circle of friends include people holding radically differ-
       ent viewpoints from your own?
O   How far does your organization encourage people from diverse
       backgrounds to mix together?
O   What processes or routines do you have for 'car-parking' ideas that
       are of no immediate value?
O   How can you arrange your organization so that you increase the
       probability and frequency of 'planned luck'?

A final thought

> To develop a complete mind
> Study the science of art
> Study the art of science
> Learn how to see
> Realize that everything connects to everything else.
> (*Leonardo da Vinci*)

2

CREATIVITY AND THE ORGANIZATION

> Economic success depends more than ever on the brain
> power and creativity of the workforce.
> (*Dominic Cadbury, Chairman of Cadbury Schweppes*)

Creativity does not often appear at the 'top of the charts' of organizational performance indicators. Yet the outputs of creativity, that is innovation, competitiveness and rapid change, are highly prized results. Here, we seek to redress the balance by establishing why creativity should be valued as a strategic resource in future-oriented organizations. As creativity is an intangible asset, it is inappropriate to do this only through traditional means (such as balance sheets and other rational valuation approaches). It is a fundamental mistake to assume that things which cannot be measured easily are not important to the future of an organization. This point is well illustrated by the 'Macnamara fallacy', as quoted by Charles Handy (1994) in *The Empty Raincoat* (Hutchinson):

> The first step is to measure whatever can be measured easily. This is OK as far as it goes. The second step is to disregard that which can't easily be measured or to give it an arbitrary quantitative value. This is artificial and misleading. The third step is to presume that what can't be measured easily really isn't important. This is blindness. The fourth step is to say that what can't easily be measured really doesn't exist. This is suicide.

THE 'DEMAND' FOR GLOBAL CREATIVITY

MACRO CHANGES

The changing cost base for manufacturing has meant that many industries have moved from the Western world. As a result, the West is attempting to move from an industrial manufacturing economy to a high technology service- and knowledge-based one. Economics is also driving the full-time workforce towards part-time labour and many functions that were previously maintained on a full-time basis are now sent out to subcontractors.

The pace of change is ever greater and types of change are less predictable. We can no longer look to the past to our collective futures. Becoming complacent in business is a very dangerous practice, as IBM discovered in the 1980s with the rise of personal computers, which nearly cost the company its existence.

New technology is increasingly having an effect on social trends, such as the shift towards a more independent workforce and the tendency to develop more fluid forms of organizations, including virtual companies.

The rise in rapid and effective communications has meant that the world is 'shrinking'. From a global 'village' consider now a global 'village green'. It is now far easier to access new ideas from around the world; as a consequence, the time to market and shelf-life of many products and services has been reduced dramatically.

Information is available to all via the Internet. Managers and executives are having to rethink the basis on which they can influence others by operating from different power bases.

In the Western world we have witnessed the rise of individualism as standards of living have improved and the visibility of improved product/service offerings has increased through mass media. In the UK in particular, people are no longer as willing to wait in queues as they used to be. Undoubtedly, increased individualism has been influenced by the rise of consumerism, supported by political 'permission', with gestures such as the Citizen's Charters which have legitimized individual rights.

For those in employment, there is a shift from a 'career for life' towards a 'lifetime of careers' with information being seen as a key resource for growth.

We have become more aware of the systemic nature of world problems. Far from adopting the position that problems in other parts of the world do not affect us, we now need to assess carefully the effect of even minor changes on the macro-environment. Decision-making under these conditions is complex and we need to ensure that the decisions we reach are the best possible outcome for our long-term future rather than the lowest common denominator. A rise in pressure group activity and a collective consciousness that we cannot continue to act in ways that are killing our planet now mean that these pressures are being acknowledged and acted upon by world leaders through the influence of mass media.

We can expect the ratio of young to older people to alter, with consequences for caring, leisure activities, insurance policies and, ultimately, political decisions.

Amongst the most rigorous observers of the future, Spyros Makridrakis (1989) has predicted that there will be five key growth areas: travel, health, entertainment, marketing and education. All five are service-based industries rather than manufacturing-oriented ones and will require a fundamental shift in thinking and action.

CURRENT AND FUTURE ORGANIZATIONAL RESPONSES

Organizations must remain in harmony with their environment and the most pro-active of them are considering how to respond, particularly in the following areas:

O   The ability to deliver value based on economies of scale (where this is still achievable).

O   The ability to form partnerships and alliances to deliver services rapidly, developing synergistic relationships with other parts of the world.

O   The identification of areas where organizations are able to deliver specialist products and services more rapidly and to a higher quality.

O   Competitive advantage through innovative products/services, especially where these can be integrated with other customer needs.

O   Leaders as creativity facilitators.

O   The need for continuous organizational re-invention where change is the norm.

O   Organizations are making consumer choice a competitive weapon. People now expect that goods will be unique, and creative marketeers have capitalized on the growing awareness that 'one size doesn't fit all'.

As these changes take place, there is an ever greater need to work across professional and geographical boundaries and to address national and cultural differences. The need for flexibility demands ever more creative responses to complex problems.

In *The Age of Unreason* (Hutchinson), Handy (1989) points out that discontinuous change requires 'upside-down' thinking to deal with it. He argues that discontinuity requires re-thinking the way in which we do things, building on the knowledge and responsibility of the elders of society but also questioning whether these ways should continue and whether the rules are adequate. It means exploration and experimentation – which is viewed as rebellious. However, revolutions unblock societies and galvanize organizations. Handy cites Copernicus, Galileo and Jesus Christ as 'arch-exponents' of upside-down thinking in the past. Freud, Marx and Einstein are more recent examples, along with Crick, Watson and Wilkins (the discoverers of DNA).

THINKING IS 'IN' – THE BUSINESS CASE FOR CREATIVITY

> Our mission is to build the most educated, skilled,
> adaptable and creative country in the world.
> (*Tony Blair*)

Creativity is no longer a quality which is 'nice to have' found in a few 'cranky' individuals – in the context of business survival and the need to stay ahead of the opposition it is talked about within leading organizations. It is mentioned as a source of competitive strength within organizations facing discontinuous or chaotic environments or where there is little or nothing to differentiate the product or service of an organization from its competitors.

KEY BUSINESS DRIVERS FOR THE 21ST CENTURY

In *Corporate Strategies of the Top 100 UK Companies of the Future*, the Corporate Research Foundation (CRF) (1995) lists six **key drivers** of future success:

O   Structural flexibility
O   Human resources
O   Innovative power
O   Growth markets
O   International orientation
O   Quality of management.

Creativity is at the heart of structural flexibility and innovative power. The report goes on to say that it is likely that many of the companies deemed 'excellent' under the current paradigm will have difficulty surviving in the future. We cannot just accept this 'formula' as a recipe for lasting success, and creative organizations will do well to develop and review the **key drivers** as they apply to their own environments.

Points to ponder

O   What currently drives performance within your key markets?
O   What differences do your competitors exhibit from your observations and intelligence?
O   What do you see changing in the next 10, 50 and 100 years?

VALUING CREATIVITY

As an intangible asset, creativity is difficult to value accurately. Accountants have worked unsuccessfully for years to devise a useful way of accounting for intangible assets. Most approaches have been of theoretical value. However, an impression of the value of intellectual capital may be seen in the following formula:

$$\text{Market Value} = \text{Book Value} + \text{Intellectual Capital}$$

If we compare market value (based on share price) for knowledge-based companies such as Microsoft, with value based on fixed assets there is a huge difference. Crudely, this difference may be equated to the value placed on the intellectual capital of the company.

Other indicators of the value of creativity include the high value placed on spending on global research and development (R&D). The *Financial Times** reported that the world's 300 top companies increased R&D spending and sales by 7 per cent in a period when overall sales growth was 8 per cent. The conclusion drawn from this is that more R&D means better growth and better profit.

Since creativity is an intangible asset, it is more useful to use a 'balanced scorecard' approach to assess its effect on performance, that is **direct** and **indirect** benefits.

Direct benefits

The **direct** benefits of creativity to an organization are in performance improvements. These may be achieved through cost reduction or by wealth creation. Systems redesign is essentially intended to achieve cost reduction. Innovation is more connected with wealth creation. Creativity is implicit in **both** approaches since both involve either rethinking existing practices or thinking totally differently.

A number of company 'snapshots' serve to illustrate direct benefits of creativity to organizations.

3M Corporation   3M aims to invent new products which change the basis of competition. This philosophy involves making a double leap forward. In practice this means that 3M has a high product turnover, yet is immensely successful and one of the most admired companies in the world. Examples of its success in double-leap competitive advantage include products in the fields of non-woven materials, adhesives, abrasives, fluorochemistry, coating (process technology), sealing compounds, electronic microinterconnects and cables.

First Direct Bank   First Direct Bank has shown consistent rapid growth as the UK's first telephone banking service. This is impressive enough, but especially so when one considers the fact that First Direct was started by a traditional banking organization. Its developmental milestones are as follows.

*Source: The R&D Scoreboard – *Financial Times* Survey, 26 June 1997.

O   June 1988   Project team initiated, code named 'Project
                      Raincloud'.
O   October 1989   First Direct is officially opened.
O   December 1990 50,000th customer joins First Direct.
O   May 1991   100,000th customer joins First Direct.
O   March 1993   250,000th customer joins First Direct.
O   December 1993 First Direct moves into operating profit for the first
                      time.
O   December 1994 Achieves break-even for the financial year.
O   April 1995   500,000th customer joins First Direct.
O   January 1997   Number of customers rises to over one million fol-
                      lowing the take over of Forward Trust Personal
                      Finance.

The First Direct organization has rewritten the meaning of distance banking
and has created a significant advantage that is visible through a number of
indicators:

O   Eighty-seven per cent of First Direct customers were extremely/very
     satisfied with their service compared with an average of 49 per cent
     for the high street banks.
O   Eighty-seven per cent of customers have recommended First Direct
     compared with an average of 11 per cent for the main high street
     banks.
O   Ninety-four per cent of customers believe that First Direct is better
     than most other banks.
O   It takes, on average, 20 seconds to answer an incoming call to First
     Direct.
O   First Direct is recommended every five seconds.

This is an extremely good performance in an industry where most of the
opposition has relied on high levels of customer apathy.

The Body Shop International plc   The Body Shop is an example of a
company that has refused to become complacent in the face of what many
other organizations would see as an unprecedented leader in changing the
way business is done. This has enabled it to expand to a £622.5 million business over 21 years.

Unlike other 'mature' businesses, the company is still experimenting in
the face of rising copy-cat competition (for example, by bringing aromatic
body or head massage into the high street). Internally, The Body Shop has
managed to protect itself from the usual 'growing pains' associated with success in traditional organizations. To refocus itself in a changing marketplace,
it is currently experimenting with a new retail concept called the 'Doorway'.
This is a de-stressing retreat offering customers a wide range of therapies for

mind, body and soul. Anita Roddick, founder of The Body Shop, says, 'We've always believed in the healing touch of an aromatherapy massage. By offering this alongside reflexology, make-overs, facials and other treatments, I think we're helping to meet modern needs that are largely ignored.'

In its continuous drive to raise the standards of ethical business, The Body Shop ran a campaign called 'Think, Act, Change' to encourage customers to think about issues of the day (for example, environmental protection, animal protection and social issues) and do something about it (for example, write a letter to their MP, sign a petition or go on a protest march). It has also set up an academy for socially responsible business, designed to raise the standards of ethical global business.

Psion Computers plc   Psion Computers has consistently demonstrated a commitment to creativity in its new product development process. In 1981 its strategy consisted of the following:

O   Vision: microcomputer technology will create a substantial industry.
O   Purpose: to market microcomputer-based products; to gain a 'rocket science' development capability in microcomputer software and hardware.
O   Key values: innovation, self-belief, 'can do' attitude.

Evidence of the success of the strategy can be seen through the performance of the company (Figure 2.1). This can be matched to Psion's technology history (Figure 2.2). The Psion story is detailed further in Chapter 5.

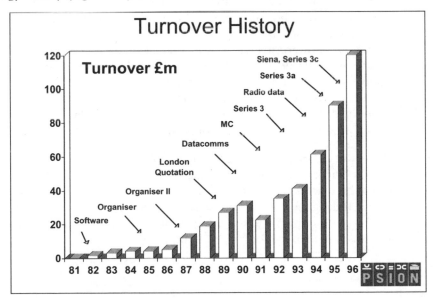

FIGURE 2.1   Psion performance results.

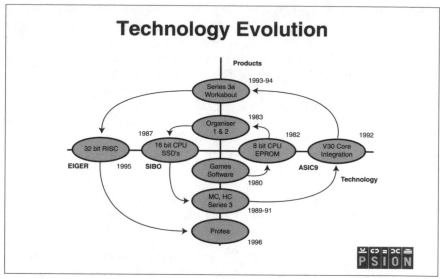

FIGURE 2.2   Psion technology history.

Examples of creativity in action as product innovations include:

O   Games: flight simulator on a Sinclair ZX81; 3D chess on the Sinclair QL, and memory-saving techniques generally.

O   Organizer: the whole concept; Lotus 1-2-3-compatible spreadsheet on a two-line organizer.

O   Series 3 hardware: battery power management – powering down things we don't need and co-operation between software and hardware; software control of LCD contrast.

O   Series 3 software: a pre-emptive multi-tasking operating system on a handheld device; elegant memory management; fully functioning word processor on a palmtop computer.

SmithKline Beecham plc   The *Financial Times** identified SmithKline Beecham as a company that seeks to acquire 40 per cent of its sales from products that have been introduced in the last five years. Thus, the company is constantly challenging itself to find better ways to produce products that are valued by its customers and has a big commitment to creativity and its successful exploitation in the form of innovations.

*Source: *Financial Times* survey, 26 June 1997.

Indirect benefits

Company profiles also illustrate the **indirect** benefits of creativity in organizations.

Hewlett Packard   Hewlett Packard provides an excellent example of a company which has been able to challenge the boundaries of its existence. The company has the encouragement of flexibility and innovation as one of its key organizational values. The best example of creativity in action within Hewlett Packard UK comes from its development of the printer business. This has grown from a very small percentage to a market share of almost 70 per cent (1997 figures) in less than 10 years. Hewlett Packard is mentioned further in Chapter 5.

Skandia life insurance   Skandia life insurance regards innovation as a critical ingredient for business success, and recognizes this through a Board-level post, the Director of Intellectual Capital, thus acknowledging the key role of ideas and information management for gaining advantage in the 21st century.* The key role of information management is discussed further in Chapter 9.

Other indirect benefits that creative organizations enjoy include:

O   Retention of key staff – this can be measured by comparing the cost of hiring key people with that of retaining them, through creative career, reward and recognition strategies.

O   An enhanced ability to cope with the unexpected. Post Office Counters Ltd cites the use of scenario planning as a way of rehearsing the future. When an unexpected event happens the company has an increased response repertoire and the 'normal' response (of doing the same things harder and faster) is avoided when a problem appears on the horizon.

AUDITING THE POTENTIAL FOR CREATIVE ADVANTAGE IN YOUR ORGANIZATION

The questions in Table 2.1 are intended to provoke your thinking about where there are opportunities to create value in your organization. Numbers are not the whole story. There are areas where social responsibility and compatibilty with company strategy dictate a tolerance of less than 100 per cent financial efficiency. Nevertheless, it is wise to be aware of the options. Use this checklist as a guide to make an assessment of the potential for creative leverage. Complete the grid as follows:

---

*Source: *Customer Service Management*, June 1997.

1.   Column 1 contains a number of generic improvement options. You may wish to adapt them to suit your own organization and its context. You may also wish to add new options.
2.   In Column 2, assess whether this option is open to you.
3.   In Column 3, identify targets that could be achieved if you answered 'Yes' in Column 2.
4.   In Column 4, make an assessment of the effect of these targets on organizational performance and state when you expect to see these benefits.

TABLE 2.1   Assessing the potential for creative advantage

Improvement option	Is this option potentially open to you? (Yes/No)	If 'Yes', what specific targets could you achieve that are related to this option? (for example, double the number of new product innovations per year)	Estimate of the effect on performance of your organization if you were to achieve these targets (High/Medium/Low or a quantified response); when will the benefits accrue?
Increase number of patents registered each year			
Increase number of new product/service innovations per year			
Reduce time taken to get new product/ service ideas to market			
Gain greater market share in existing markets			
Enter new markets where you could sell existing products/services			
Reduce unit product/ service costs			
Increase reliability of operations so that the need for quality checks is obsolete			

TABLE 2.1 *continued*

Improvement option	Is this option potentially open to you? (Yes/No)	If 'Yes' what specific targets could you achieve that are related to this option, for example double the number of new product innovations per year	Estimate of the effect on performance of your organization if you were to achieve these targets (High/Medium/Low or a quantified response); when will the benefits accrue?
Increase number of employee suggestions that result in profitable innovations per year			
Increase conversion rate of enquiries to sales			
Increase customer referral rato			
Reduce customer returns and complaints			
Exploit your 'know-how' further, for example, technology, information			
Structure sales and marketing reward and recognition to reflect a balance of short- and long-term margin goals			
Eliminate unprofitable or time-consuming activities which genuinely do not support your star products/services			
Increase level of customer involvement in product concept and design			

TABLE 2.1   *concluded*

Improvement option	Is this option potentially open to you? (Yes/No)	If 'Yes' what specific targets could you achieve that are related to this option, for example double the number of new product innovations per year	Estimate of the effect on performance of your organization if you were to achieve these targets (High/Medium/Low or a quantified response); when will the benefits accrue?
Increase your customer responsiveness index, that is reduce the number of customers who are indifferent to products and services they have purchased/used			
Increase your customer advocacy index, that is convert customers who are willing to give passive referrals about your products/services to proactive company advocates			
Increase your customer targeting index, that is reduce the numbers of your customers who buy products/services that they don't really want or need			

ARENAS WHERE CREATIVITY IS VITAL TO SUCCESS

Creativity is not a panacea for all organizational problems. There are certain areas of organizations that are most able to benefit from a creative approach. The following list illustrates arenas where creativity adds competitive strength. Many of these are detailed as case studies in subsequent chapters.

O   Continuous product and service innovation: the development of the Dyson vacuum cleaner and its impact on the existing vacuum cleaner market (see Chapter 3).

O   Changes in organization structure: the restructuring of Navico to provide radical increases in productivity and innovation (see Chapter 5).

O   Troubleshooting: some Total Quality approaches that have been followed through properly, for example the approach to continuous improvement by Post Office Counters Ltd (see Chapter 6).

O   Introduction of new technology: cellular manufacturing by Navico and the invention of the Dyson vacuum cleaner and its subsequent launch into the market (see Chapters 3 and 5).

O   Improved working climate: Glaxo-Wellcome's approach to the location of functions, leadership and the built environment (see Chapter 5).

O   Image building: the Body Shop's high-profile campaigns.

O   Defining direction and envisioning a potent and desirable future that drives commitment: strategy development to improve effectiveness and efficiency at the College of Guidance Studies (see Chapter 6).

O   Developing corporate culture: the two-way 'issueometer' process to rapidly identify and address blockages within the change process by the National and Provincial Building Society (see Chapter 7).

O   Re-engineering and work re-design: the turnaround strategy for Navico (see Chapter 5).

O   Sales and marketing improvements: the reframing of the Mars chocolate brand as an ice-cream product, of Lucozade as a 'health' not a 'sickness' product; giving extended product lifecycles and opening up new markets for existing products.

O   Consultation approaches where there are multiple stakeholders: Kent County Council's approach to involvement in strategic planning (see Chapter 6).

SUMMARY

The rational case for creativity is not the only or, indeed, the most important reason to encourage it. Yet, there are some indicators that illustrate its value. These range from modern accounting approaches which include the issue of intellectual capital to the examination of the performance of creative organizations.

Although the benefits of creativity are mostly associated with long-term intangible value, it is possible to 'account' for the effect of creativity on organizational performance through the examination of organizations that rely on creativity for their competitive advantage.

You will find it useful to consolidate your reading by reviewing the following questions.

About what you have learned

O   What has reading this chapter confirmed in your mind?
O   What new curiosities has it raised, especially about ways of creating meaningful measurement of the value that creativity offers?

About putting the ideas to work

O   What information can you gather to present the case for using creativity within your organization?
O   Where are the outcomes of creativity most observable in your organization and how long is the time between creative thought and meaningful outcomes?
O   Where and when would creativity be unhelpful in your organization?

A final thought

> If you think creativity is expensive, try ignorance for a change.
> (*Adapted quotation from Anita Roddick,*
> *Body Shop International*)

PART TWO
CREATIVITY IN PRACTICE

❖

3

MODELS AND CONCEPTS OF PERSONAL CREATIVITY

All our dreams can come true – if we have the courage to
pursue them.
(*Walt Disney*)

It is now time to turn our attention to a number of models of creativity which can be applied to individuals in organizations. Much of what is discussed here has been used successfully within organizations to unblock creativity or identify performance gains. There are no magic formulae for creativity – just paradoxes – there is no strong evidence to suggest that it is possible to have a deliberate strategy to produce creativity. Furthermore, some practices mentioned by very creative organizations are contrary to conventional wisdom on what encourages creativity. Consider the following quotations from leaders in creative organizations:

'Stage managed' creativity does not work – if you gave the
people half an afternoon to be creative, they might just use
the time to doss.

If someone comes up with a crap idea, we tell them so.

Thus 'enforced daydreaming' may not work and negative feedback may not hinder the creative person, reinforcing the notion that creativity may emerge where there is a suitable psychological contract despite what some gurus and theorists would argue are unsupportive practices. Furthermore:

Creativity exists where chaos and structure meet within the
organization.

This comment implies that it may be counter-productive to sanitize organizations so that they might be more creative.

We shall identify strategies to overcome personal blocks to creativity, according to a number of discrete levels: environment, behaviour, capability, beliefs and identity. These levels are often linked either in a mutually reinforcing or dissonant way. For example, a person who **believes** him/herself to be creative, but who possesses poor listening and questioning **behaviours** will find it hard to work effectively as part of a creative team. The effect of the organization culture, structure and systems and the external environment will be examined in Chapter 4.

A TRANSACTIONAL MODEL

Rosemary Stewart (1982) proposed a model that can be used to describe the nature of work. This separates jobs into three components:

O   **Demands** or **ends**.
O   **Constraints** or **can't do's**.
O   **Choices** or **degrees of freedom over means** of achieving the ends.

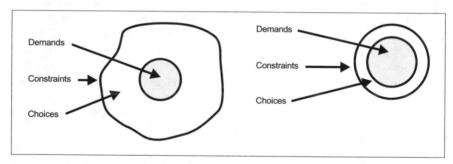

FIGURE 3.1   Demands, constraints and choices. (Adapted from an idea by Stewart R (1982) *Choices for the Manager*, McGraw-Hill.)

We can envisage a continuum of jobs, ranging from those with a wide number of choices, on the left, to those where there is very little discretion over means of reaching the demands on the right (Figure 3.1).

When I first came across this idea it occurred to me that the job with a high degree of choices looked rather like a fried egg. By analogy, the highly constrained job resembled a boiled egg cut through the centre as viewed from above. I have discovered that many other people find the egg metaphor helpful when exploring what motivates people and how jobs can be designed to exploit these desires.

THE 'FRIED EGG'

A stereotypical 'fried egg' job would be that of a research scientist working in the pharmaceutical industry: the prime demand is to discover a novel chemical which may be used therapeutically in a chosen area of disease. There are usually some financial constraints to free expression, but these are relatively unimportant if a drug is being sought for a major disease (for example, cancer or heart disease). The scientist is given a considerable discretion over **what** work is done, **how** it is done and **when** it is done.

THE 'BOILED EGG'

A stereotypical 'boiled egg' job would be a traditional manufacturing operation, where the specified demand is to produce a number of items. There are many constraints in the form of precise systems for manufacture, safety rules and the machinery used may only allow one way of manufacture. The manufacturing operative has a very low degree of choice over **means**.

COMBINING PEOPLE AND JOBS

Taking this notion one stage further, individuals may also be characterized by use of the egg metaphor. Some people require a high level of choice over certain elements of their work and others less so, thus we can envisage a number of person–job **transactions**.

Good 'fit'

Figure 3.2 shows a high degree of fit between person and job. The job–person combination on the left is open to more creative activity, whereas the combination on the right is highly constrained. In both situations the individuals concerned are likely to derive a high level of satisfaction from their work because there is a good fit between job design and individual's needs.

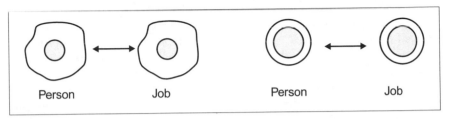

FIGURE 3.2   Good 'fit'.

Poor 'fit'

Figure 3.3 shows a creative person in a highly constrained job (the 'fried egg' person in a 'boiled egg' job). The individual who needs higher levels of discretion in his/her work will continuously find barriers to creativity imposed by the nature of the job. This situation is likely to lead to dissatisfaction and poor performance. However, people are sometimes prepared to work in this manner. In some cases, individuals see their job as an economic necessity that provides income to fuel more creative pursuits elsewhere. *In extremis* an individual may become a source of 'guerrilla creativity', trying to find ways of circumnavigating the constraints imposed by their job.

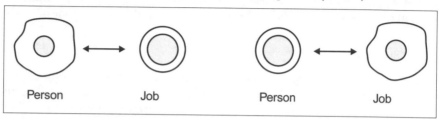

Person   Job   Person   Job

FIGURE 3.3   Poor 'fit'.

'GUERRILLA CREATIVITY' IN ACTION

A good example of what happens when a fried egg person has 'unacceptable' demands placed on him was provided by an ex-work colleague who was employed in pharmaceutical research. He rarely saw his boss and was content to work with few defined boundaries. At that time, his employers operated a corporate policy that required all employees to 'clock in' using a flexitime system. He saw this as an unnecessary interference with his freedom and he devised a way of connecting the clocks to instrumentation which had the effect of making them run at several times normal speed. He made this 'innovation' known to others so that everyone could show the company just how many hours they had worked. It is possible to ascribe this 'industrial sabotage' to laziness. However, this was not the case since the individual concerned was highly committed to his work and always worked many more hours than were required. It is better explained as a result of his frustration with a system that reflected a lack of trust in staff, coupled with a typically scientific way of illustrating the absurdity of the situation.

Consider the situation of the constrained individual in an open-ended job ('boiled egg' person–'fried egg' job). This person may well find the degree of uncertainty involved in the job frightening and often fails to deliver the performance required.

Is it possible to change boiled egg people into fried egg people and vice versa? My experience suggests that it is, although the ways of achieving this transition are very different and results, in terms of performance, also differ.

Constraining a 'fried egg' person into a 'boiled egg' job

Persuading a fried egg person to accept a boiled egg job may be achieved on an instrumental level by coming to an agreement about the constraints inherent in the job and accepting that opportunities for creativity lie outside the organization. At best, a mediocre performance may be expected from this situation and it may be argued that it would have been better to employ a boiled egg person in the first place. In some cases, projects may be identified that utilize the individual's need for discretionary choice to gain greater motivation from them.

Developing a boiled egg person in a fried egg job

Developing boiled egg people in fried egg jobs requires nurturing, support and the provision of appropriate opportunities. It is possible, given time, for these individuals to express discretion and flexibility. However, a 'sink or swim' approach is not likely to be successful here.

Another important point about choice within jobs is that a person's need for choice tends to be domain-specific. For example, many graphic artists have a high need for choice in the specification of equipment that is central to their job, but little or no interest in voicing opinions about how personnel systems impact them (except to complain when it impedes progress). The research scientist considered earlier only had an interest in management to the extent of securing the resources needed to do the job, and he was quite happy to exist with limited discretion on managerial issues. The way to find out in which domains people value choice is by **asking them**. It is easier to write this than do it in practice, since good rapport and an ability to get beyond the obvious answers are needed to be successful.

The egg metaphor can be extended. I have worked with groups which considered the way in which the egg was 'cooked' related to its environment and how this affected the person and the job. Others have suggested that their jobs are 'scrambled'. Like all metaphors, it is important to work on your own meaning rather than to transpose that of someone else. I will therefore leave this section only partly cooked!

Points to ponder

○   Know what sort of 'eggs' you have in your organization and use them to the best of their abilities.

○   Find out in which domains people require choice and give it to them wherever or whenever possible.

○   Where do you need to set out demands and constraints when they are genuinely not available for creative negotiation?

THE IMPACT OF PERSONALITY ON CREATIVE BEHAVIOUR

ASPECTS OF CREATIVE THINKING

There are many models that are helpful when considering creative thinking, which serve to demonstrate that thinking is an entirely individual process.

Koestler (1964) identified a set of inter-dependent dimensions that affect thinking within individuals:

1.   Degrees of consciousness.
2.   Degrees of verbalization.
3.   Degrees of abstraction.
4.   Degrees of flexibility.
5.   Type and intensity of motivation.
6.   Realistic versus autistic thought.
7.   Dominance of outer or inner environment.
8.   Learning and performing.
9.   Routine and originality.

Consider this example: have you ever been talking to someone about their ideas or a problem and found that their ideas seem to be in 'outer space' compared with your own views on the same subject? What aspects of the way you think would you have to change to convey your ideas in a way that the other person would understand?

Taking this one stage further, it is helpful to separate two key approaches to thinking that are relevant to creativity.

Divergent versus convergent thinking

In the context of creative problem-solving, it is recognized that a number of stages are generally involved:

O   Problem/opportunity definition.
O   Generating ideas.
O   Choosing ideas.
O   Solution implementation.

Two fundamentally different thinking styles are required throughout the process:

O   Convergent thinking: focusing on an issue in depth, to specify it precisely.
O   Divergent thinking: looking at the issue from the widest possible set of perspectives.

Divergent thinking is characterized by a playful free-thinking state, whereas convergent thinking is characterized by constructive critique and 'adult' behaviours. Some people also find it easier to switch between thinking styles than others.

Both are necessary, but there can be a tendency for individuals to value convergent thinkers more highly and treat them as the only 'creatives'. In the absence of divergent thinking there would be no closure and thus no innovation. In other words, **both thinking styles are creative**. This idea is developed in Chapter 11, since the different thinking styles are more valuable at different phases of the creative process.

TO ADAPT OR INNOVATE? – THAT IS THE QUESTION

Creative people are often viewed as having 'wild' ideas that are not relevant to immediate concerns. However, much creativity in organizations can be minor as well as major and often manifests itself as incremental continuous shifts in the way products and services are designed, produced and delivered.

Professor Michael Kirton (1989) devised an inventory that typifies the continuum of styles, ranging between the creative behaviour of high adaptors to that of high innovators.

The Kirton Adaptor–Innovator gives a two-fold description of creative thinking style, based on a continuum from adaptive to innovative tendency. The two creative types may be typified as follows:

Adaptors

O   Provide sufficiency of ideas based on original problem and original likely solutions.

O   Develop ideas that are more readily accepted by most people.

O   Are likely to provide more comprehensive searches of one or a few ideas.

O   Seek a solution within the structure of the problem and in ways tried, understood, safe, sure and predictable.

O   Develop ideas with minimal risk and maximum continuity and stability.

Innovators

O   Provide a proliferation of ideas, many of which may not address the problem.

O   Reconstruct or reframe problems and provide less expected and potentially less acceptable solutions which challenge accepted practice.

O   Present many less carefully worked out formulations.

O   Present ideas that may be far away from the prevailing paradigms which are likely to be more strongly resisted.

Individuals may be categorized along a linear scale which follows a normal distribution. Broadly speaking:

O   Adaptors habitually try to solve their problems by the use of rules.

O   Innovators frequently try to solve their problems by bending or breaking the rules.

Both are required for successful innovation, yet Kirton (1989) pointed out that there is potential for conflict in groups where individual KAI scores are more than 20 points apart. This does not mean that these situations should be avoided since conflict is valuable for creativity. It is also important that a radical change agent or leader has a 'displaced' score for success, for example an adaptor in a group of innovators and vice versa. Kirton is adamant, however, that we are all change agents.

Adaptive and innovative behaviour can be inferred from observation of key business leaders.

RICHARD BRANSON

Despite the wide variety of his business ventures, Richard Branson could be said to be adaptive in nature. The principles behind most of his ventures are those of improving an existing product or service in an industry where advantage can be gained through calculated risk-taking.

STEVE JOBS

Steve Jobs, who started the Apple Corporation (sales increased from $2.7 million in 1977 to $331 million in 1981) was reputed to be enthusiastic, hardworking and full of ideas. But he was restless, easily bored and blunt to the point of tactlessness. All these elements are characteristic of a high innovator.

THE JUNGIAN VIEWPOINT

The Myers Briggs Type Indicator (MBTI) aims to measure preferences relating to Jung's theory of personality types, according to four bipolar types.

1. Where do you prefer to focus your attention? The EI scale.

E – Extraversion	I – Introversion
Focus is on the outer world of people and things	Focus is on the inner world of reflection

2. How do you acquire information? The SN scale.

S – Sensing	N – Intuition
Focus is on the realities of the situation, careful with detail	Focus is on the big picture grasping overall patterns

3. How do you make decisions? The TF scale.

T – Thinking	F – Feeling
Focus is on objective	Focus is on person-

decision-making, analysing
and considering

centred values, seek
harmony

4. How do you orient to the outside world? The JP scale.

J – Judging

P – Perceiving

Focus is on structure, planning, Focus is on understanding,
regulation and control   flexibility and spontaneity

Looking at the MBTI preferences, each type can irritate the opposing type if
people forget that different concerns derive from different working styles.
Where differences are accommodated, each type usually benefits from working with individuals with opposing preferences. Each type will attend to the
areas that their opposites are inclined to forget or minimize.

Table 3.1 gives a simplified view of type conflicts and synergies as they
relate to creativity:

TABLE 3.1   Myers Briggs type conflicts and synergies*

Conflict	Synergy
S finds N: impractical, hard to follow	**S needs N**: to prepare for the future, offer innovative ideas
N finds S: materialistic and pessimistic	**N needs S**: to remind them of facts, be realistic, have patience
T finds F: illogical, over-emotional	**T needs F**: to connect with feelings, persuade, reconcile
F finds T: critical, insensitive	**F needs T**: to be tough and weigh costs and benefits
E finds I: withdrawn, cool	**E needs I**: for reflection and depth of understanding
I finds E: superficial, intrusive	**I needs E**: to make contacts and take action
J finds P: disorganized, irresponsible	**J needs P**: for adaptability and information-gathering
P finds J: rigid, inflexible	**P needs J**: for organization and for completion

*Adapted from materials produced by the Oxford Psychologists Press Ltd, Lambourne House, 311–321
Banbury Road, Oxford OX2 7JH.

A good example of differences in action is provided by the example of Ray Cooper and Ashley Newton, who are joint managing directors of Virgin Records.* They prefer to share the role because each is only interested in one aspect of the business. Newton sums up the relationship as follows, 'I'm an arty family man, and Ray's a party animal. Whenever we go out, Ray always wants another drink at one o' clock in the morning and all I want to do is go home.'

Points to ponder

O   Creativity rests on the generation of a large number of choices. Instant judgements are likely to prevent opportunities for inventive search. This has important consequences for the management of creative individuals, since a good deal of management is concerned with decision making and judgement.

O   Individuals with strong judging characteristics can minimize the effects of instant judgement by starting projects earlier and leaving space for the fermentation of ideas, making final decisions at the last possible moment.

THE FOUR Ps

> Your limitations are your expectations.
> (*Richard Wardle*)

Jane Henry (1991) articulated a model of creativity in the Open University Business School MBA programme 'Creative Management' which involves four 'Ps' (see Henry J (1991) *Perspective* Milton Keynes: Open University Press, part of the Open University Business School MBA programme on creative management):

O   Positivity: the consistent habit of seeing problems as opportunities. The ability to recover rapidly from setbacks and tolerate criticism. An unwillingness to let blockages impede progress.

O   Playfulness: drawing on the resources of childhood by taking risks, using fun and humour in thinking, resulting in flexibility of thought and deed. Involves feeling comfortable outside mainstream thinking and action.

O   Passion: driven by a consuming purpose. An obsessive will to achieve goals. Some people prefer to use the word 'purpose' to passion.

*Source: *Financial Times*, 26 June 1997.

○   Persistence: this is the difference between the saying, 'If at first you don't succeed, try try again' and saying, 'If at first you don't succeed, try something different until you do succeed.'

The Dyson story illustrates these principles in action.

THE DYSON STORY

The story of the launch of the Dyson vacuum cleaner is a story of persistence, passion and flexibility in the face of a wide range of external blocks to creativity and innovation. It sums up a number of strategies used to overcome or minimize these blocks.

The fundamental breakthrough made by the Dyson lies in its ability to outperform all other vacuum cleaners by its suction performance remaining the same regardless of how much dust it has collected (Figure 3.4).

This breakthrough was achieved by removing the conventional vacuum cleaner dust bag and replacing it with a cyclone system which separates dust particles down to 0.1 micron. Like many creative ideas, the origins of the Dyson can be traced to the inventor's dissatisfaction with the performance of existing vacuum cleaners:

> I noticed that the cleaner wasn't sucking, so I took the bag
> out and emptied it. But it still didn't suck.
> *(James Dyson)*

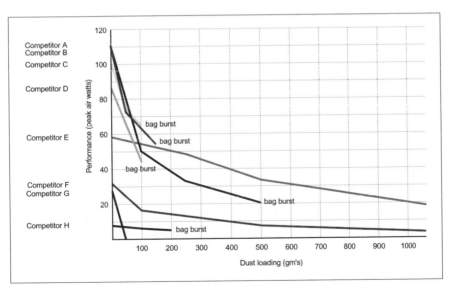

FIGURE 3.4   Dyson versus conventional vacuum cleaners.

On further investigation James Dyson found a thin layer of dust on the inside of the bag and by dismantling the machine he realized that the airflow that goes through the cleaner had to go through the pores of the bag. This problem became the stimulus for the development of the Dyson Dual Cyclone vacuum cleaners. The time from conception to launch was 15 years, and from launch to commercial success another 10 years. During the development phase Dyson produced 5127 prototypes, using the Edisonian method – only making one change between tests so that he could perfect the invention.

Dyson working methods

O   Everyone who starts at Dyson makes a Dyson vacuum cleaner in their first few days which they then take home for their own use.
O   Engineering and design are not viewed as separate disciplines. Design staff are as much involved in testing as engineers are in conceptual ideas.
O   The final assembly of Dyson vacuum cleaners is done entirely by hand.
O   People do not wear suits and ties.
O   All staff use the Dyson café, which only serves fresh food and has a wide vegetarian selection (but no chips).
O   People talk to each other rather than send memos. Dialogue is the founding principle for progress.
O   Dyson employees are encouraged to be different on principle.
O   Everyone is encouraged to generate ideas.
O   The designers and engineers aim to design everything flawlessly. This is apparent in the working environment as much as in the product.
O   Dyson does not use advertising or publicity agencies.
O   Many Dyson employees are recruited straight from university because their minds are open to new ideas and working methods.

External blocks

Experts proved to be a constant source of frustration. Most of James Dyson's approaches to vacuum cleaner manufacturers did not receive a written response. Some examples serve to illustrate the point:

O   1982 – a large American manufacturer would only meet James Dyson if he agreed to sign over the rights to anything he revealed to them in conversation.
O   1992 – the Secretary of State for Wales rejected Dyson's application for a development grant, insisting that if there really was a better type of vacuum cleaner then surely one of the big manufacturers would be making it.

Venture capitalists were equally ambivalent about the opportunity, being risk-averse to a manufacturing venture and James Dyson's design capability. It seemed as though they were only interested in marketing, and failed to recognize these traits in people whom they labelled designers, inventors or manufacturers.

It took continuing persistence to eventually find a manufacturer and a bank loan of £600,000 from Lloyds to bring the invention to the market place.

A further complication was that market research suggested that the clear dust collection bin was not desirable. This was based on the suggestion that people would not like the dirt being visible in case neighbours saw how much dirt had been picked up in their homes. Dyson decided to ignore this information and was successful in persuading the users of the advantages that it offered. This serves to demonstrate that market research cannot always adequately predict what the customer wants, including satisfaction with seeing the results of all your hard work!

Dyson also faced a number of attacks on his product from existing manufacturers. In spite of the fact that his product was nearly twice the price of the nearest competitor, demand for the Dyson vacuum cleaner has increased. This demonstrates the competitive edge that can be gained from creativity and design where it leads to clear advantages over existing products.

Reflections

The Dyson story demonstrates the four Ps model of creativity (passion, persistence, positivity and playfulness) in action; in particular, passion and persistence. At the organizational level, it is also clear that much flexibility was needed to navigate skilfully various external barriers to the successful launch of the innovation.

It also illustrates the following issues regarding personal creativity:

O   Myopia – a complete lack of understanding of the commercial potential of the product, even by 'experts'.

O   Extended timescale – the need to maintain momentum and focus over a highly protracted process.

O   Legal challenges – new technology that leapfrogs the competition will be resisted strongly. Although this is a 'non-surprising' outcome, most inventors and creative people seem blind to this problem and are completely unable to do anything about it.

O   Lack of customer vision – people only want what they already have, until they can see and try something different.

O   Market research does not always offer useful information for innovation, especially where people's knowledge of the innovation is low.

(Dyson Appliances Limited, Tetbury Hill, Malmesbury, Wilts SN16 0RP, UK)

EXTENDING THE FOUR Ps

The four Ps model has been developed into an inventory for use by individuals and organizations in order for them to gain an understanding of what

they are doing well already and where there are potential areas for improvement. Figure 3.5 shows organizations with very different profiles which
undertook this analysis.

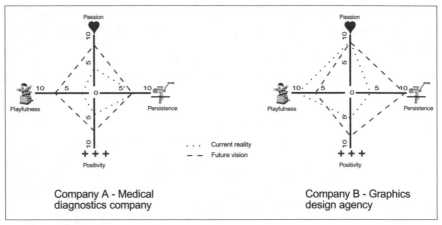

FIGURE 3.5   The four Ps of creativity.

The crucial point is that the four Ps are a **balance**, that is it is not always
'good' to have all four dimensions scoring 10/10. For example, in Company
A, the nature of the environment tended to drive the persistence score
upwards (high levels of regulation etc.). Although Company A desired more
playfulness, it had to be domain-specific. It was important to identify specific
areas and types of project where playfulness would lead to better results
otherwise the organization would not produce any output.

SELF-ASSESSMENT USING THE FOUR Ps FRAMEWORK

Using the grid in Figure 3.6:
1.   Develop your own understanding of what each of the four 'Ps'
       means in your environment.

Positivity

Playfulness

Passion

Persistence

2.   Give yourself a score on each dimension as you are now and
       join up the scores.
3.   Give yourself another score on each dimension according to how
       you would like to be within a specified time and join these up.

4.   Analyse the key differences and devise a number of actionable steps to reduce the differences between the profiles.
5.   Repeat the exercise for your organization or a relevant part of it. Persuade others to complete the assessment and compare your reasons for the scores you give.

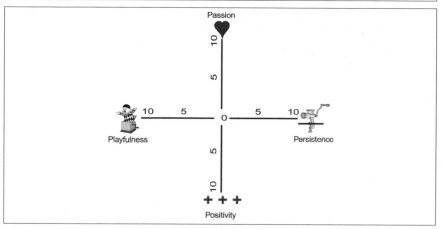

FIGURE 3.6   Self-assessment of the four Ps.

Points to ponder

○   Creative people generally require higher degrees of freedom in the things they are passionate about.

○   Creativity is assisted by intelligence **across** a number of fields of expertise and non-expertise can be of value. It is believed that Alexander Graham Bell would not have attempted to invent the telephone if he had been an electronics expert. How can you have access to a wide range of intelligence's in your personal and work life?

○   Set unattainable goals to create tension for ideas and increase the eventual levels of achievement.

○   Work hard at your chosen obsession.

○   Visualize your desired outcomes rather than becoming engrossed in the 'here and now'.

○   Scan a variety of media for new ideas, even if they seem unconnected with your creative focus.

○   Make time for play, daydreaming and relaxation.

○   Create a micro-environment that assists creative thinking.

○   Carry devices to capture ideas as they occur (perhaps a tape recorder and a notepad).

○   Use sleep and other 'dead times' for idea processing.

○   Think whilst doing routine things – ironing, baking, leisure activities etc.

O   Work with others, particularly those who bring another perspective, even if this conflicts with your own ideas.

BLOCKS TO PERSONAL CREATIVITY

Blockages to creativity mostly present themselves as **symptoms**, which are presumed to be the causes of difficulty. This is rarely the case and it is important to discover the **causes** of creativity blockages before moving on to devise strategies to minimize or eradicate them. These blockages may be classified by increasing difficulty, from those that are visible to deep-seated issues associated with identity (Figure 3.7).

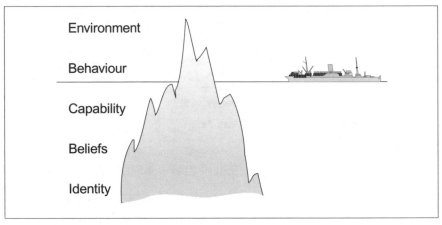

Environment

Behaviour

Capability

Beliefs

Identity

FIGURE 3.7   The organizational iceberg.

ENVIRONMENT
The 'Martini' syndrome

The wrong place and the wrong time.

Lack of opportunity is often caused by the climate being unsuitable for creativity, that is creativity is absent for a variety of reasons: timing of the idea, inadequate idea 'packaging', a physical environment not conducive to creativity or unsupportive leadership.

BEHAVIOUR SYNDROMES
'Premature evaluation'

People who make snap judgements are prone to premature evaluation. They tend to have a preference for judging ideas rather than generating them and often exhibit an inability to relax, incubate ideas and sleep on them. This tendency can arise from a pressured work environment or from personality traits.

Good judges are aware of the range of factors that distort their impressions. They recognize that their beliefs are simply tentative ideas.

'Interpersonal vacuum'

Broadly speaking, poor listening, questioning, summarizing and challenging behaviours are often linked to a lack of skills (capabilities) in these areas and a belief that such behaviours are only good for counsellors and therapists.

CAPABILITY SYNDROMES

'Stay in our box'

Caused by stereotyping, or our need to put things in filing cabinets in our mind. For example, if we see the issue of 'communications' as including only communication 'devices' (such as telephones and computers) we are unlikely to develop ideas about the effect of cultures on communications.

'Limited capacity'

Research shows that most of us find it impossible to hold more than seven discrete pieces of information in our conscious minds at any one time. This results in information overload when we are presented with large volumes of information.

'Ambiguity'

Faced with 'new thinking territories', I observe a wide tendency to retreat mentally from the ambiguity that this situation creates. Many people in organizations exhibit a lack of flexibility in the face of chaos and uncertainty.

'Hammer and nails'

Mostly connected with approaching the situation with a single technique or skill. This syndrome is typified by people who **always** use brainstorming or who **always** ask questions when faced with a problem.

BELIEF SYNDROMES

'Old dogs'

Arises from different perceptions about what creativity is and can be (adaptive or innovative, concepts or practical ideas etc.). It is also supported by an invented belief that thinking capacity diminishes with increasing age. Since the belief is invented, it is also clear that the inventors are, by definition, creative.

'I'm not qualified'

A frequent beliefs-based blockage is that of assuming that creativity only comes from those who are qualified, sometimes disguised through statements such as

'I don't have the proper credentials' or 'I don't have a high IQ'. Also compounded by a lack of awareness of the value that people without specific expertise can contribute to a given situation (the 'fish out of water' syndrome).

'Fish out of water'

Presupposes that to be creative, one must be an expert in the field. As explained in Chapter 1, there is plenty of evidence to suggest that novices are extremely valuable in creative activity, even if this provokes conflict. We shall explore the theme of creative conflict in Chapter 7.

'Fear of insanity'

Some people have observed the fine line that exists between highly creative people and insanity. This may set up a belief that it is dangerous to think in this way.

'Archaeology'

Much organizational thinking is typified by the use of the past to inform decisions about the future. Traditional habits and limiting mindsets (where individuals are not able to perceive possibilities due to a belief that the old way was better) are quite common even in very modern organizations. This belief is quite independent of age, many young people adopt it in order to succeed in companies.

'Passivity'

Typified by the fear of what other people might think, a fear of failure (or success), an unbalanced view of one's right to be heard, a low tolerance of conflict etc.

IDENTITY SYNDROMES

The Freudian explanation for identity blockages is based on conflicts between the id (the instinctive animal part of ourselves), the ego (the socially aware and conscious aspect) and the superego (moralistic part that forbids and prohibits). Whilst this is helpful as an explanation, it also tends to limit possibilities for change by giving credence to the blockage. Since I have never actually **seen** an ego, it can be more helpful to assume that it does not exist, opening up the possibilities for change.

'Projection'

Often comes out in statements such as 'I work for an organization – I can't be creative', or 'I'm a woman – men are the ingenious ones'.

'Rational ego'

If the ability to be rational in all situations is wrapped up in the person's ego, it is likely to be very pervasive indeed. Whilst it is possible to change, this involves persuading an individual to challenge his/her deepest emotions and should not be attempted without great skill and ethics.

OPTIONS FOR REMOVING OR MINIMIZING CREATIVITY BLOCKS

The obvious solution to the problem of creativity blocks is to change it. Thus, if the environment is a problem, one needs to change the environment and so on! To achieve the right change requires some thought. Some options and ideas to act as thought starters are given below.

MODIFYING THE ENVIRONMENT

Extreme examples of individuals who manufactured a personal environment that inspired them include Schiller, who filled his desk with rotten apples. Dr Johnson surrounded himself with a purring cat, orange peel and tea. Kant worked in bed at certain times of the day, with the blankets arranged around him in a way he had invented himself. Organizational versions of environmental modification include:

O   Going for a walk.
O   Playing sport, music.
O   Bringing creative artefacts to the office.
O   Having 'field days', where you choose to go out to the country to work outside.

MODIFYING BEHAVIOUR

O   Use techniques and routines that bypass or minimize the particular creative blocks that you are prone to, for example, if you tend to make snap judgements, ensure that you schedule creative meetings so that decisions **have** to be made later in the process.
O   Don't be afraid to act when you don't have complete understanding.
O   Spend time understanding the problem or opportunity.

MODIFYING CAPABILITY

This is the domain of training and development activities in the main. However, training does not necessarily mean attending a course. The subject is discussed in greater depth in Chapter 10. Some options for overcoming capability blocks include:

O   Develop skills of mapping uncharted territory using 'complexity organizers', such as systems mapping, rich picturing etc.

O   Look for connections between diverse problems.
O   Recognize that good thinking is yet another asset to be developed.

MODIFYING BELIEFS

> If you play at being a genius, you become one.
> (*Dali*)

O   Act as though you are creative. This involves modifying your impression of the truth for a time so that you can test whether your behaviour changes. A practical strategy involves a decision to be creative at the next meeting requiring this quality and then following through with action.
O   Work with others who do not have the same creative blockages and elect an 'official conscience' to scan the blocks and flag them up if they materialize.
O   If working with others, agree ground rules to minimize blocks to creativity. Most of the ground rules that are used in 'brainstorming' sessions are intended to achieve this.
O   Practise doing things that require you to adopt alternative belief systems, for example, if you have a strong 'perceiver' quality, make decisions by a thorough analysis of all the options from time to time. *In extremis*, try reading logarithmic tables and analysing the connections between sines, cosines and tangents!
O   Recognize that good intuition comes after a period of concentrated thought and hard work.
O   Raise awareness of the value of conflict and set requirements for it.

MODIFYING IDENTITY

O   Question the validity of the identity-based statements, for example, if the block is 'I work for an organization – I can't be creative', ask about organizations that are creative or go out and visit one.
O   Identify situations where this block is appropriate and where it imposes limitations. Identify new strategies for overcoming limiting situations.

SUMMARY

Practical models of creativity (as it applies to individuals and the roles which they adopt in organizations) have been examined and a framework for identifying and tackling personal blockages to creative thought and action has been provided. The main points are:

ASSESSING YOUR OWN BLOCKAGES TO CREATIVITY AND DEVISING AN ACTION PLAN (TABLE 3.2)

1. Examine each of the blockages and make a priority list of the top three that affect your own creativity and are important to your work. Discuss your assessment with others who work with you to improve your own assessment.
2. Use the ideas in this section as a starting point to design at least 10 options for minimizing or overcoming these blockages.
3. After a period of reflection, critique your list constructively and select those strategies that you will put into action. Identify up to three specific steps that you are able to take in the next 30 days to realize your plan.

O People and their jobs can be viewed as transactions and the role of the creative manager is to find good balances between people and their changing jobs.

O Creativity can arise from adaptation of existing ideas or more radical leaps forward.

O The four-stage model of creativity (the four Ps) may be applied to individuals or organizations to gain an understanding of where effort may best be targeted to enhance creativity.

O The iceberg model identifies sources of personal creativity blockages by use of five interconnected levels, ranging from environment to identity.

O Once creativity blockages have been identified it becomes much easier to devise a strategy to minimize or eradicate them.

You will find it useful to consolidate your reading by reviewing the following questions:

About what you have learned

O What has reading this chapter confirmed in your mind?
O What useful contradictions has it raised?
O What new curiosities has it identified?

About putting the ideas to work

O Where can you find the support of a variety of people (adaptors and innovators) that will improve the quality and robustness of your decisions?

O By how much does your organization deliberately hire people who are likely to see things differently?

O What processes or routines can help delay important decisions where there is more than one solution?

○   How can you arrange things so that your organization's 'four P' matrix is in tune with the needs of the environment?

A final thought

A man would do well to carry a pencil in his pocket and write down the thoughts of the moment. Those that come unsought are commonly the most valuable and should be secured, because they seldom return.

(Francis Bacon)

TABLE 3.2   Assessing and addressing blockages to personal creativity

Top three creativity blockages (rank three on the list)	How does the block manifest itself?	Options for improvement	First steps forward
Martini			
Premature evaluation			
Interpersonal vacuum			
Stay in our box			
Limited capacity			
Ambiguity			
Hammer and nails			
Old dogs			
I'm not qualified			
Fish out of water			
Fear of insanity			
Archaeology			
Passivity			
Projection			
Rational ego			

4

MODELS AND CONCEPTS OF ORGANIZATIONAL CREATIVITY

> We are trying to sell more and more intellect and less and
> less materials.
> (*George Hogg, Vice President Strategic Planning, 3M*)

We now turn our attention to organizational creativity. Whilst creativity may be different for each individual, the real payoff comes when creativity is leveraged at the organizational level, as illustrated by the 3M quotation above. Organizational creativity does not mean the removal of individual flair by the use of standard approaches. However, there are undeniable tensions between individual creative activity and the needs of an organization to systematize work. Creative organizations manage these tensions – not by removing them, but by encouraging and managing the inevitable paradoxes.

We begin here with a strategic view of organizational creativity and then examine creative subsystems in Part III. As well as looking at what helps organizational creativity, we have already identified a need to remove blockages to creativity. This is a key role of leadership in developing an organization. Paradoxically, the removal of blockages is often sufficient to start more creative approaches rather than importing techniques.

WHAT IS ORGANIZATIONAL CREATIVITY?

> We used to use iron oxide to make cave paintings, and now
> we put it on floppy disks.
> (*Paul Romer*)

The raw material we have to work with has been the same throughout history – there is the 'stuff' in the earth's crust and the 'stuff' in the atmosphere. So, when we think about growth, the only way it can happen is by finding better recipes for rearranging the fixed amount of 'stuff' we have.

> Think of a manufacturing process with twenty steps. The
> number of possible combinations is ten to the power
> eighteen, equivalent to the number of seconds which have
> elapsed since the big bang.

Creative organizations realize that the future will come from rearranging the 'stuff', not from making the same old cave paintings, or executing 20 steps in exactly the same order for the next 3000 years.

DEFINITIONS OF THE CREATIVE ORGANIZATION

Organization creativity can be seen as a **process** whereby creativity is the **input** to the processes that lead to innovation and competitiveness. This may be described thus:

> Creativity is the ability to identify some technology that will
> give us a leading edge over our competitors

and is the approach adopted by leading edge companies, such as 3M, which seeks innovative products and services that change the basis of competition.

Many companies formalize the creative process through a research and development function. It is helpful to view the R&D process as a 'pipeline', where ideas enter at one end and increased market share and/or return on investment (ROI) is generated when a successful product or service emerges at the other end (Figure 4.1).

The time spent in the pipeline varies for different industries, for example, in software applications it may be months; in the aerospace industry it may be decades. Any shortening of the pipe 'length' or improvements in the number of ideas converted to innovations will produce financial benefit for the organization.

In non-profit-seeking organizations the notion of increased market share or return on investment may be replaced by more appropriate outcomes, such as contribution or enhancement of strategic positioning.

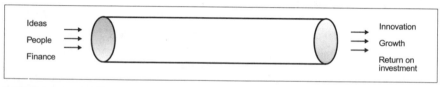

FIGURE 4.1   An input–output view of the creative organization.

Other definitions of organizational creativity were outlined by participants in the research for this book. These included '**infection theory**':

> Creative people stimulate creativity in naturally uncreative
> people.

Infection theory relates to the concept of 'cognitive dissonance', that is the creative person stretches someone else's thinking like an elastic band and the other person (or organization) has to adjust their thinking in order to reduce this stretching. If the creative person overstretches the capacity of the other to adjust, their ideas are ditched (and the person who formulated the idea may also be regarded as foolish or dangerous). A number of contributors mentioned that they believed that a good deal of courage and assertiveness on the part of creative individuals was needed to operate in this way.

Creativity also concerns the '**climate**' of the organization:

> Drusillas define creativity as the freedom, encouragement
> and involvement to feel part of something that the public
> want.

Aspects of climates will be explored further in Chapter 9.

Creative organizations may be defined through the use of metaphor. Consider the creative organization as a nuclear reactor. Nuclear reactors are controlled by the insertion of graphite as a moderator to ensure that the plant does not run out of control. In the case of a creative organization, the 'reaction' (idea generators) also needs to be moderated (by people who can mop up the ideas and develop them into innovations) to ensure that the organization does not become critically overloaded with ideas and no output.

The creative organization has been described in terms of 'banana throwers' and 'banana catchers'. Banana throwers are individuals who generate ideas without necessarily having any concern for their practical value. These people often throw their bananas without considering how appropriate the timing is or whether their audience is receptive. Banana throwers must be mixed with banana catchers, who capture ideas and obtain resources to develop them at the right time.

RECIPES FOR CREATIVE ORGANIZATIONS

There are no universal 'recipes' for building creative organizations. However, it is possible to specify the requirements that make organizational creativity **more probable**. A number of leading writers have described models for organizations where creativity is a core competence.

Handy (1985, 1989, 1994) mentions the 'triple I corporation' as being the organization of the future, where:

$$I^3 = AV$$
$$(I = \text{Intelligence, Information and Ideas; } AV = \text{added value.})$$

Handy is a leader amongst those who suggest that traditional organizational skills are being replaced by softer competencies, such as creativity, which shows itself through the generation of ideas that transform the organization.

Twiss (1974) suggests that possibilities open to organizations wanting to develop the conditions that encourage creativity include:

O   Obtaining and keeping creative people within the organization.
O   Generation of a working environment that encourages creativity.
O   Use of techniques that develop creative problem-solving capacity within the organization.

Thus, Twiss sees a role for technique as well as the right 'raw materials'.

My own studies of creative organizations suggest a 'formula':

The 80/20 'formula'
(Creativity is 80 per cent context and 20 per cent technique.)

To build a creative organization, as a minimum, you need two components.

Context (80 per cent)

'Context' is the permission/encouragement for creativity in an organizational sense. Creative organizations establish a suitable context for creativity to emerge and context includes some or all of the following:

O   Culture, leadership style and values.
O   Structures and systems.
O   Skills and resources.

Each of these will be explained in greater detail in Part Three.

Technique (20 per cent)

'Techniques' are the processes used to push individual/group thinking beyond the constraints often imposed within routine organizational work. Whilst some organizations make use of proprietary creativity 'toolkits', they are insufficient to generate a creative culture. The emphasis needs to shift towards the creation of contexts where innate creativity can emerge. Techniques have their place when an appropriate context has been created but cannot be used to 'force' creativity. In other words, if the organization does not espouse the context of creativity, it will be a waste of time and money to send individuals on a 'creativity course'. Where training is appropriate, a variety of techniques is recommended, so that individuals may fit a technique to the issue or even design their own that fits the context, rather than having to force-fit organizational issues to techniques. Debates about appropriate use of creativity techniques are raised in Part Four.

In some cases the 80/20 formula can be modified to allow less emphasis on context. In other words the context for creativity is positive and there is a genuine need for techniques to enhance the level and nature of creative thinking. However, my experience (as a manager of creative people and as a consultant to a number of organizations seeking to generate more creative approaches) suggests that too much faith is placed in technique. The 80:20 ratio offers a guideline for most organizations.

Many 'learning organizations' encourage creativity. Organizational learning requires people to challenge the 'givens' and develop new strategic choices, so their organization is constantly in tune with the world in which it operates. There are many definitions of a learning organization; this concept is explored in greater detail in Chapter 10.

WHAT SORT OF CREATIVITY?

Much organizational creativity has been the result of incremental shifts in thinking; relatively few 'big breakthroughs' occur. Organizational creativity is traditionally **adaptive** rather than **radical**. This is understandable, since most organizations are rational goal-directed institutions and the collective motives of those working for them also mitigate against risk-taking. If we take a strategic viewpoint, although there is a higher risk associated with taking radical steps, competitive advantage is the business of gaining a posi tion that others find difficult to copy or compete with. Thus, there is a powerful argument for radical change in circumstances where there is little or nothing to differentiate others in the market and the market is itself receptive to the change.

Examples of **adaptive** organizational creativity include:

O   Colonel Sanders' development of Kentucky Fried Chicken.
O   Kent County Council's overhaul of the Special Needs section in the Education Service that led to improved customer service (see Chapter 6).

Examples of **radical** organizational creativity include:

O   The invention of the photocopier by Xerox, which killed off the need for carbon paper and fundamentally changed the nature of office work.
O   The invention of the Post-it™ note by Art Fry and 3M's subsequent marketing of the product.
O   Edwin Land's invention of the instant camera for Polaroid.

A two-dimensional grid (the product/service destiny matrix) can be constructed to weigh the relative risks (according to how radical the product/service idea is) against the nature of the market. The 'animals' in the matrix are viewed as metaphors for products, services and even entire organizations or their subsidiary business units (see Figure 4.2).

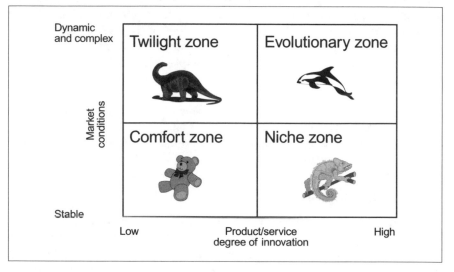

FIGURE 4.2   The product/service destiny matrix.

Taking each box in turn:

○   **Dinosaurs:** live in the twilight zone. Although they may have been innovative in the early stages of life, competition has leapfrogged them and the markets in which they operate have become more sophisticated. Dinosaurs may either change or risk extinction. The re-invention of Lucozade as a health drink shows how a dinosaur can turn into a dolphin.

○   **Teddy bears:** live in the comfort zone. The key message here is 'if it ain't broke, don't fix it'. Teddy bears come to life when the market threatens. A UK bathroom supplier faced difficulties recently when an important customer demanded a more environmentally sound product that was cheaper. This prompted a value engineering exercise to meet these requirements. In this way, the teddy bear became a dolphin and not a dinosaur. As in real life, many people (consumers) eventually grow out of the teddy bear stage.

○   **Lizards:** live in the niche zone. These are highly innovative products or services that tend to be over-engineered and the domain of the 'wacky' professor. Lizards must blend in with the environment in order to survive or attempt to reach a more innovative market. They cannot survive for long in the niche zone and need to meta-morphose into dolphins or teddy bears. Examples of lizards that failed to do this include the Sinclair C5 and Howard Hughes' flying boat which broke up on take-off. The Sony Walkman is a good example of a lizard which changed into a dolphin by changing the dynamics of its market.

O   **Dolphins:** live in the evolutionary zone. These are products and services which exploit the opportunites provided by dynamic com-plex markets. Dolphins thrive in turbulent waters and current exam-ples include organizations such as Microsoft and Intel.

Clearly, it is important to have a product/service portfolio in order to avoid risking all whilst recognizing the need to resource key projects adequately.

ASSESSING YOUR PRODUCT/SERVICE DESTINY MATRIX

1.   Identify the important products and services that your organiza-tion provides and place them in one of the four boxes of the product/service destiny matrix (Figure 4.2).
2.   Indicate with an arrow where you would like each product/service to move to within a given time.
3.   Devise a plan of action that will help you to take the first steps.

HOW DO CREATIVE ORGANIZATIONS DO IT?

A range of approaches used by a number of creative organizations offer per-spectives on the issues involved:*

3M

O   **Small is beautiful:** when a Division becomes too large, it is divided.
O   **Accept failure:** Divisions must derive 30 per cent of sales from products introduced in the last four years and 10 per cent from products that are less than one year old. 3M estimates that only two in every 100 ideas reach the customer.
O   **Encourage champions:** when a 3M employee devises a product idea, he or she recruits a team to develop it. Salaries and promo-tions are tied to product progress.
O   **Involve the customer in design:** customers routinely help to shape product ideas.
O   **Share ideas:** technology belongs to everyone, wherever it originates.

*Adapted and updated from the April 10, 1989 issue of *Business Week* by special permission. © 1997 by McGraw-Hill Companies.

O   **Don't kill a project:** if an idea does not 'fit' in one of 3M's divisions, an employee can devote 15 per cent of his/her time to prove it is workable. Grants are awarded each year to encourage this.

In practice, it is said that some 3M employees use much more than 15 per cent 'bootlegging' time and others use none at all. What matters is the fact that the 15 per cent rule exists as visible permission/encouragement to creativity.

Hewlett Packard

O   **Bootlegging is OK:** researchers are urged to spend 10 per cent of their time on pet projects.
O   **Open all hours:** facilities are open 24 hours a day.
O   **Small is beautiful:** keeps divisions small to maximize collaboration.

Johnson & Johnson

O   **Failure is OK:** the freedom to fail is a built-in cultural prerogative.
O   **Autonomy is beautiful:** uses many autonomous operating units to encourage innovation.

A DAY IN THE LIFE OF A CREATIVE ORGANIZATION

The following metaphor is based on a combination of experiences of creative organizations.

THE JAZZ BAND METAPHOR

The jazz band is a loose association of individuals that need no sheet music, since they share a common love for the music; achieved by careful selection of musicians, based on ability and empathy within and on the edge of the band's style. Within the jazz band musicians can blow their own trumpets whilst recognizing the need for the 'solos' to be consistent with the band's musical direction.

The informal band leader helps band members to reach new heights of musicianship and encourages the swapping of instruments to broaden skills. The band is paid on the basis of quality of performance, although random bonuses from a 'slush fund' are allocated by group consent for outstanding individual performances.

The repertoire of the band is wide and both well-rehearsed and unstructured, for the performance has both elements of formal musical structure and improvised chaos. Some performances are unremarkable, yet there are moments when the band seems to know exactly what to do to take its music in a new direction that has never been rehearsed formally.

Although the band members derive great enjoyment from playing their music when practising or performing, off-stage they often disagree vigorously about many issues concerned with the music. In some cases, individuals are not great personal friends, yet differences are subservient to the greater 'task' of music. For example, the guitarist may be gregarious yet aloof, whereas the bass player will often be the one to arrange social events. The drummer is always late for rehearsals as he has to beg a lift from the piano player and is never organized enough to buy a car.

Competitiveness manifests itself in a positive way, in so far as soloists attempt to outdo each other with the aim of moving the general level of performance upwards. Although each individual could probably play a very impressive piece, the results achieved by the band are greater than the individual players could achieve on their own. The band also has to compete with others for bookings and one of the members will have responsibility for obtaining them, through advocating the band to club owners and trying tricks to make it more visible than rivals.

Occasionally, the band is asked to play requests. Although performed dutifully, they often lack the sparkle achieved when the band is in 'free flow'. The musicians claim to be unaware of anything around them, including the audience, and they could be said to be creating music in a highly selfish way at such times.

The jazz band metaphor contains the following aspects of creative organization design:

O   The need to balance structure and chaos according to the needs of the various stakeholders.
O   The ability to learn continuously and adapt to change through the use of signposts which are understood by the whole organization.
O   Use of unconscious processes to guide the direction of the organization, that is using both logic and intuition.
O   The emergence of a collective consciousness that informs the organization about its performance.
O   The notion that creativity needs to be 'crept up on'. It is impossible to force, but technique helps. No amount of engineering will necessarily produce the intended result.
O   The use of risk-taking within a safe environment.
O   Personality differences made irrelevant by a consuming passion with a shared purpose.
O   The idea that the strategy arises from synthesis of collective capability and that strategy emerges rather than being thoroughly planned.

By comparison, one organization I visited represented its current level of creativity thus:

> There is a great deal of sheet music in our company (procedure) ... some people want to play folk music (culture) ... rewards flow to those with the loudest instruments ... etc.

Point to ponder

○   Do you let people play their own solos or do you insist that they use the sheet music you prepared for them?

DESIGNING THE CREATIVE ORGANIZATION

> Look to the future, listen to the past, but act now!

There have been numerous attempts to build creativity into organizations through tactical initiatives. These rarely produce long-lasting and significant results and are of importance only where the need for creativity may be sensibly diverted to one particular unit or subculture of an organization.

When designing creativity into an organization a strategic and systemic view must be taken. A **systems view** of strategy requires that the culture, leadership style and values, structures and systems, and skills and resources of the organization be aligned to provide the necessary synergy. A useful model is that of a three-legged stool (Figure 4.3). All three 'legs' need to remain in balance if the stool is to remain upright. Any modifications to one

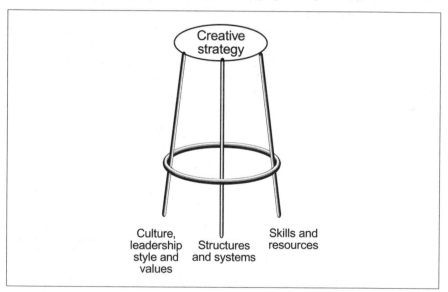

FIGURE 4.3   A strategic and systemic view of the creative organization.

element (leg) of the system (stool) must be balanced by corresponding changes in the others.

It is important to define each of the 'legs':

○   **Culture, leadership style and values:** the 'way we do things here', leadership role and style, and the espoused and realized values that the organization lives and breathes.

○   **Structures and systems:** formal organizational structures, informal structures (networking, information structures), and the shadow side of the organization). Systems include rewards, recognition and career pathways.

○   **Skills and resources:** attraction, development and retention of creative talent, supported by information, finance and an appropriate climate for creativity.

Some of these elements ('legs') are more important for creativity in different types and sizes of organization. Different organizations pay more attention to some elements than others. What is particularly important is that the chosen strategies **fit** the particular organization.

Each of these components are examined in greater detail in Chapters 7, 8 and 9.

BLOCKS TO ORGANIZATIONAL CREATIVITY

All the blockages that impede individual creativity are present in organizations. However, the organizational blockages are compounded by a tendency for organizations to have a collective consciousness which accepts certain ideas and not others. (More will be said about this in Chapters 7 and 10.) Any moves to improve organizational creativity must therefore take account of the 'corporate immune system' if they are to succeed. The behaviour of the corporate immune system can be neatly summed up by Clark's Law of Revolutionary Ideas:

> Every new idea, be it in science, politics, art or any other
> field, evokes three stages of reaction: 'It's impossible. Don't
> waste my time.' 'It's possible, but it's not worth doing.' 'I
> said it was a good idea all along.'*

The case of Dyson Appliances Limited referred to in Chapter 3 illustrates Clark's Law in action. Dyson's achievement was to move from step two to step three in the above sequence.

*Cited in Leboeuf (1990) *How to Develop and Profit from your Creative Powers* Piatkus.

When examining organizational creativity we must look at the **ends** of the process, that is a successful product/service innovation. It is, therefore, important to look at both internal and external blockages. Internal creative blocks relate to factors that reduce product or service development, whereas external blocks relate to factors that reduce the likelihood of successful innovation.

INTERNAL CREATIVE BLOCKS

Our three-legged stool model may be used to identify internal blocks to organizational creativity.

From culture, leadership style and values

In terms of the relationship with the personal creative blocks identified in Chapter 3, culture, leadership style and values relate to the levels of **beliefs, behaviour** and **identity** in the 'iceberg' model. The main blocks are:

O   **Inappropriate leadership style:** for example, autocratic leadership valuing only its own ideas and not rewarding others.

O   **Lack of appropriate behaviours:** for example, a culture with poor listening and questioning behaviours is unlikely to hear let alone develop even the most creative ideas.

O   **'Unwritten rules':** for example, there can be powerful pressures to prevent someone working for a computer company from saying that a manual system is better.

O   **Values that encourage conformity:** for example, if reason, logic and practicality are good then, by implication, intuition, qualitative judgements and playfulness are bad.

O   **Overseriousness:** Koestler (1964) mentions three domains of creativity: artistic originality (the 'ah' reaction); scientific discovery (the 'a-ha' reaction); and comic inspiration (the 'ha-ha' reaction). If humour is considered out of place, creativity will suffer.

O   **Groupthink:** causes the problem of people not wishing to 'be first' in a situation where new ideas are under discussion, for fear of ridicule.

From structures and systems

Structures and systems relate to the level of **environment** in the 'iceberg' model. The main blocks are:

O   **Lack of effective co-operation and trust:** particularly relevant amongst colleagues and between business units, usually due to a lack of horizontal co-ordinating mechanisms.

O   **Encouraging conformity and deference to positional authority:** can include poorly designed appraisal systems and career development pathways.

O   **Lack of psychological contracts of trust:** this can occur when organizations undergo frequent structural re-arrangements since people tend to require a bond of trust before they will share ideas and network effectively.

O   **Inappropriate reward systems:** obvious, as shown by the example below.

HOW NOT TO REWARD YOUR MOST TALENTED WORKERS

The example concerns a laboratory of technologists. Their employers had a simple reward strategy which promoted people who obtained a degree through part-time study at a university or college. This also conferred the status of 'Senior Technologist' and was 'marked symbolically' by the provision of a desk rather than having to write at the bench.

One year, a number of technologists gained their degrees at the same time. This presented their manager with a problem since another technologist who had acquired his degree two years previously complained that he would have nothing to show for his extra time and effort at the enhanced grade. The problem was explained (foolishly in hindsight) to the group by the manager. After some deliberation, a decision was made to buy the newly appointed senior technologists small self-assembly desks (the accepted norm was for a full-sized oak variety). There was a good deal of resentment at this petty differential. The situation was made worse when the manager attempted to appease the senior technologists by ordering a junior member of staff to assemble the desks as a gesture to the technologists' new seniority. It was not surprising when many of the desk legs fell off ...

From skills and resources

Skills and resources relate to the level of **capability** in the 'iceberg' model. The main blocks are:

O   **The wrong tools or the wrong use of the tools for the job**: inflexible or inadequate use of problem-solving strategies. This often arises from the use of 'brainstorming' to fix all organizational problems when this technique may be inappropriate for the particular problem.

O   **Information blocks**: barriers to the free flow of ideas and information to improve the quality of learning.

O   **Financial blocks**: lack of development capital and revenue or the absence of organizational resources to 'fast-track' promising projects.

O   **Poor climate**: can destroy all chances of creativity and innovation, as demonstrated by the following example.

IT CAN TAKE 20 YEARS TO BUILD A CLIMATE OF TRUST AND FIVE SECONDS TO DISMANTLE IT ... HOW TO DESTROY A HEALTHY CLIMATE

The following is an extract from a memo sent to a number of staff in a medium-sized organization that espouses a culture of encouraging ideas – with devastating effect. Names have been changed to protect those involved.

To: Craig, Neil, Mike, Jim, Paul, Fred
From: John

The 1997 budgets are now being finalized. High but achievable targets have been set.

I will personally be paying close attention to our achievements against these targets which we must make this year. Non-achievement of our monthly targets will result in a strong involvement from me as to why they were not met.

I shall be extremely critical if I discover that turnover has been lost through shoddy or careless customer service. Mistakes are NOT acceptable.

In the past there has been strong criticism from Sales about errors being made by Distribution and I intend to ensure that these errors are eliminated.

Every Monday morning I want a report on my desk from each Distribution Manager informing me of any errors that were made in the previous week. This report must contain brief details of the error and most importantly who was responsible for the error. It must also state what action was taken to resolve the problem.

Whilst I accept that mistakes occasionally occur in any normal business, the sheer volume of mistakes currently being made is totally unacceptable.

I expect to see the first reports on my desk next Monday. If I am out of the office on a Monday the reports will be monitored by Paul or Fred.

I want you to copy this letter to all your staff who are responsible for order taking, picking and delivery. Sales staff should also be copied.

Mistakes are a cancer in our business which will eventually threaten all our livelihoods unless we cut them out. Eliminating mistakes also increases profits, which is in everybody's interests with our new profit sharing scheme.

Regards
John

EXTERNAL CREATIVE BLOCKS

The main external barriers may be categorized as follows:

O   **Access to finance to bring ideas to market:** a lack of ability to persuade fundholders, such as banks and venture capitalists, of the value of the innovation.

O   **Product/service fit with market needs:** relates to the product/service destiny matrix.

O   **Inappropriate timing:** launching products and services too early or too late.

The following example of a patent that never reached the market illustrates these barriers to exploiting creativity in action (see Figure 4.4).

THE VIRTUAL BOOKREADER – PATENT SUMMARY

Background

Whilst the personal computer may have improved office productivity it has not reduced the use of paper copies of documents. A major reason for this is that is long documents are tedious to read on a computer screen. This applies to an even greater degree when reading books. Despite the current availability of computer technology, many people still prefer to read hard copies of books. Other reasons for this include: fear of technology; environment (books are often read in places where there is no access to electricity); books are not generally read in a 'linear' fashion (that is, readers flick pages and cross-refer). A traditional computer screen is therefore a particularly unfriendly way of reading a book. This invention brings existing technologies together in a novel way that overcomes the sociological and technological barriers to using a computer screen for reading books.

THE PROBLEM THAT THE INVENTION SOLVES

This invention relates to a user-friendly way to read books by use of computer-based technology. This will be of particular use to frequent travellers who wish to save on luggage space; libraries for multiple book loans and book publishers wishing to enter electronic book distribution.

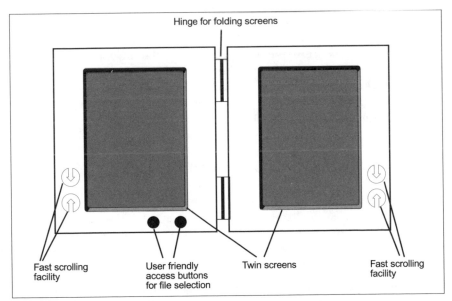

FIGURE 4.4   The virtual bookreader patent (schematic).

ESSENTIAL FEATURES

The invention consists of the following items:

A mini computer, with twin screens, designed to have the outward appearance of a medium-sized book.

A fast-scrolling facility that enables two pages of the book to be displayed simultaneously, even when these pages are not in logical sequence.

A means of transferring data to the system, for example, an integral floppy disk drive or a CD ROM device.

User friendly access buttons for file selection from the data transfer system.

Battery support to enable the unit to be used on journeys and in remote locations.

This patent can be analysed in terms of its successful and less successful features that led to its failure to get to the market.

Successes

○   **User orientation:** there was a good potential fit with practical needs of the market at the time. In other words, the invention had been thought out from the user's point of view and there was a clear market segment that was worthy of further research.

Failures

○   **Poor timing:** the innovation did not fit the prevailing technical direction of the industry at that time.

○   **Persistence:** a lack of persistence on the part of the inventor. No prototype was ever made and there was an expectation that funding would flow from the organization to the inventor due to the expected returns on the finished product.

○   **Marketing myopia:** a lack of vision of the target organizations, possibly compounded by being overly focused on their own strategic direction, that is a lack of emergent strategy.

OPTIONS FOR REMOVING OR MINIMIZING CREATIVITY BLOCKS

It would be all too easy to suggest that all one needs to do is to reverse the source of the blocks and creativity would be released. Whilst this is true, the implementation process is often easier said than done. A host of approaches for removing or minimizing creative blocks is contained in the separate chapters on our three-legged stool. The key options are summarized here.

○   Sensitize the organization to the need for high-quality listening skills. Encourage the 'Socratic' style of enquiry through the use of questions rather than the traditional communications style, based on advocating one's own ideas.

O   Hire creative leaders with appropriate styles for the groups they will work with.

O   Challenge 'unwritten rules' and values.

O   Institute comic rituals to introduce tension.

O   Reward behaviours that disturb 'group think' and add co-operation across units.

O   Use team development across functions to increase trust.

O   Get rid of all unhelpful systems.

O   Use 'boundary crossers' to integrate disparate functions that have to co-operate.

O   Operate from a wide repertoire of creative problem-solving tools.

O   Set up information transfer mechanisms and make sharing of ideas a rewardable activity.

O   Introduce ideas rooms/padded cells where anything goes, supported by spray paint, Post-it notes, crayons, systems thinking tools, drinks etc.

O   Create environments where informal mixing occurs.

O   Change the climate.

O   Introduce 'slush funds' to fuel speculative ventures.

O   Ruthlessly screen ideas for their fit with the market whilst remaining open to letting a few 'wild cards' through the net in case they turn out to be ahead of their time.

O   Time the introduction of new products and services carefully.

ASSESSING ORGANIZATIONAL BLOCKAGES TO CREATIVITY AND DEVISING OPTIONS FOR ELIMINATING OR MINIMIZING THEM (SEE TABLE 4.1)

1.   Form a small group and engage in a dialogue with the aim of prioritizing the top three blockages to organizational creativity.

2.   Using the ideas in this section as a starting point, design at least 10 options for eliminating or minimizing these blockages.

3.   After a period of reflection, constructively critique the list and select those strategies that you will put into action. Identify up to three specific steps that you are able to take in the next 30 days to begin your plan. Commit to producing three more steps in 30 days' time that take account of what you learned with the first actions and so on.

TABLE 4.1   Assessing and addressing blocks to organizational creativity

Top three creativity blockages (tick three on the list)	How does the block manifest itself?	Options for improvement	First steps
Inappropriate leadership style			
Lack of appropriate behaviours to bring ideas into action			
The 'unwritten rules'			
Values that encourage conformity			
Overseriousness			
Groupthink			
Lack of effective co-operation and trust			

TABLE 4.1   Concluded

Top three creativity blockages (tick three on the list)	How does the block manifest itself?	Options for improvement	First steps
Systems that encourage conformity and deference to positional authority			
Lack of psychological contracts of trust			
Inappropriate reward systems			
The wrong tools or the wrong use of the tools for the job			
Information blocks			
Financial blocks			
Poor climate			

SUMMARY

We have looked at a strategic view of creativity – where it can be leveraged for greater levels of innovation and other organizational results. The main points that arise from this view are:

O   Organizational creativity is connected with finding improved ways of doing things, be they minor continuous changes or more radical leaps forward.

O   Much organizational creativity is adaptive which is consistent with the levels of risk the organization is prepared to take.

O   To maintain competitive advantage, organizations need to manage a balanced portfolio of creative risks. The product/service destiny matrix is one way of categorizing the risks by thinking about the ends of the creative process.

O   Creative organizations set much greater store by generating a context where creativity can emerge. Only when this is right will creativity techniques have any effect on the levels of creativity in the organization.

O   The creative organization is one that has balanced the three elements of: culture, leadership style and values; structures and systems; and skills and resources in such a way that creativity is allowed to emerge. There can be no 'standard' here. Each organization needs to adopt a position that is appropriate to its environment.

O   Once creativity blocks have been identified, it becomes much easier to devise a strategy to minimize, eradicate or ignore them.

You will find it useful to consolidate your reading by reviewing the following questions.

About what you have learned

O   What has reading this chapter confirmed in your mind?
O   What useful contradictions has it raised?
O   What further questions does it raise?

About putting the ideas to work

O   How far does your organization change its strategy in line with its environment? Is strategy formulation a formal process that produces a plan which is then implemented in spite of changes externally?

O   How do the key decision-makers in your organization see the various 'legs' of the stool? Which ones are given greater emphasis, for example, is all change delivered through restructuring, or do skills come into the equation?

O   Are all your products and services 'dinosaurs'? What pressures are
there to change some of them into 'dolphins'?

A final thought

It's all very well having lots of 'dolphins' in your product/service destiny
matrix, but ...

> Groups with guitars are on their way out.
> (*Decca Records, turning down The Beatles, 1962*)

5

ORGANIZATIONAL CREATIVITY IN THE PRIVATE SECTOR

Innovate or evaporate.

This chapter presents a number of case studies of organizations which encourage creativity for competitive advantage. It is not possible to generate a general 'recipe' from these cases, as creativity is context-dependent, that is practices that work for one organization would not transfer directly to another.

CREATIVITY IN THE PRIVATE SECTOR

We have seen that in the private sector creativity is an **input** which leads to the **output** of innovation. There can be a tendency to treat creativity like any other resource, such as finance or information, but creativity is far more fragile than other organizational resources and requires special treatment.

CASE STUDIES

3M CORPORATION

The 3M Corporation is synonymous with creativity and innovation. The company thrives on continuous product development and has a catalogue of ground-breaking new product innovations, including the world-famous 'Post-it' repositionable notes. Less obviously, 3M has been successful with innovations in a number of fields, such as non-woven materials, adhesives, abrasives, fluorochemistry, coating (process technology), sealing compounds, electronic microinterconnects and cables.

3M is renowned for its ability to innovate on a continuing basis. The following example illustrates this process in action in the field of a technology application known as 'microreplication'.

Microreplication is the art and science of applying to various materials an engineered surface microstructure or topography with precise dimensions and configurations. Microreplicated surfaces:

O   Retro-reflect light to create materials for highway signs that are three times brighter to the eye than any other reflective signs, improving roadway safety through better visibility.

O   Transport light from one place to another. Remote-source lighting guides motorists along a mountain curve in Italy and replaces fluorescent lighting in the tunnel between Boston's Logan Airport and downtown.

O   Increase interior light levels naturally. A microreplicated lens system on the roof increases ambient daylight in the horticulture exhibit at Minnesota Zoo by two to five times.

O   Collect solar energy for more efficient conversion into heat or electricity.

O   Create brighter images on screens of laptop computers and video camcorders whilst reducing battery drain.

O   Reduce friction drag, speeding up the flow of fluids inside a pipe or the flow of air across an aircraft wing surface.

O   Create new generation abrasives that work faster and better to polish metal parts from golf club heads to hip implants and even plastic eye-wear.

O   Produce mechanical attachment systems that outperform glue for jobs such as mounting abrasive pads to their backings.

About three dozen 3M laboratories are experimenting with microstructured surfaces. They are seeking not only immediate applications but also to gain an understanding of the phenomena that occur when surface structures are changed. For example:

O   Refraction governs the behaviour of a fresnel lens with relatively large surface structures. Divergent light rays are collected and focused to create a bright image on a screen, as with an overhead projector.

O   Make the surface structure smaller and diffraction occurs. Light is no longer focused but is broken into its component colours.

O   Make the surfaces still smaller, and neither refraction nor defraction takes place. Instead, other properties, such as increased adhesion, suddenly occur.

3M scientists routinely build structures down to a micron in size. This involves bringing together six complex enabling technologies:

O   Structure design to produce precise angles and spacing measured in angstroms. The light-reflecting grooves in 3M Scotchlite Diamond Grade Reflective Sheeting work only when they are at exactly the correct angle to each other.

O   Structure generation to create moulds using proprietary ultra precision micromachining techniques.

O   Metrology, or, more commonly, the science of measurement. 3M had to develop technology and tools to measure microstructures before these structures could be made.

O   Replica tooling, since mould making is expensive and complex, and manufacturing requires more than one mould.

O   Materials and composites – to find materials that can be used with the microreplication process.

O   Systems integration, which combines all the others to make the actual microreplicated product.

The manufacturing process is compact, requiring a space no larger than three or four ordinary offices. It is a single-step process. Raw materials arrive at one end and the finished products roll out at the other. Production can be shifted from microsurfaced abrasives to reflective sign materials quickly and easily, which gives 3M great flexibility in responding to changing market needs. There is no run up waste; quality remains consistent from the first inch to the last foot.

One example of an application of microreplication technology is 3M Scotchlite Diamond Grade Reflective Sheeting, which is visually three times brighter than the traditional glass-bead products. It is based on cube-corner or prismatic technology instead of glass beads. Each square inch of Diamond Grade sheeting contains about 7000 unique prismatic cubes. These prismatic cubes improve reflection of light even if a sign is located at a severe angle to oncoming headlights. Highway engineers call this capability 'angularity'. Angularity is important because older drivers need more light to see at night; also because the headlights of trucks and cars are not at the same height. Angularity is a feature of Scotchlite Series 980 Conspicuity Sheeting. This product is used to outline the shape of tractor trailers for highway safety. The film reflects at angles to almost 90° which means that trucks can be seen while making a wide turn or backing out of driveways. Turning and backing up are when most accidents occur.

The story began in the early 1960s; 3M wanted to expand sales of overhead transparencies and supplies by reaching into the important education market.

Microreplication technology began when Roger Appeldorn, an optics scientist, developed an innovative plastic fresnel lens that was light, cheap, easy to make and made possible the first practical overhead projector. Grooves in the plastic and reproducing them were key to this invention. It replaced heavy glass lenses that were very expensive to make. The new machine established the position of 3M as the leading maker of overhead projectors and supplies.

From that base, Roger and others looked into the interesting phenomena that occurred when microscopic changes were made in the surface structure of materials. That led, first, to light pipes and to what today is our most reflective highway sign material, as well as other product areas.

This is an example of how a technology evolves at 3M, from one application to many existing and potential applications throughout the company. (3M has a rule: 'products belong to divisions; technologies belong to the company'.)

The business drivers for the technology may be summarized as follows:

O   It is a growth driver not only for today – the short term – but also of promise for the near-term and long-term future.
O   The technology strengthens 3M's position in existing markets and provides entry into new markets.
O   It demonstrates the fact that 3M's tradition of technical innovation remains active and vital.

And it shows how 3M gets the most out of technology.

The contributory factors that led to Roger Appeldorn's success were:

O   The 3M 15% rule.
O   Bootlegging.
O   Personal qualities of passion and persistence.

> Without all these, micoreplication technology advances
> probably would have ended with the overhead projector.
> (*Henry G Owen, 3M Corporation, USA.*)

Themes illustrated in the case study

O   Structuring 'looseness' into a large organization.
O   Passion and persistence in action.
O   Finding multiple commercial outlets for creative product ideas to ensure that creativity is a valued resource.
O   Use of technology to overcome current barriers to exploiting an idea.

GLAXO-WELLCOME RESEARCH AND DEVELOPMENT

Glaxo-Wellcome is one of the most successful pharmaceutical companies, with a strong commitment to innovative drug discovery. This is articulated through its mission statement, company report, strategic plans and values. It is also evident through the investment in research and development activity (14 per cent of annual sales in 1997), specific targets in terms of the percentage of inventions successfully converted to viable products (of all compounds selected for full development, only one in five survives to the market place) and the number of patents filed per year.

Glaxo-Wellcome has a variety of subcultures and uses a variety of approaches to creativity rather than seeking to slavishly adopt one single 'recipe', that is, one size doesn't necessarily fit all.

Culture, structure and systems

The long timescales and significant initial investments in speculative R&D activity give the R&D organization a long term, high-risk perspective.

Much of the organization is decentralized and its structure was flattened following integration of the two separate companies. In the short term flattening can cause difficulties with morale and creative contribution, yet over the longer term the potential for more rapid and effective communications is likely to facilitate the sharing of ideas.

The following systems are instrumental in supporting creative behaviours:

O   Customer involvement in new product/service design.
O   Appraisal systems.
O   Use of 'venture groups' for exploratory projects.
O   Self-set goals.
O   Continuous learning policy.

In addition to systems that support creativity, resources must be targeted towards the most promising projects. A key 'trick' is killing off unpromising projects without demotivating staff. Project reviews and champions are used to concentrate on commercial potential.

Skills and resources

The following methods are used to develop organizational creativity:

O   Training and development in creative problem-solving techniques.
O   Out-of-role 'cross-functional' moves of staff.
O   Self-study/open learning.
O   Attendance at 'expert' seminars.
O   Scanning specialist journals.
O   Coaching.

Individual perspectives on creativity

Keith Truman, Manager, Inhalation Product Development   The manager's role in this unit encompasses both leadership and project management, requiring a clear understanding of the differences in role and the ability to adopt a flexible approach. During 1995/6 the organization of Inhalation Product Development changed so that there is much more mixing between scientific disciplines, that is, analytical chemists and formulation scientists.

As a result of this mixing Keith has developed his link role (boundary crosser) to ensure adequate standards and partnership arrangements guarantee a high-quality approach to external bodies such as the Food and Drug Administration.

Much work has been done to gain a shared understanding of the group's purpose, operating principles and five- and 10-year vision, using processes that involved **everyone** in the department. A number of clear objectives have emerged, in terms of:

O   Science.
O   Partnerships.
O   Skills and attributes.
O   Working environment (hard and soft).

In each case there are action-focused groups working on making each of these happen.

Defining creativity   Creativity is the ability to identify technology that gives us a leading edge over our competitors. Creativity is very important in producing inhalation devices that outperform the competition in terms of:

O   Patient acceptability.
O   How reproducible the device is.
O   How effective the device is.
O   How expensive it is.
O   How many added value features can be incorporated from a marketing point of view.

A specific example where creativity has been important was a dry powder delivery system which was designed within the Inhalation group. The device is regarded as a class leader, having won several awards.

The following factors were felt to contribute to creativity within Inhalation Product Development:

O   **Environment**
        Externally, a big pressure is the competition which is intense and continuous. Intellectual property and patent information is fed in weekly and there are planned improvements to improve the flow of this information.
        Internally, leadership ethos is very important – managers being visible, 'walking the job', encouraging new ideas, making sure that staff are aware of opportunities. There is a greater emphasis on creating a context for creativity, where people feel safe to experiment within a broad direction. There is still some way to go in terms of arranging the geography for close contact between groups. This is an his-

torical result of the previous structure which arranged groups by functional scientific disciplines.

○ **Behaviour**
The role of the creative manager is to facilitate decision-making by teams by operating an 'upturned pyramid'. Some staff may still prefer a traditional hierarchy. In particular, it takes time for people to believe that their ideas will be valued. 'Walking the job' is a regular occurrence. The philosophy behind this is discussion of problems, provision of resources and idea generation rather than control of work. Inevitably, some areas are further ahead than others – not all leaders walk the job, their staff feel that their manager is too remote. Strong leadership is required in terms of direction setting (**ends**), but there is choice over **means**. News groups are being discussed as a means of recording learning for idea transfer and adaptation.

○ **Capabilities**
All of our people have the ability – 'what we need to do is to unlock the key'. Training courses have some value but creativity is released over a longer timescale, via a stimulating environment, opportunity, contributions being recognized, people feeling valued, and adequate rewards. In a high-technology environment intellectual skills are a **given** – the challenge is to get people to use their intellect. Trying to strike a balance between individual and team recognition is a challenge – and the ability to learn from mistakes is very important. The move towards a learning organization is a contribution towards this. Training in team work is currently practised outside the working teams – this could be extended to in-tact teams.

> To use tools like Kepner Tregoe, 'you must be in the mood' – tools are less important than the way in which they are used (environment, culture).

Bill Brickell, Head of Chemical Analysis Department   The Chemical Analysis Department is part of the Chemical Development Division, with responsibility for analytical support to new chemical processes *en route* to their commercial supply. The department consists of 55 people, from school leavers to PhD scientists, and has a very flat structure. Recently (at the time of my research) people from the Beckenham, Dartford, Research and Pharmacy areas had been merged. Since the study there has been further restructuring. The mixing of disciplines providing a high potential for creativity through difference.

Creativity within the department is connected with totally original thought combined with a strong risk-taking element. Because creative ideas are not tried and tested individuals need a lot of assertiveness/confidence.

The following factors were felt to contribute to creativity within the department:

○ **Environment**
The Stevenage site provides lots of opportunities for bouncing ideas off others due to the conscious design of the building. The building was designed to include a number of 'nodes' which signify the meeting points between various scientific disciplines – these spaces are calm, controlled, functionally efficient and quiet and include a number of specially commissioned works of art to maintain an ethos of 'quiet quality'. The premises are open 24 hours a day, seven days a week, to enable people to work when they are most energized to be creative. The information environment is important. A number of intranet sites are available for people to drop in ideas – these sites are not moderated and are left for people to develop their own approach. There are a number of 'robust' conversations on the Web sites and these are encouraged. Disagreements and conflict are tolerated since these lead to better ideas in the long run. Several technique groups concentrate on pushing specialist knowledge by scanning the external environment. Collaborations with academia and industrial areas are also used.

○ **Behaviours**
A measure of successful leadership is the recruitment of individuals who will challenge leadership and the system rather than people with whom we will be comfortable. A culture of creativity emerges since individuals see themselves as being expected to challenge and not accept what they are asked to do without question. This is just as creative as having an 'off the wall' idea. Team meetings use a rotating Chair system, which includes the Secretary, they run whether the head is present or not. Creativity is part of every role specification against which individuals are assessed. There is a balance to be struck between individual and team reward for creative behaviour. The use of a 'dual ladder' career system (technical and managerial) is helpful to give greater choice over careers. There are numerous improvement initiatives which provide opportunities for people to take a blank sheet of paper and contribute at a different level to their existing job. In this sense, integration of the two companies has provided a number of opportunities for creative management.

> We have developed the understanding that you expect
> your own ideas to be challenged.

○ **Capabilities**
Creativity is **hired in** by selecting people who challenge the system.

An active policy of secondment is used, both to challenge what goes on and to learn from it. This operates on a local and international level. Secondments vary in length from a week to six months and encouragement is given to take six months. The Division uses a portfolio of creative thinking tools in order to provide a wider choice – the main ones in use are 'sticky walls', Kepner Tregoe and brainstorming.

O   **Beliefs about creativity**
'Creative people provide the "germ" (seed) of new ways of working' – the creative person can plant the seed within the shaper and completer–finisher. A bit like throwing bananas.

> We need more banana throwers. We also need people who
> can pick the bananas up and turn them into policy and
> action.

Creative people stimulate creativity in naturally uncreative individuals (people who are reticent about offering their own ideas). The creative person stretches someone's thinking like an elastic band and the other person has to adjust their thinking in order to reduce this stretching.

Themes illustrated in the case study
O   Diversity in action – walking the talk about encouraging difference.
O   Use of the built environment as an enabler of creativity.
O   Creative leadership – thinking and acting outside the box.
O   The need for initiators and creativity champions to ensure that ideas are converted into successful innovations.

HEWLETT PACKARD

Hewlett Packard does not single out creativity as a separate issue, but it is woven into the fabric of the organization and is expected; creativity is valued highly as integral to their people and processes. The company was founded in 1939 by Bill Hewlett and Dave Packard, two Stanford engineers who combined their product ideas and unique management style to form a working partnership. Their first product was an improved audio oscillator used to test sound equipment. The company stayed in the market for testing and measuring equipment until the 1970s when it created the hand-held calculator market. More recently, Hewlett Packard has moved into computers, medical devices, electronic testing equipment and instrumentation.

Hewlett Packard operates from a fundamental set of principles which have remained largely unchanged over the years. These were moulded into 'the HP way' in 1957 and cover values, corporate objectives, strategies and practices. Aspects of the HP way are reproduced at the end of this case study.

> The HP way, when you really come down to it, is respecting
> the integrity of the individual.
> (*Bill Hewlett 1987*)

Today, the traditional HP practices such as 'management by wandering around', 'management by objectives' and the 'open door policy' are supported by others such as a Ten-Step Business Planning Process, Total Quality Control and Hoshin Kanri.

More specifically, creativity has been important to Hewlett Packard in the development of the computer printer business. This has grown from a very small percentage to a market share of almost 70 per cent (1997 figures) in less than 10 years.

THE HP WAY
ORGANIZATIONAL VALUES

We have trust and respect for individuals

We approach each situation with the belief that people want to do a good job and will do so, given the proper tools and support. We attract highly capable, diverse, innovative people and recognize their efforts and contributions to the company. HP people contribute enthusiastically and share in the success that they make possible.

We focus on a high level of achievement and contribution

Our customers expect HP products and services to be of the highest quality and to provide lasting value. To achieve this, all HP people – but especially managers – must be leaders who generate enthusiasm and respond with extra effort to meet customer needs. Techniques and management practices which are effective today may be outdated in the future. For us to remain at the forefront in all our activities people should always be looking for new and better ways to do their work.

We conduct our business with uncompromising integrity

We expect HP people to be open and honest in their

dealings to earn the trust and loyalty of others. People at every level are expected to adhere to the highest standards of business ethics and must understand that anything else is totally unacceptable. As a practical matter, ethical conduct cannot be assured by written HP policies and codes; it must be an integral part of the organization, a deeply ingrained tradition that is passed from one generation of employees to another.

We achieve our common objectives through teamwork

We recognize that it is only through effective co-operation within and among organizations that we can achieve our goals. Our commitment is to work as a world-wide team to fulfil the expectations of our customers, shareholders and others who depend on us. The benefits and obligations of doing business are shared among all HP people.

We encourage flexibility and innovation

We create an inclusive work environment which supports the diversity of our people and stimulates innovation. We strive for overall objectives which are clearly stated and agreed upon, and allow people flexibility in working towards goals in ways that they help determine are best for the organization. HP people should personally accept responsibility and be encouraged to upgrade their skills and capabilities through ongoing training and development. This is especially important in a technical business where the rate of progress is rapid and where people are expected to adapt to change.

Corporate objectives

Profit

To achieve sufficient profit to finance our company growth and to provide the resources we need to achieve our other corporate objectives.

Customers

To provide products and services of the highest quality and

the greatest possible value to our customers, thereby gaining and holding their respect and loyalty.

Fields of interest

To participate in those fields of interest that build upon our technology and customer base, that offer opportunities for continued growth, and that enable us to make a needed and profitable contribution.

Growth

To let our growth be limited only by our profits and our ability to produce innovative products that satisfy real customer needs.

Our people

To help HP people share in the company's success which they make possible; to provide employment security based on performance; to ensure them a safe and pleasant work environment; to recognize their individual achievements; to value their diversity; and to help them gain a sense of satisfaction and accomplishment from their work.

Management

To foster initiative and creativity by allowing the individual great freedom of action in attaining well defined corporate objectives.

Citizenship

To honour our obligations to society by being an economic, intellectual and social asset to each nation and each community in which we operate.

(Ian Ryder, Hewlett Packard UK)

Themes illustrated in the case study

O   The importance of values in driving people forward with a shared purpose.

O   Creation of a strong culture that still permits 'looseness' in terms of being able to move into new markets.

NAVICO

Navico Navigation and Communication Systems is a well-established manufacturer of quality marine electronic products, such as automatic pilots, tiller and wheel pilots, navigational instruments and devices and a variety of radio models, including a hand-held waterproof radio. Products have a short life-cycle and customers are constantly seeking increasingly sophisticated new features. As a result, the company is constantly innovating, and places great emphasis on research and development. By the end of 1998 all products in the Navico range will be less than three years old. Since 1993 the number of full-time staff has grown from 65 to 109.

Here, we look at the creative transformation of the company towards a modern organization with a high degree of flexibility and responsiveness to continuous change.

The business need for change

Almost a decade ago, Navico moved from assembly line manufacturing to cellular manufacturing. At the same time, it introduced a more flexible approach to staffing production. A number of reasons prompted these changes. Key among these were:

Nature of the market Navico's market is seasonal. For example, sounders or paddle wheels need to be fitted into the bottom of the boat. The market tends to peak in March and April and is exhausted by Easter, once boats are in the water. On the other hand, auto pilots are mainly cockpit-fitted instruments, and can be fitted while the boat is afloat. Their market, therefore, continues until the end of June. After this most people are just interested in sailing rather than purchasing new kit, so the market tails off. Traditionally, Navico used the slack end of the year to build stock in order to cover the peak burst of selling in the spring and early summer months. The problem was that this tied up capital and resources for a substantial period of the year, during which little profit was made. The goal was, therefore, to reshape the company culture and restructure production, to focus on the sales curve, so the company could build in line with the peaks.

Work organization Labour was being used ineffectively. The factory had also reached its capacity with the technology available at the time. Furthermore, the beginning of the recession meant that the company had more labour than the market now warranted. The market was also changing its philosophy, demanding shorter and shorter response times, and limiting its forecasting. As a result, the company made a third of its workforce redundant. The concept of changing company culture was already in hand, and the redundancies became a turning point to concentrate attention on the need for multi-skilling and greater efficiency. Everyone recognized that this was fundamental to survival.

Moving to cellular manufacturing

Navico has moved from an assembly line system to one based on a cellular structure, with cell leaders replacing line managers.

Although not directly involved in taking the decision to move to cellular manufacturing, all the staff were involved in the implementation stage in 1990. The factory was shut for a few days. All the staff took part in off-site discussions in a hotel, where the proposed changes were presented to them and they were given an opportunity to express their views. It was made clear that the survival of the company depended on these changes being made.

There are, on average, between four and six members in a cell, with the largest having 11 members. Cells operate more as family units, with the role of the cell leader being to monitor rather than police. Members float between cells, whereas cell leaders remain in post and have ultimate ownership of the products and processes within their particular unit.

Selecting cell leaders   Before cellular manufacturing was introduced supervisors tended to be appointed using the traditional approach of selecting somebody who was good at their job. Cellular team leadership requires particular strengths in interpersonal skills rather than technical expertise; people who could grow with the concept, and who possessed good motivational skills. Defining and using these criteria was crucial in ensuring that cell leaders had the right abilities.

Changing the company structure

Moving from a functional structure   In 1991, Navico had a highly functional production structure. Additional functions, such as service, tended to be added on when a need was recognized, and reported to the functional manager considered most appropriate.

When Mike Bowerman joined the company, he separated the production engineering function, which was formerly under the auspices of the test manager. Components progressing was introduced so that parts were managed through a cycle. Surface mount technology was introduced and the company became very product-focused. The introduction of this new technology, which replaced manual mounting of components, had a drastic effect on the number of employees. Previously 20 people could build 100 radios a week; now five people can produce between 150 and 200 radios a week.

Flexing the workforce   The aim was to structure the workforce to meet the peaks in demand. This took place in two stages. The original approach was to reduce the level of year-round core staff, and the question was how to build during the periods of peak demand. The solution was to take on a number of staff for a six-month period. These workers were given identical training to the core staff. Instead of being allowed to take holidays, however, they were given an 8 per cent bonus at the end of their employment – equivalent to payment in lieu of holidays. Since a number of those available to work this way had commitments (such as children at school) they were also allowed to work shorter shifts, from 09.30 to 14.30. The use of creativity in flexing the workforce ensured that Navico retained good people and kept motivation alive.

At the end of the six-month contract, the company gave a commitment to contact these temporary workers again in October. Most chose to come back. About 25 contract workers were taken on in this way, which, at one point, actually represented more than half the workforce.

Lessons were learned from the changes, however. Not least, the first time Navico tried this experiment, it found that it lacked the supervisory resource to train and manage this rapid influx of assembly workers. This meant that things began to get out of control and the company had to use the annual shutdown period to bring routines and planning back in line.

Absorbing a flexible workforce   As the company has grown, it has absorbed the contract workers into the full-time staff, the last short-term contract being offered two years ago. Apart from the cell restructuring, improvements in efficiency mean that Navico now copes with market peaks using the same level of full-time staff. A key contributory factor was the increase of business in a more stable market, which has meant that the level of core staff can now remain quite high all year round.

The increase in demand for navigation parts in March and April is now dealt with by additional overtime. In effect, improved efficiency and the greater use of subcontractors has enabled the company to bring the number of low-season staff closer to that of the high season, maintaining a higher core staff level. The advantage is that resources can be devoted to training the core staff, rather than being diverted to induction for temporary workers.

Culture change – continuous improvement   At Navico a culture of continuous improvement is embedded at the highest levels and has spread throughout the rest of the organization. Mike Bowerman takes the view that individuals work within their own 'bubble', which represents their personal sphere of influence. Empowerment is seen in terms of empowering individuals within their personal spheres of influence.

Quality circles   Individual cell members express their views at regular quality circle meetings, held once a month, and cells are expected to deal with their own problems as part of the continuous improvement philosophy. Two staff members have a role of co-ordinating continuous improvement within the cells. In one instance, the involvement of the quality co-ordinators resulted in a problem being solved within three days, leading to a sudden improvement in that cell's achievement level.

Team training   A strong emphasis is placed on training, backed up by financial investment. The assembly manager points out that multi-skilling process has to be controlled, or quality will suffer dramatically. This means achieving a balance between moving people between cells, to stop them getting stale when they want a change, and not moving them too quickly, thus destroying stability.

Navico takes the view that, if a system is not uniform, multi-skilling is difficult to achieve. Techniques are the same throughout the factory, even if different cells use different processes in producing a part. The multi-skilling element lies in the product knowledge and the ability to transfer skills to other products.

Information systems

Although information technology has enabled scheduling systems to be computerized to a high degree, the shortcomings of over-reliance on the information this generates have been clearly recognized. Navico found that with constant changes to production requirements, owing to the nature of the business, and a large number of lines to progress, production schedules were never fully worked through without change. Flexibility has, therefore, been built into the system, by use of a mixture of computer-generated information and a manual system of writing the daily and weekly production requirements for each cell on a board which can easily be amended. Production targets are written on the boards. It is up to each cell to decide how to achieve them.

Staff rewards

The company pays the highest wage rates in the area for shopfloor work and prides itself on how staff are rewarded. This year the training review has been formalized, with the workforce being graded in terms of dexterity, which leads to workmanship and time standards. This means that the pay structure can reward those who deserve a higher hourly rate.

The company has introduced a profit-sharing scheme, under which 10 per cent of pre-tax profit goes into a pool. The first £10,000 is shared equally between all members of staff, with the exception of one or two senior staff who are not in the scheme. It is then paid pro-rata across the shopfloor. The scheme rewards the performance of the company as a whole and is based on the view that if the company makes a profit everyone can share in it. Navico believes that this approach provides a more sustained motivation than bonuses, which are quickly forgotten once spent. It is also a fairer approach than rewarding team performance, given that cell membership is fluid, with the possibility of some people joining or leaving a particular team during any one period.

Lessons learned

The change process was assisted by the following:

○   A strong external driver for change which was made visible to all the workforce.

○   A combination of a good theorist (the R&D engineer had a passion for learning about how businesses made these sorts of changes) with someone who had practical experience of making change happen by adapting 'theories' into the particular context.

○   Visiting other companies to discover how they had implemented these changes, with the specific intention of discovering what does work and what does not. This intelligence could then be adapted to Navico ('creative swiping').

○   The ability to be brave and speak your mind. Being prepared to be criticized and admit mistakes at the highest level.

○   The importance of giving individuals the chance to make mistakes. If somebody is not allowed this freedom, they will be unwilling to work again in a particular cell where they may have made an error.

○   The key to success is not believing that you have ever reached the finishing line. There is always one more thing that you can do to take the change forward.

(Mike Bowerman, Navico.)

Themes illustrated in the case study

○   The need to undertake structural and cultural change simultaneously.

○   The need to mobilize dissatisfaction with the way things are.

○   The need to identify obstacles to progress and make these priority issues for change.

○   Redesigning the organization from a blank sheet to allow radical change.

○   Ensuring that reward systems synchronize with desired goals and performances.

PSION COMPUTERS PLC

The principal business role of Psion is to design, manufacture and supply products that serve customer needs for portable computing and data communications. The company aims to address volume international markets for individual, professional and business needs. Psion's key values are quality, innovation, self-belief and a 'can-do' attitude. Psion has consistently demonstrated a commitment to creativity in its new product development process.

The company has a group structure, divided between product companies and distribution companies, depicted in Figure 5.1.

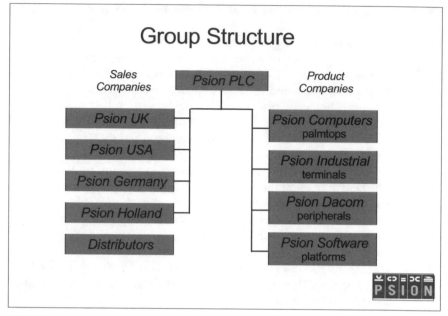

FIGURE 5.1   Psion structure.

Psion's results are shown in Chapter 2.

The innovation process

Psion regards innovation as doing something that someone else has not done before. This includes having new ideas (creativity) **and** implementing them (innovation). It requires conception plus invention plus exploitation. However, it does not imply research, that is one does not have to create a technology to be innovative, although research is one way which is beyond the reach of most companies. Innovation often involves harnessing technology rather than creating it to produce a different and beneficial result.

Psion sees innovation as providing the basis for survival and sustained competitive advantage, especially through two of the four marketing Ps:

O   **Product** differentiation through product innovation leading to higher gross margins.
O   **Price** leadership through manufacturing process innovation.

In addition, necessity is the mother of invention. Psion has utilized this approach on a number of occasions, for example Huffman compression arose from the problem of bursting the ROM budget.

How Psion arranges innovation

The company believes that the requirements for innovation are:

O   Good people.
O   The right culture and values.
O   A management style that lets things happen.

Good people are:

O   Driven and energized 'creatives.' These people are both talented
         and hardworking. They possess analytical and deep thinking capa-
         bilities and the ability to reflect. They are also intuitive.
O   People who are passionate about what they do.
O   People who develop themselves – personal mastery as Senge (1990)
         would describe it.
O   Free thinkers.

The right culture involves:

O   Different personality types – bio-diversity.
O   Tolerance of uncertainty.
O   Encouraging risk-taking.
O   Natural authority rather than positional authority   intellectually
         tough and creative.
O   A desire to do things – an ambitious quality – 'insanely great', a
         desire to delight the customer rather than just meet expectations.
O   Passion is an accepted cultural norm.

A management style that lets things happen:

O   Not too much command and control – avoiding bureaucracy, loose
         ambiguous structures, lots of dotted lines, getting people to ques-
         tion the status quo, need to tolerate and even encourage the right
         kind of confrontational behaviour; paradoxically, a bit of discipline
         sometimes helps.
O   A tendency to leadership rather than management – stretch goals,
         risk-taking, trust, giving people their head, leading by example –
         creative leaders.
O   Gets the different specialists to work together on problems.

Along with the positive features, there are some difficulties, for example:

O   The need to kill unpromising projects.
O   Too much innovation can lead to an unbalanced view.
O   The tension between innovation and planning – innovation, almost
         by definition, cannot be planned for.
O   Chaos, confusion and informality are the seedbeds of creativity.
O   Some things just 'emerge' which upsets planning.
O   Balancing innovation and discipline.

Examples of Psion product innovations

O   Games (Flight simulator on a Sinclair ZX81; 3D chess on the Sinclair QL; memory saving techniques).

O   Organiser (the whole concept; Lotus 1-2-3-compatible spreadsheet on a two-line organizer).

O   Series 3 hardware (step-up switching allowed the use of two AA batteries rather than a nine-volt PP3; serial protocol for a two-wire serial interface).

O   Series 3 software (a pre-emptive multi-tasking operating system on a handheld computer; elegant memory management; a fully functioning word processor on a palmtop; Huffman compression – after bursting the ROM budget).

Interestingly, the company is also willing to acknowledge that it has had a number of innovations that did not quite work, and it learned from them:

O   The TRS80-based development system that switched the memory from a ZX81.

O   Gull-wing SSD drive doors on the MC.

O   Pager on the Organiser.

Structural considerations

The strategy that Psion considers to be a consistent winner is the one that integrates marketing and technology. This must be coupled with a recognition of customer demand for successful innovation. Although R&D and Marketing depend on each other for new product innovations, there are frequent misunderstandings and conflicts. A new product development study of 56 firms and 289 new product development projects found:

O   Forty-one per cent of firms had harmony between R&D and Marketing with only 13 per cent new product development failure.

O   Twenty-one per cent of firms had mild disharmony between R&D and Marketing with a 23 per cent new product development failure.

O   Thirty-nine per cent of firms had severe disharmony between R&D and Marketing with a 68 per cent new product development failure.

Psion sees this as an argument to co-locate R&D and Marketing. Having said this, the company has functioned without a product marketing department for most of its history, having had 'lay' marketing input from engineers and top management.

In terms of design, Psion believes that this should be left to engineers. Design involves the translation of requirements (**benefits**) into a product specification (**features**). Marketing speaks the language of benefits and engineering speaks the language of features. Good engineers should learn the language of benefits and translate it into features which add the desired value.

Contrary to conventional wisdom, Psion does not see the marketing department as having sole responsibility for customer input and market estimation. This is because marketing people may emphasize less risky new products that are minor improvements in existing products and product managers tend to produce incremental range extensions to maintain existing lines rather than introduce new business opportunities.

(*Charles Davis, Development Director, Psion Computers plc*).

Themes illustrated in the case study

O Giving tangible example to the need for tolerance of failure.

O Integration of functions that need to communicate, and the tolerance of conflict.

O Using diversity to produce ideas.

O The need for ambiguity tolerance and opportunity spotting (seeing the glass half-full rather than half-empty).

O Passion and persistence in action.

REFLECTIONS AND SUMMARY

The 'recipes' for creativity are different in each organization, reflecting different sizes, market conditions, internal cultures etc., yet some recurring themes emerge, reinforcing the various models presented in earlier chapters. These may be summarized as follows:

O The role of the creative leader is to find the **maniacs with a mission**, provide them with the resources to create, to inspire and support them and then get out of their way.

O Respecting and modelling the integrity of individuals is key to encouraging creativity. Drastic surgery to organizations, such as re-engineering and flatter structures, can be disruptive to creativity in the short term, but if handled sensitively, the organization can recover more quickly. In the longer term, leaner and flatter structures can assist creativity if coupled with suitable means of informal communication.

O Cultural myths should be managed in ways that reinforce the need for creativity. This is likely to include the encouragement of a 'shadow side' of the organization.

O The built environment can be a helpful influence to encouraging creativity.

O Informal communications are the main arena where creativity is released.

O The over-zealous application of organizational systems can hinder creativity.

○   A limited number of creative thinking techniques were in use. This required individuals and groups to force-fit the available techniques to the problems/opportunities under consideration. A larger menu of techniques from which to draw, and an understanding of which techniques suit particular types of problem/opportunity is essential to creativity.

You will find it useful to consolidate your reading by reviewing the following questions.

About what you have learned

○   What has reading this chapter confirmed in your mind?
○   What useful contradictions has it raised?

About creatively swiping the ideas

○   What ideas from the case studies are most easily adapted to suit the context of your own organization?
○   What organizations do you know that you could research in order to benchmark your own?
○   How can you utilize some of the ideas in this chapter to influence the direction of your organization so that it becomes more successful?

A final thought

> If you want to succeed, double your failure rate.
> (*Thomas Watson*)

6

ORGANIZATIONAL CREATIVITY IN THE PUBLIC SECTOR

❖

This chapter describes a number of case studies of creativity within the public sector, and outlines the transferable lessons from these cases. There are certain differences between the public and private sectors. These may be seen as problems or opportunities, depending on the viewpoint taken. The public sector organizations mentioned here have seen the differences positively and managed to make progress in the face of apparent blockages where others have remained on the starting grid.

THE CONTEXT FOR CREATIVITY IN THE PUBLIC SECTOR

Differences between the public and private sectors that affect creativity may be summarized as follows:

MULTIPLE ACCOUNTABILITIES

Too many stakeholders thicken the broth.

One of the key differences between public and private sector organizations is the diversity of stakeholders that exert an influence on public sector bodies. 'Stakeholder consciousness' may have both positive and negative effects.

On the negative side, the multiplicity and potentially conflicting demands from these groups can act as a restriction on freedom of action. In many cases there is a reduction of creative activity. In other cases, stakeholder consciousness becomes a crippling disease whereby, despite positive efforts to please all stakeholders, the outcome is one of huge inefficiency and the design of hybrid services which do not meet the needs of any single stakeholder group. Put simply:

A camel is a horse designed by a committee.

A more positive viewpoint suggests that the confusion created by multiple stakeholders results in no one group having a strong influence on the organization. This, in turn, allows a good deal of room in the organization for 'pockets of creativity' in which local bespoke solutions are devised to meet needs effectively. The organization needs to have a central core that is tolerant of diversity to function in this fashion.

Organizations that have successfully incorporated creativity into a public sector setting have, in the main, adopted the second, positive viewpoint.

UNLIMITED DEMAND

Another consequence of operating in the public sector is the unlimited demand for the services offered. For example, despite specialisms within the health profession, the end user of services is relatively unaware of this aspect of healthcare and sees a hospital as a place where illness is cured, whatever this means in practice.

INTANGIBILITY

Unlike organizations that produce tangible products, many public service organizations deliver services which are nebulous and therefore harder to assess in terms of their innovative quality. Key measures of service innovation are: perceived quality by the target customer group, responsiveness, reliability and value. In such circumstances, it becomes important to assess changes in service innovation as a measure of performance. Market research is also hampered, since service 'prototypes' are less tangible.

THE 'LONG TERMISM' ASSET

Paradoxically, public service organizations have the advantage of being able to take a longer term view than many private enterprises. Although many public sector managers tend to take the 'fashionable' view that it is harder to be creative in the public sector, the ability to plan in the longer term is a very important asset. In some cases this is affected by political changes, yet even these are predictable in terms of timing and likely effects of change.

CASE STUDIES

POST OFFICE COUNTERS LTD

Since the separation of the various business units of the Post Office, there have been different approaches to creativity, consistent with the needs of the different units. For example, Royal Mail went down the 'process' driven route, whereas Post Office Counters looked at a cultural change approach, most recently supported by the European Foundation for Quality Management framework.

Post Office Counters is divided into seven customer-focused regional business units supported by a Head Office and two commercial business centres. The review focused on the South Wales and South West region.

Arenas for creativity

Post Office Counters Ltd (POCL) encourages creativity at two levels – **personal** and **systems**.

Personal   One of the crucial areas recognized by POCL in becoming a customer-focused organization was the role of **leadership** (not management). The leadership commitment emphasizes key **behaviours** – such as innovation and enthusiasm – of effective leaders and measures these in a meaningful way. It applies across the organization. All managers collect leadership commitment **feedback** from their teams, and produce an **action plan** addressing the top three areas for improvement **identified by their team**. An example of the format for collecting this information is shown in Table 6.1.

By introducing the process, POCL moved away from an earlier version which described leadership in short phrases, such as 'recognition', 'two-way communication' etc., towards more meaningful descriptions of what leadership is and can be. The company has also consistently measured these elements so that trends may be identified. This allows the organization to do several things:

O   To transfer best practices within regions and across the various businesses.

O   To identify areas for improvement and creatively 'swipe' (acquire and adapt) approaches practised elsewhere.

O   To involve and encourage the contribution of team members in improvements to the way the team itself, and the organization is managed.

An example of the format used for the personal action plan is shown in Table 6.2.

The emphasis on leadership has an important effect on team performance. POCL uses a process called 'Team Route to Excellence' to help teams to focus on performance improvement. This technique is powerful in administration teams as it reinforces the internal customer concept. The process involves answering six questions:

TABLE 6.1   Leadership commitment

Value	Behaviour
Customer focus	Focusing on, understanding and satisfying customer needs
Integrity	Communicating and dealing with others with complete trust, honesty and fairness
Teamwork	Maximizing the contributions individuals can make to the team through effective communications co-operation and listening to, and supporting, one another
Respect	Setting a strong personal example of respect and recognition and actively co-operating with others
Innovation	Showing enterprise and welcoming change by taking sensible risks and learning from mistakes
Enthusiasm	Demonstrating a positive spirit and enthusiasm for the mission and driving towards achieving business goals
Professionalism	Working efficiently to get it right first time, managing by fact and eliminating personal prejudice
Continuous improvement	Concentrate on finding solutions rather than simply stating problems, and identifying and acting on improvement opportunities

TABLE 6.2   Personal action plan

Name

In order to demonstrate visibly my personal commitment to excellence, I will personally change my behaviour by:

Action	How action will be measured
Embracing change (innovation) Discuss with the team any planned changes to working practices within the centre that may have an effect on individuals within the stock team	Discussions minuted and agreed
Identifying ways to improve (continuous improvement) in line with business objectives, any regional initiatives to improve service levels will be discussed with the team and any that are agreed by the team will be introduced	Discussions minuted and agreed. Any improvements to be monitored and results to be fed-back to the team at monthly meetings

TABLE 6.2   *concluded*

Action	How action will be measured
Development (teamwork) Team members to be coached through new tasks as the need arises	Check back with the individual to ensure coaching delivered the necessary skills
Discretion (integrity) Any personal information disclosed to the line manager will be kept in confidence unless permission is given by the individual concerned	Check understanding with individuals at all times to ensure compliance
Signed	
Date	
To be updated (month/year)	

- ○   Who are our customers?
- ○   What are our outputs?
- ○   What standards do our customers expect of us?
- ○   How well are we performing?
- ○   What do we need to do to improve?
- ○   How do we affect business goals and targets?

An example of the format used for the Team Route To Excellence is shown in Table 6.3

This is an effective tool for teams to trial improvements to processes and to measure the effectiveness of those improvements. Successful improvement activities can then be shared with counterparts in other business units.

Systems   A variety of tools and techniques to enable these processes is provided, leading to original ideas and involvement. These link into a quality improvement database where individuals log what they are doing. Activities can be tracked and good practices transferred both through a formal process driven by information technology and through informal processes, such as chance corridor meetings, internal network meetings etc. There is a danger of making such systems too bureaucratic since this is felt to hinder individual flair, but in contrast, some bureaucracy is needed in order to ensure that ideas can flow round the organization in an efficient manner.

TABLE 6.3   Team route to excellence

1. Team purpose		Outputs	Link to regional top objectives
2. Team Outputs	3. Customers	4. Measures of performance for customers	5. Agreed performance/ satisfaction targets	6. Performance against targets	7. Quality improvement activity	8. Team objectives

This team contributes to

Critical process (Business Processes)

Team members:

Post Office Counters Ltd

> The registration and sharing of quality improvements can be perceived as a chore rather than a means of sharing and building on individual and team success.

> The more you try to collect information on ideas and improvements, the more it switches people off. When you are trying to embed a culture of 'continuous improvement' as the normal way of working, forcing people to record all their improvement activities sends out a signal that improvement is anything but 'Business As Usual'.

For this reason, whilst staff are still encouraged to log their improvements, POCL is currently exploring its ability to capture effective (i.e. measurable) improvements through existing but less obtrusive means.

There is also a formal system called IDEAS (Ideas Delivering Excellence And Success). This is a vastly improved 'suggestions' scheme, which encourages people to trial things in low-risk ways. The scheme formalizes the process of testing and implementing staff ideas and ensures that line managers effectively evaluate suggestions raised by their staff. A recent review has meant a move away from the recording of locally implemented IDEAS, to a central collation of IDEAS with national impact. This is another example of an improvement initiative evolving into 'business as usual'.

The role of training and development

Training and development is used to reinforce the culture in the following ways:

O   At the induction stage, there is intensive effort to transmit the tools and techniques required and provide a common language for continuous improvement.

O   A number of events concerning leadership are organized, which seek to provide continuous challenge. These include events for middle managers where they are encouraged to use a range of tools and techniques to create innovative solutions to common management/leadership problems. In addition, events are run mixing people from the various POCL businesses to address key strategic issues involving the use of creative approaches such as scenario 'Blue Sky' planning. These events are specifically designed to encourage 'out of the box' thinking and to equip managers to apply these approaches back in the workplace.

Where does creativity contribute to business performance?

Examples of creativity making a difference include:

O   Self-managed teams – the effect of de-layering has required people to work more autonomously. The need for individuals to make more local decisions has been received differently by different individuals. Various supports have been provided to help people overcome the fear of having more discretion. In some cases, individuals moved between teams to meet their personal needs. The main outcomes have been: teams taking ownership and responsibility for implementing improvements through an increased understanding of where they are going; an increased willingness to loan staff across teams; increased effectiveness and efficiency from 'average' teams, where they have been able to make up for individual weaknesses due to the lack of a 'star' performer.

O   In order to draw the attention of administrative teams to their role in growing sales a creative approach was adopted. This involves individual teams competing in the 'Handicap Stakes', using the analogy of a horse race. Teams must overcome hurdles to pass the finishing line and win a prize.

O   Cross-functional steering groups are regularly used to tackle the issues that do not fall into neat functional headings. These groups have flexible membership (based on skills required) and the authority to make decisions on problems they are dealing with. One example is aligning the work of personnel and training to directly support the delivery of business objectives through the retail network.

How is progress monitored?

Measuring the cultural components of a business, such as innovation and creativity, is difficult. The implementation of a measurement system (when one is required) must not kill the creativity it is there to support!

POCL tracks its normal business performance through Key Performance Indicators (KPIs) which are embedded in national and regional business plans. KPI teams are used to convert plans into action. This has resulted in numerous incremental improvements, some of which have been implemented locally, others nationally.

At regional level the emphasis is on incremental change within the businesses' strategies and policies. There is scope for radical change, but this tends to be concentrated at business level. Within POCL practices should be consistent across the country.

Radical changes – such as the implementation of Europe's largest information technology project – are generally limited to three or four in any given planning period in order to ensure a clear focus and commitment to achievement.

Rewards and recognition

There is a formal recognition policy and the aim is to offer recognition that is meaningful to the recipient (e.g. not by offering a bottle of whisky to a teetotaller). Over time, POCL has learned that people do not value T-shirts and mugs and have moved away from these symbolic rewards, towards recognition based on the contribution that the individual has made.

The company has dispensed with the improvements budget and now considers ideas to be part of 'business as usual'.

Summary

The factors considered by POCL to enhance creativity are:

O   Company commitment from the very top.
O   Clearly directed long-term vision.
O   Effective two-way communication.
O   Empowering staff to take personal responsibility.
O   Use of a variety of improvement methods/initiatives.

(Paul Maisey, Head of Management Process, South Wales & South West Region; Andrea Harwood, Management Process Manager, South Wales & South West Region; Jane Leach, Retail Quality Manager, South Wales & South West Region; David Pilkington, IDEAs Co-ordinator, South Wales & South West Region)

THE COLLEGE OF GUIDANCE STUDIES

Strategic planning has traditionally been considered to be a linear process involving the analysis of the pressures facing an organization, consideration of the choices open to it and the implementation of a strategy. However, it is widely acknowledged that many strategies are not implemented. This suggests that plans are frequently adapted in reality or the world changed in ways that confounded the planners and prevented implementation. In a discontinuous organizational environment, the linear approach to strategic planning is increasingly questionable.

The example given by the College of Guidance Studies used processes to tackle discontinuity and is indicative of a more creative way to organize strategic thinking in a rapidly changing world.

Background

The College of Guidance Studies is a specialist higher education college with a mission to be the guidance community's centre of excellence in education, training, research and development. It offers high-quality opportunities in initial training, continuing professional development, research and national resources.

The strategic management process

The strategic management process of the College consists of three elements:

O   **Analysis**: internal and external.
O   **Choice**: identification and selection.
O   **Implementation**: systems, values and structure.

Creativity is used to surface and overcome blocks to thinking at each stage. Some examples of the approaches taken are given.

Strategic analysis   Projective techniques were used to analyse the organization – one approach involved seeing the organization as an animal. This produced a number of pictures which were used to reveal underlying assumptions about the College and its environment. The assumptions implicit in the 'cygnet' were:

O   The College had grown.
O   A cygnet can grow into a swan.
O   A lot of activity goes on beneath the surface.
O   It is loyal.
O   It looks after its young.
O   It has few predators other than man.

This process rapidly revealed assumptions about how the College saw itself; these assumptions were subsequently investigated.

Strategic choice   Generic strategic choices are easily identified by use of a model such as the Ansoff matrix. However, there is a need to evaluate and choose between these options. Previous experience at the College was that of sitting and talking at length about matters without necessarily reaching a decision. An 'election' was arranged where people were asked to vote on the strategic options using a scoring mechanism with defined criteria of feasibility, acceptability and suitability. The results were then factorized and collated to give a priority ranking. This provided a rapid way of sorting the 'wheat from the chaff' and was supplemented by a much more focused dialogue. This procedure did not eliminate the need for an emotional component to the decision-making process, but did significantly reduce the time required to get to the final choices.

Strategic implementation   Once the best options were established the College switched towards what was needed to make the strategies happen. The process used encouraged 'thinking outside the box' by imagining what the College would be like four years on by thinking about:

O   Our belief systems.
O   Our behaviours.

O   What we had 'let go' of.
O   What we had changed.
O   Our physical appearance.

To encourage the strategy group in this type of thinking, music and a guided imagery sequence was used to create an atmosphere which was conducive to visionary thinking. The result was that everyone had pictures that reflected whom and what we wanted to be. An example is shown in Figure 6.1.

FIGURE 6.1   The octopus vision.

The octopus vision
O   Fast moving, quick to respond.
O   Can be predatory.
O   Niche market (sea).
O   Capable of reproduction – baby octopuses (franchising).
O   Can cover its tracks if necessary (ink).
O   Cold and warm water.
O   Lots of arms (products or markets).
O   Reaching out.
O   Central resource.

From these high-level visions, a range of operating strategies and objectives were developed.

Reflections

> The whole process left me thinking at a deeper level about the organization and has enabled me to challenge some old assumptions which I believe we all have to do to achieve

that future place we want for ourselves.
(Alaine Sommerville, Chief Executive,
The College of Guidance Studies, Hextable, Kent)

Themes illustrated in the case study

O   Participative strategy formulation.
O   Processes for questioning the status quo.
O   Use of projection to bypass rational approaches to strategic thinking.

KENT COUNTY COUNCIL

This case is presented in the form of a personal reflection by Danny Chesterman, Corporate Advisor in Learning and Development at Kent County Council (KCC).

Something I know really clearly about my work in local government is that during my 20 years spread over three different authorities, I have come to see things very differently. During the early part of my career, when I was studying for professional qualifications and learning how things were done in a big metropolitan council my ideas about creativity were very influenced by models of professional excellence. I needed to learn the language of management in order to survive in my trade and get on. So what I saw as creativity and innovation were examples of good practice within a dominant and established view of how things should be done. As my career has developed I have seen creativity more and more as working outside the dominant paradigm of the way things are done. That experience has led me to believe that maximum creativity is created in the flux between doing known things excellently and doing new things inexpertly. Practising both simultaneously may sound paradoxical but that is the stuff of creativity.

Kent County Council is by any standards a large and diverse organization with a fluctuating political direction and a mass of competing objectives. Looking back over my nine years, it seems to me that the most exciting and enduring changes brought about in that time have not come from carefully planned strategies with known outcomes, but have arisen from individuals taking a risk in doing something new or different. It is a homeopathic rather than surgical model of organizational change which seems to have worked best. Homeopathy depends on adding very small doses of difference into a system in the belief that the system will use its own energy to incorporate the change within it. Surgery, on the other hand, may be effective in emergency situations but also runs the risk of stimulating resistance from the very system it seeks to help. Incremental changes can often turn out to be the most radical ones. Reformatory changes often turn out to be the least radical. It is much less risky for living systems to try minor variations than big mutations.

An example of creativity starting with one person taking a risk in doing something different is the Kent Job Club. This is now a comprehensive service for all those in transition from one job or career to another. It is available to those at risk of redundancy from the County Council, and is resourced by staff of the central Human Resource Group, Social Services, the Adult Careers and Guidance Service, and other associates bought in as and when needed. Its services have developed from a basic redeployment service to a fully fledged career counselling service, with help in preparing CVs and interviews, a resource room, access to a confidential counselling service to deal with the trauma of job loss, outplacement support and financial counselling. These services have been developed to meet demand and have attracted funds as they have gone along (since all Human Resource Services in Kent are fully costed). But it all started with one of the consultants in the central Human Resource Group finding that her skills in one-to-one support were being sought out by those in transition. She then thought she could develop a niche for herself in developing the service more widely. This service has now developed its reputation to the point where it is in demand from outside organizations as well as KCC. Having the pressure to recover costs through fee earning has contributed to creativity and innovation. Developing an environment in which people are free to act, combined with having a clear and measurable target from the organization means, in my experience, a fertile environment for creativity, because people will use their own talents to secure their own futures and not be constrained by how things are currently done.

Creativity has also been encouraged by the deliberate practice of importing difference from outside in the form of external consultants and trainers. These are used very selectively and sparingly, where there is genuine added value to be gained by transferring capability internally. In several cases they have provided just that little bit of leverage and confidence boosting for staff inside KCC to go that one bit further and take a risk, whilst getting support from others in the process.

An example involved the engagement of some consultants to develop the skills of business re-engineering in house. This led, amongst others things, to a project in our Special Needs section in the Education Service. At the outset the presenting problem appeared to be that Special Needs statements were taking too long to process. Applying a business process re-engineering methodology, parents of special needs children were widely consulted at the diagnostic stage about what was the problem that needed to be solved. It turned out that of much more concern to parents was not the length of time taken but the degree of involvement that the parents had in the process. In due course the length of time taken to produce the statements did in fact reduce but more importantly the whole process of state-menting children was overhauled and transformed in a way which met much more closely the needs of the stakeholders.

Geographically, Kent's position on the edge of Europe and on the edge of England has a bearing on its propensity to innovate. Kent has invested in its links with Europe very successfully over the years by creatively developing partnerships with other agencies across the Channel and successfully applying for European funds. Eurocast, a joint funded project to provide curriculum support and advice, came about through one person having a bright idea and developing links with other countries to the point where a proposal was finally successful. In the early stages of the idea there were lots of ripples in the organization since it did not pass through the traditional hurdles in the right order. If it had, it probably would have been stopped somewhere.

This exemplifies the notion that it is easier to act your way into a different way of thinking than it is to think your way into a different way of acting. It is about engaging both heart and mind in the process. In both the Job Club example and the Eurocast example there was a degree of corporate tolerance in the system and a nurturing environment in the immediate management structure where people felt that the inevitable anxiety and risk associated with a new idea could be shared, and they would get supported if there were snags on the way. We cannot legislate or set standards for creativity. What you can do is help people to sustain higher levels of anxiety in a constructive way so that new possibilities and new innovations can emerge. After all, success is 95 per cent failure. Without failure there is no success.

As well as new ideas for doing different things there is a route into creativity through doing the same things differently. In part of the Human Resource Group we found that we could manage with much less management once we started to pay attention to the process of our management meetings. We engaged an internal consultant from another department at KCC to help us learn more about our own processes. We developed a practice of having a 10-minute break in our management meetings to give space for people to say what they observed about our own processes. This resulted in a much richer level of understanding and a much more meaningful level of dialogue. When we communicated like this we felt that there was much less that needed discussing or managing. We developed a greater level of trust and rapport, and a sense of community where we felt we needed less rules to govern our behaviour.

People have a need to express their individuality, but they also have a need to belong. One of the ways of fulfilling the need to belong is to conform to the norms of the way things are done in an organization. But it is non-conformance to the way things are done that often creates new ideas. So a key to encouraging creativity and innovation is to explore how membership of a particular section or organization need not be dependent on conformance. Thus we developed a culture within our central consultancy unit in which attendance at management team meetings was optional. We recognized that there were different ways in which people could contribute to a community and that not everybody likes to give their contribution at meetings. People can fulfil their obligations to a community in many different ways. The notion of people having obligations to a community as well as expectations from it is important in creating freedom without anarchy, and order without oppression.

Other examples of creativity and action include a group of careworkers who developed their own appraisal system to replace the one KCC promoted as standard, and a group of roadworkers who decided to take turns to stop and talk to the general public about what they were doing when they were digging potholes. The result was that complaints went down rapidly and job satisfaction increased. These examples indicate what happens when management does not over manage. MBWA used to be known as 'management by walking about'. Perhaps creativity is better encouraged by adopting a maxim 'management by walking away', thus creating 'possibility space'. This is not an abdication of management responsibilities, but a way to define them differently. It leads to the inverted pyramid, where those in the highest paid positions in the authority are at the bottom of the pyramid, there to support those above them. The most productive teams in the organization are those which have built into their management processes really good support systems. It is this combination of high challenge (from both within and outside the organization) and high support, which provides the conditions under which creativity flourishes.

I cannot write about KCC's examples of creativity without acknowledging that there are many examples within the same organization of repeatedly conforming to existing patterns of behaviour which stifle creativity. For example, excessive monitoring or endless structural reviews stimulate huge amounts of anxiety which would otherwise be put into creative problem-solving.

These dominant patterns of behaviour often seem to present a defence against change and innovation. But such resistance to change also has its place. Familiarity with 'the way things are done around here', even if they do not look as if they are working, is an important part of the way people construct their identity, and as dissatisfaction with the existing order of things builds up it fuels creativity and a determination to try something different. Seen in this way, blocking behaviours provide an important fuel for energizing the shadow side of the organization; there, play and experimentation can stimulate innovation. But it may need to grow a root system underground for several years before it is strong enough to show itself in daylight.

(Danny Chesterman, Corporate Advisor
– Learning and Development, Kent County Council)

REFLECTIONS AND SUMMARY

We have considered organizational creativity in the public sector. Contrary to the popular notion that creativity is an irrelevant quality in public sector organizations it is clear that it has a place there. It may be that the level and type of creativity used has to accommodate constraints imposed by context, nevertheless, there are a number of good examples of the ability to think and act differently producing valuable results for the organizations involved.

The main insights that emerge may be summarized thus:

O   Creativity is intimately involved with the process of strategic think-ing under conditions of change. Strategy moves from being a plan based on what was done before towards a flexible 'direction' which can respond to unplanned changes in the environment.

O   There is room for some bureaucracy within a creative organization. The level of bureaucracy will inform the level of creative activity within the organization.

O   Creativity is concerned with making sense of paradoxes, not by choosing between issues (either/or mindset) but learning to toler-ate multiple realities (and/also mindset). A model that represents both possibilities is shown in Figure 6.2.

O   Creativity exists where chaos and structure meet within the organi-zation. In a chaotic environment, expressions of standards and value are useful not because they inform action, but because they represent something fixed and solid which it is possible to agree/disagree with. A metaphor for this is an organizational 'dart-board' which people may channel energy towards (positive and negative).

O   There are problems associated with launching radical ideas due to the issue of cognitive dissonance (ideas which are far removed from the dominant presentation of the present reality are 'disposed of').

O   It is also connected with the asking of naïve questions. In transac-tional analysis terms, this involves a cycling between 'free child' and 'adult' states. Leaders could be typified as 'nurturing parents' in their role to encourage creativity.

O   It may also involve starting processes differently, that is from a non-traditional place. Creativity may be something that needs to be 'sneaked up' on. Ideas to escape from mental tramlines included bringing in someone off the street to formal meetings to act as a disturbance and using children to question the 'obvious'.

O   In terms of creative change management, we should learn to create 'stability zones' within organizations. These are akin to an oasis in a desert, to which people would return on an occasional basis. Other organizations have mentioned personal development as one such

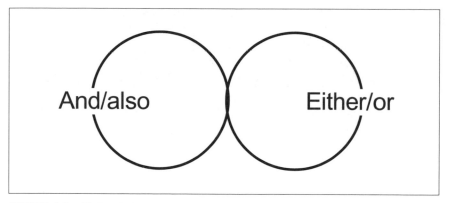

FIGURE 6.2   Not only but also.

stability zone. These could be provided by the organization (pater-
nalistic mode) or, more likely in an age where lifetime employment
is highly unlikely, these need to come from within individuals.

You will find it useful to consolidate your reading by reviewing the following
questions.

About what you have learned

O   What has reading this chapter confirmed in your mind?
O   What useful contradictions has it raised?

About creatively swiping the ideas

O   What ideas from the case study are most easily adapted to suit the
context of your own organization?
O   What organizations do you know that you could research in order
to benchmark your own?
O   How can you utilize some of the ideas in this chapter to influence
the direction of your organization so that it becomes more successful?

A final thought

> You have to systematically create confusion – it sets
> creativity free – everything that is contradictory creates life.
> (*Salvador Dali, presumably commenting on Chaos theory*
> *before it was invented*)

PART THREE
DESIGNING THE CREATIVE ORGANIZATION

❖

7

CULTURE, LEADERSHIP STYLE AND VALUES

❖

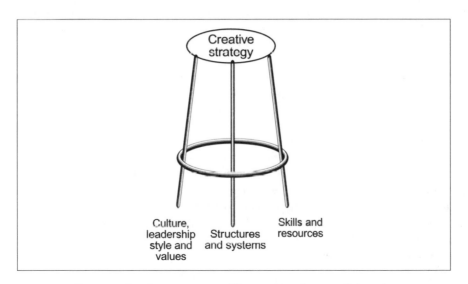

Farmers don't grow crops. They create the conditions in
which crops can grow.

The culture of an organization is a major factor that determines
whether the enterprise flourishes on a continuing basis or withers and
eventually dies. Unfortunately, culture is an intangible asset (or liability) which is only seen via tangible manifestations; it cannot be easily quanti-
fied on a company balance sheet or other 'bean-counting' devices. This is
why I sometimes feel nervous about letting **some** accountants and information technologists become involved in culture change programmes, even
though the differences they bring to such matters are of immense value.

This chapter examines the influence of culture, leadership style and values on creativity, and identifies the cultural conditions in which creativity is more likely to emerge. There are no instant recipes here and it is counterproductive to 'over cook' the design of culture in some respects. Nevertheless, cultures can and should be designed with care and flair so that both desirable and unexpected creative behaviours emerge.

CULTURE SPOTTING

You never stand in the same river twice.

Culture is a word that has slipped into common usage, but it seems that the word is generally misunderstood. This is neatly illustrated by the following story.

I was invited to visit a medium-sized company some time ago, and was faintly impressed when the Personnel Director told me that they were 'doing culture change'. Somewhat foolishly (with hindsight) I became interested and asked him what the existing culture was like, how it might be changed and to what form. After a rather lengthy pause, he looked at me sternly and said, 'We are doing culture change'.

This story illustrates the difficulty experienced by many intelligent people in grasping what culture is and being able to describe their own organizational culture(s). Chaos theorists amongst us may be outraged and say, 'We cannot predict the outcome of an intervention in a complex adaptive system', and I agree. Yet I found it paradoxical that a Personnel Director was prepared to spend considerable amounts of time and money to hire me to fix something that he wasn't even sure was broken. The sales people amongst you will look puzzled at this point and say, 'Why didn't you offer him an extensive organization-wide programme of focus groups and questionnaires to help him articulate the change and send in the first bill?' Well, that's another story, as they say!

DEFINING CULTURE

Metaphors are useful as a means of describing intangible assets. One for culture is 'glue'. When viewed in this way, culture has a positive effect in holding the organization together and maintaining a shared vision. Organizations that view culture as glue tend to adopt processes that are intended to be their 'adhesive', such as high-profile internal company media, briefing groups, team development activities and values workshops. These cultures can become very 'strong', in the sense that there is a high degree of alignment with the values and purpose of the organization.

There is an alternative, more sinister view of 'glue', which involves properties associated with preventing an organization from responding to change
through becoming 'stuck' in a number of unconscious patterns of behaviour. In essence all cultures have the weaknesses of their strengths. Some
companies have responded to the problems produced by a strong culture
by making·change the number one value.

THE PROBLEM OF VISIBILITY – GETTING BENEATH THE 'ICEBERG'

One of the biggest difficulties in deciding what organizational culture should
be like rests on the problem of 'seeing' the culture and its associated
strengths and weaknesses. This is because much culture is wrapped up in
unconscious assumptions about the 'way we do things around here'.

Another metaphor for culture is 'wind'; you know it is there, and it can be
described using concepts such as velocity and direction, yet wind cannot be
seen or touched. It is possible to 'see' wind through observing its effect on
trees and other objects on the landscape. Similarly, it is possible to 'see' the
culture of an organization through its effect on things that are **visible** on
the organization's landscape:

O **Environment** – this includes 'high-' and 'low-profile' symbols.
   High-profile symbols include the mission statement, company logo,
   annual report and uniforms. Low-profile symbols include the stories, myths, slogans, buildings, dress code, furniture and specific jargon that influence the way people work.
O **Employee behaviour** – especially when the organization faces a
   critical moment in its history, such as a take-over or financial crisis.
   It is often most apparent to an outsider (for example a consultant or
   a new starter) who has not adopted the habits of the organization.

At a deeper level, culture involves the values and collective beliefs about the
organization and its identity. These elements are generally **invisible**. The iceberg metaphor can be revisited here – environmental and behavioural aspects
are visible above the water line and everything else is invisible (Figure 7.1).

There are at least two schools of thought arguing about the relative
importance of visible versus invisible elements.

One group claims that behaviour is all that counts and it matters little
whether people's values are consistent with their behaviour, since employment is a contract where performance (appropriate behaviours) is
exchanged for rewards (such as money).

The second group argues that one can never obtain excellent performance until people's values are aligned with all the other elements. Such
assumptions produce cultural reinforcement programmes where people are
challenged to 'live the company values'.

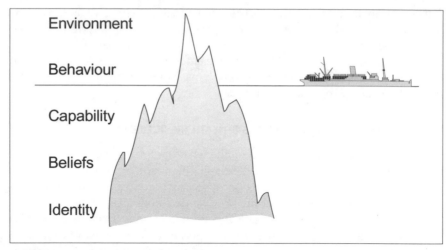

FIGURE 7.1   The iceberg metaphor.

Both perspectives are potentially correct – it just depends on what type of organization one is working for, and the psychological contract that is developed from the culture, as to which one is favoured.

There is a shift towards a greater emphasis on aligning values in many modern organizations. Examples of this include The Body Shop and Johnson & Johnson.

A HANDY VIEWPOINT OF CULTURE

A number of metaphors for culture have been suggested. Some proprietary models of culture do possess sufficient flexibility to be useful for most organizations. Of these, I believe that Charles Handy's development of Roger Harrison's typology is excellent and worthy of reproduction here. In his book, *Understanding Organizations* (Penguin), Handy (1985) offered us four culture 'stereotypes'.

The Power culture

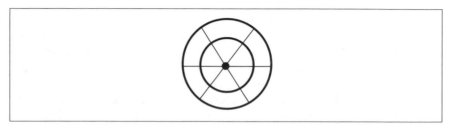

FIGURE 7.2   The power culture.

Frequently present in entrepreneurial companies. Handy points out that if this company had a patron god it would be Zeus, who ruled by whim and impulse. The power culture depends on a central power source with rays of power and influence spreading out from a central figure. They are connected by functional or specialist strings but the power rings are centres of activity and influence (Figure 7.2). Many small entrepreneurial businesses start out as power cultures.

The Role culture

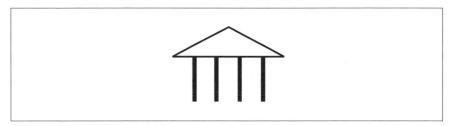

FIGURE 7.3   The role culture.

Role cultures are frequently linked to bureaucracies, and the accompanying structure reflects this as it is reminiscent of a Greek temple. The patron god is Apollo, the god of reason. The role culture has its major strengths in pillars, which are its functions or specialities (Figure 7.3). These are controlled at the top by a narrow band of senior management. Some large manufacturing concerns have role cultures, particularly where the environment is stable and where economies may be gained from large-scale operations.

The Task culture

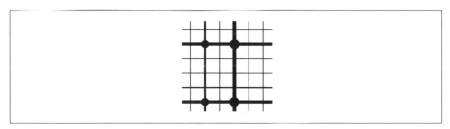

FIGURE 7.4   The task culture.

The task culture is job or project oriented, with an accompanying structure best represented as a net (Figure 7.4). Some of the strands of the net are thicker than others and much of the power and influence lies at the interstices of the net. Many project-oriented matrix organizations, for example software houses, have task cultures.

The Person culture

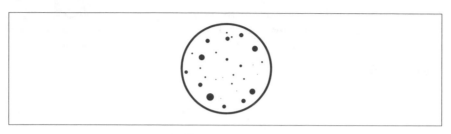

FIGURE 7.5   The person culture.

In the person culture, individuals are the focal point. Its structure is as minimal as possible and may be represented as a galaxy of stars (Figure 7.5). If it were to have a patron god it would be Dionysius, the god of the self-oriented individual. It is most commonly found in 'professional' organizations such as consultancies and architects. This type of culture is increasingly relevant in a society where individualism is growing and virtual organizations are becoming more commonplace.

All the above cultures have associated strengths and weaknesses with respect to creativity, summarized in Table 7.1.

TABLE 7.1   Handy's four cultures

Culture type	Strengths	Potential weaknesses
Power	Rapid decision making; can respond to crises well; puts faith in key individuals; creativity is rewarded to the extent that it makes the organization and key individuals in it more powerful	Finds it hard to exist without the leader; growth can present problems; 'unfocused' creativity will more than likely be punished
Role	Produces economies in stable environments; career tenure and opportunity based on time served; creativity is	Resistant to change; low incentives for mavericks; slow to change if an opportunity is noticed; over-

TABLE 7.1 *concluded*

Culture type	Strengths	Potential weaknesses
	possible provided that it is disguised in 'rational clothes'	performance or radical creativity will limit career progression
Task	Rapid adaptation to change; good in changing markets; can release high levels of productive creativity	Can lose focus if purpose becomes obscured; can be inefficient; difficulties with control
Person	High performance is possible when there is strong alignment of individual/organizational goals; can release high levels of creativity	Control near impossible; creativity can become internally focused (needs-driven)

In many large organizations, multiple cultures co-exist. Handy (1985) cites the example of GEC, which had a central power culture but managed to grow by giving maximum independence to the individual heads of linked organizations, with different cultures, requiring a common theme of financial results as the only criterion of interest to the centre.

THE PERMANENCE OF CULTURE

Culture is held together by rational and emotional forces which are self-sustaining. Many management consultants and business leaders resort to rational techniques to change culture, usually with disappointing results. Culture change is both a rational and creative process. The economist, Jay Kenneth Galbraith, sums up the problem of culture change:

> Faced with the choice of changing one's mind and proving
> there is no need to do so, almost everyone gets busy on
> the proof.

Changing ways of thinking has been a challenge from the earliest times. History is an important starting point when considering the topic. In 204 BC, the comic poet Naevius was convicted of slander for poking fun at public officials. Later on, Emperor Nero deported critics and burned manuscripts of which he disapproved. Both examples illustrate the results of thinking differently from the prevailing view.

If collective mindsets or **paradigms** are involved the difficulty is magnified. When Copernicus proposed that a rotating earth revolving with the other planets about a stationary sun could account in a simpler way for movements of the sun, moon and other planets, it took 26 years for his account to appear. Galileo also experienced severe problems in advancing the Copernican argument nearly 100 years later and was eventually forced to disavow his belief by the Inquisition. The penalties become greater as the degree of cognitive dissonance with the prevailing paradigm increases as shown in Figure 7.6.

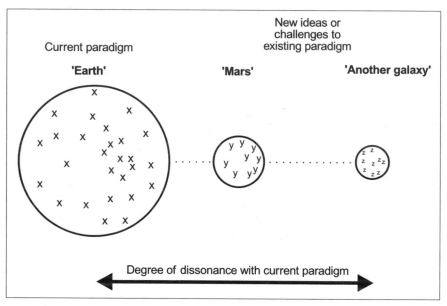

FIGURE 7.6   'Loving the alien' – the difficulty of stepping outside the current world of ideas.

Modern organizations do not have an 'Inquisition' division to forestall change, as practised in the Middle Ages. However, there are powerful psychological and practical contemporary penalties for being a 'Martian' or 'in another galaxy', by challenging the *status quo*, such as downsizing or being assigned to 'special projects'.

STRONG OR WEAK?

Strength is usually seen as something to be prized and many organizations have made significant attempts to build a strong internal culture, that is, where the norms, values and beliefs are commonly shared and tend to be unchanging over time. A disadvantage of a strong culture is that it tends to be very difficult to change if the world in which the organization operates alters.

Alternative responses to the problem of a culture that does not respond to external change include:

O   Build a strong culture based on generalized rather than specific values. This has the advantage of being receptive to multiple interpretations by staff and the corresponding disadvantage that staff may fail to identify with any of the values expressed due to their 'motherhood and apple pie' nature.

O   Build a strong culture based on a single principle or a few timeless principles. A single-principle culture would be one where the number one value is change. Such an approach is highly adaptable, but has a tendency to lose sight of the organization's goals. This culture needs a matching structure that allows for extremes of entrepreneurial behaviour, so that new businesses may spring up as autonomous enterprises.

O   Tolerate a weak culture. The strength of this approach is adaptation; a key weakness is lack of alignment and motivation due to a diffused identity.

Points to ponder

O   If you were to describe your organization's **current** and **desired** culture (or sub-culture) using a metaphor, what would they be like? What are the critical differences?

O   Visit your organization as though you are a detached observer. What do your first impressions tell you about the culture?

DEFINING A CREATIVE CULTURE

> Creativity should itself become an organizational value.
> (*Dr Gareth Jones, Senior Vice President,*
> *Human Resources, Polygram International*)

NO SINGLE PREFERRED CREATIVE CULTURE

Various writers have favoured a particular culture in order to encourage creativity in organizations. In contrast, it is a mistake to assume that creativity requires a particular type of culture. Provided the culture fits the organization's context (environment, current and future pressures) there is a possibility for creative endeavour, although **level** (how much) and **type** of creativity (adaptive or innovative) will be affected by the prevailing culture(s).

A second mistake is the assumption made by many organizations and some writers that there should be one culture throughout the organization. In larger, diverse organizations especially, there is a need to tolerate and encourage subcultures that allow particular divisions and units to maximize their contribution to the organization. Subcultures are often resisted since they tend to generate conflict between subunits. Arguably, conflict is better than toleration of poor performance from the whole organization in the interest of having a single culture statement from the Human Resources Division. Organizations that recognize the value of subcultures need to deal with the consequences of conflict if creativity is to emerge.

A third mistake is to assume that organizational structure totally defines the culture. For example, many managers suggest that bureaucracies cannot have a creative culture. Yet, some of the more positive associations of bureaucracies are good for creativity in organizations, for example promotion by merit and formalization of routine functions to free up space for more important matters. In many cases, what is being referred to as bureaucracy is the popular (and negative) understanding of the term, for example the tendency to generate 'red tape'. This contrasts with the features originally described by Max Weber, who saw positive outcomes from designing organizations along rational–economic lines.

MYTH MANAGEMENT MATTERS

Culture is one means of reinforcing the norms and expectations of the organization. This is often done by the management of meaning through identity level 'symbols', communications strategies and 'myths'. Examples of the expression of creativity through identity level symbols include:

O   The 'imagineering' concept of the Disney Corporation demonstrates the value placed on **imagination** and **action**.
O   The Wellcome Foundation's 'Unicorn' logo. This symbolized **uniqueness** in terms of bringing new cures for illnesses.

BEHAVIOURAL MODELLING

Myth management is insufficient in itself to develop a culture. It must be coupled with detailed modelling of expected behaviours. At Glaxo-Wellcome Research and Development, much of the internal communications concentrates on personal responsibility and initiative as essential prerequisites to creativity. As described in Chapter 5, the culture is modelled down to the last detail (built environments, open all hours and use of 'unrelated stimuli', such as art, to enrich the environment).

This deliberate attempt to design informality into the environment is intended to increase the frequency of serendipitous value-added conversations. Although insufficient to guarantee creativity (as some formal mechanisms for promoting creativity are needed) informality is an important contributor at both a symbolic and practical level.

INFORMAL COMMUNICATIONS PREFERRED

The number of communications channels open to organizations has widened significantly over recent years, especially due to the rise in multimedia and multiple-user configurations now available. These represent 'competition' for more traditional methods.

Within the organizations researched for this book, informal conversations were preferred as the main communications channel for creativity. One or two organizations were using electronic conferencing to 'bounce ideas around' on a nominal basis. There was some evidence to suggest that the level of anonymity and psychological distance afforded by electronic communications was helpful in gaining contributions from quieter staff.

There is also a danger of substituting information technology for communications that require a personal touch. Some managers would rather send a reprimand via e-mail to someone in the next office instead of talking to them. Use of e-mail as an 'electronic cattle prod' is unhelpful and degrades its integrity for more appropriate applications.

Creative thinking is helped by contributions that are relatively distant from the problem. The places where these sorts of conversations are traditionally held is being eroded in organizations, and the metaphorical 'smoking rooms' in organizations should be preserved – places where relaxed dialogue can take place and contributions can be heard from a wide cross-section of people.

Points to ponder

O   Pick communications channels for ideas and creative thinking carefully, according to the type of interaction being sought, rather than resorting to your 'usual' modes of communication.

O   E-mail is best used as a transmission device as it does not convey meaning in the same way as face-to-face methods. If you use electronic media for thoughtful conversations or brainstorming, ensure that e-mail and conferencing mechanisms allow you to operate from the appropriate mindset and perform the full range of functions necessary for successful creative communications.

A WALK ON THE WILD SIDE – THE NEED FOR CONFLICT

If you haven't initiated a clash of ideas recently, you need
to re-evaluate your reason for existence as a leader.

Many organization cultures or subcultures deliberately or accidentally encourage the problem of obedience, typified by a comment made by one senior manager in a corporation:

I'm **obliged** to become a World Class Manufacturer.

Obligation is insufficient to generate the required drive and is worse than outright civil war in terms of long-term productivity.

THEY'RE CREATING LIKE CATS AND DOGS

FIGURE 7.7   The diverse organization.

Heat creates ideas.
(*James Coghill*)

One metaphor for an obedient organization is a dog. Alternatively, the curious organizations could be typified as a cat. To gain the best possible result, a hybrid of cats and dogs is required. Notice how this metaphor illustrates the problem of diversity, since cats and dogs generally do not get along too well (Figure 7.7).

The consequences of adopting the time-honoured approach to staff selection (we tend to surround ourselves with people who support our own limitations) are low levels of conflict, low levels of creativity and low levels of innovation. If an organization operates in a stable market where there are no competitors it may be argued that there is no need for conflict. I do struggle to find such organizations in the current age.

One of the consequences of developing a collegiate organization culture, where positive 'can-do' values are the norm, is that creativity can suffer – the implied assumption is that conflict is bad. Hewlett Packard is mentioned by Pascale (1990) in his book, *Managing on the Edge*, as an example of an organization where the overwhelming positivity of the 'HP way' tends to result in conflict avoidance. It is not that this is inherently 'wrong' – Hewlett Packard is an outstandingly successful organization by any standards. There may be some arenas in which the habit of conflict avoidance is unhelpful to making further and faster progress.

Pascale (1990) gives the example of Dentsu, the largest advertising agency in the world, as an organization that flourishes on contention. Dentsu's founder, Hideo Yoshida, devised 10 precepts which he named his Ten Rules of the Demon. Rule number 10 reads:

> When confrontation is necessary, don't shy away from it.
> Confrontation is the mother of progress and the fertilizer
> of an aggressive enterprise. If you fear conflict, it will make
> you timid and irresolute.
> *(Pascale, 1990)**

WHAT TYPE OF CONFLICT?

> Conflict is necessary for creativity, although it is difficult
> to generate this in an organization that values co-
> operation. Where conflict has been generated in the past
> it has led to a much tighter definition of roles and
> responsibilities with the result that a better solution has
> emerged.
> *(Senior executive, large pharmaceutical company.)*

Some varieties of conflict are helpful for creativity and others are positively damaging to its long-term prospects. The range of sources of conflict are shown in Figure 7.8.

Conflict over ideas and tasks (debate) is productive in the long term as it results in improved innovations and productivity. When it moves towards conflict over personality and emotional issues, there are occasions when this is healthy for the individuals involved. However, it can become a chronic condition which can lead to decline of the climate and affects the work group and the organization badly. An unhealthy negative conflict sequence may be represented as shown in Figure 7.9.

At an organizational level, conflict over personality becomes conflict over collective personality, that is ideology. The classic example of this type of conflict is found between Sales and Personnel departments, where collective thinking styles are often diametrically opposed.

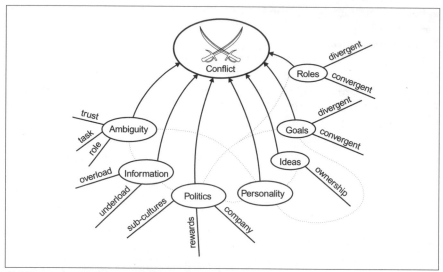

FIGURE 7.8   Multiple sources of conflict.

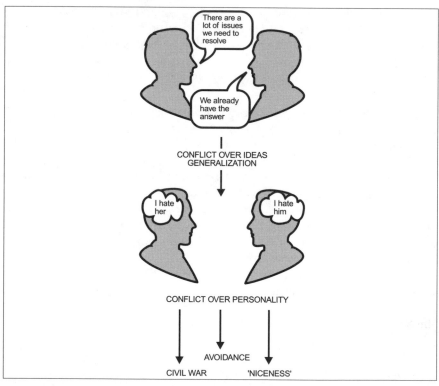

FIGURE 7.9   A negative conflict sequence.

CONFLICT IS NECESSARY FOR TRUST TO EMERGE

Conflict over ideas breeds trust which breeds risk-taking which leads to creativity. Once again, we cannot make a single prescription for addressing conflict here. Some of the options which organizations use include:

O   Integrators – people who can talk a variety of 'internal languages' and have wide acceptance across the various subcultures.
O   Move people across the subcultures outside their professional role.
O   Accept that conflict is a natural process that leads to improved ideas and allow or encourage it. This is not a passive view.
O   Encourage parallel activities with the intention of raising the general level of creativity and performance. This is akin to one interpretation of the word 'marathon', where two runners would attempt to win so that both competitors would improve their performance. It is also the nature of competition within good jazz bands.
O   Ask people to 'write down their `hidden agendas'.
O   Depersonalize conflict by using a common language based on roles to discuss conflict or relate it to the need to refocus the task.
O   Change the geographical set-up so that creative conflict is more likely (by bringing together departments with radically different subcultures).
O   Bring tension into stable organizations by importing ideas and information that generate counter-views.
O   Use dialogue and other assumption-surfacing processes to reveal the positive intentions and mental maps of people who are in conflict, so that they can come to recognize the value of their differences.

CHAOS AND DISORDER

> Innovation at 3M is anything but orderly.
> (*Dr William E Coyne, Senior Vice President,*
> *Research and Development, 3M*)

> You've gotta roll with it.
> (*Oasis*)

Most prevailing approaches to strategy are no longer adequate. They attempt to identify ends and then construct detailed plans to get there. This approach is a legacy of the Industrial Age and the kind of traditional science that made it possible. As we leave the Industrial Age traditional science no longer provides an adequate context for long-range planning. In a complex system, ends or objectives are seen as parts of adaptive processes. These processes permit the emergence of continuity and novelty and allow the organization to respond to the unexpected. Currently, organizations are facing the challenge of creating organizational environments in which emergent strategies can develop. The difference between the various approaches to strategy can be summarized as shown in Figure 7.10.

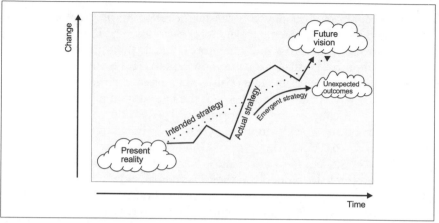

FIGURE 7.10   Emergent strategy in action.

Emergence is possible in larger organizations where there is no strong ethos of corporate standardization. In some cases, this is matched by breaking the organization into a number of small autonomous units. Important insights from Chaos theory and related topics include:

○   The danger of proclaiming the intention to change the culture or build a creative organization. This tends to mobilize the opposition and reduces the chance of reaching the intended outcome. It is sometimes wiser to undertake change as a 'business as usual' activity and pronounce what has happened some time after the change has become part of the fabric of the organization.

○   The possibility that one can use relatively small changes in the organization to produce massive and radical changes.

○   The need for leaders to create meaning out of apparent disorder, in order to engage people to move in a direction.

○   Actions speak louder than words – if your organization wishes to become a learning organization, it may be more powerful to start acting in ways that demonstrate your belief that failure is a valuable asset.

NOT ONLY BUT ALSO ...

Whilst Chaos theory has attractions for complex organizations, it requires a high tolerance of ambiguity on the part of individuals. This can be summarized as a shift (see Figure 7.11):

From 'either/or' thinking   **To** 'and/also' thinking

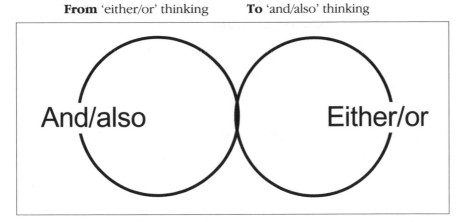

FIGURE 7.11   Not only but also revisited.

An example of this in action is the need to tolerate failure **and** avoid critical mistakes by ensuring that risk-taking is confined to specific areas of activity.

One response to complexity and ambiguity is simplification. Other (more useful) alternatives include:

O   Learning to be curious and tolerate (or even enjoy) uncertainty. This is perhaps the most robust personal strategy for addressing complexity.

O   Use of information-processing mechanisms that preserve the rich-ness of complexity whilst providing overview and insight. This is the domain of effective information management. Techniques such as outliners, systems mapping and rich picturing are of assistance in addressing complexity.

The tolerance of ambiguity and paradox is most important for complex problems and issues. It is a pointless habit when conducting routine tasks such as deciding when to go to lunch. Creative leaders have the ability to synthesize apparent opposites. They also recognize the necessity of contra-dictions as a means of gaining leverage for change. One practical routine that can be adopted by people wishing to develop this capability is to habit-ually use the and/also response to dilemmas and paradoxes.

Points to ponder

O   Next time you are faced with an important decision or a dilemma, commit to setting yourself a goal of allowing the opposite sides of the argument to reside together for a significantly longer period than you would habitually tolerate.

O   Find at least five new rituals in your organization that make contradictions **discussible** and **liveable**. For example, fill a large soapbox with concrete and use it to stand on at team meetings as a routine for allowing people to 'bitch' in an unfocused manner for up to three minutes. Insist that this is followed by a problem-solving phase to address the issue or concern.

INFLUENCE OF LEADERSHIP ON CREATIVE POTENTIAL

I must follow them. I am their leader.
(Bonar Law)

Successful new product and service development depends to a large degree on the role of leadership in creating a climate where ideas can arise and germinate. **Leadership** is being distinguished from **management** in the following way.

Leadership

Behaviour on the part of some members of a group or organization that creates or changes basic assumptions and values in the group.

Management

Behaviour on the part of some members of a group or organization that helps the group to achieve some goals, but **within** the assumptions or values previously agreed on by the group. (Definitions from Schein E (1988) *Process Consultation* Vol. 1 (second edition), pp. 84–85. ©1988 by Addison-Wesley Publishing Co., Inc. Reprinted by permission of Addison-Wesley.)

WHERE DOES YOUR BASIS FOR LEADERSHIP COME FROM?

If leadership and influencing behaviours are what is visible to others, the supporting system is a power base to act from. Some further definitions are helpful here:

O   **Power** is the **ability** of a person or a group to influence other people or groups.

O   **Influence** is the **process** of affecting what another person or group does and/or thinks.

O   **Authority** is the **right** to exercise power.

The principle of **elegance** in creative leadership arises from the use of the minimum amounts of all three of the above. In other words, what are the necessary and sufficient conditions for obtaining the desired result?

Influence rather than dictatorship is the most legitimate mechanism of getting things done in creative organizations, although this will be affected by the prevailing culture, the expectations of the led and the urgency/complexity of the task.

FLEXING YOUR POWER SOURCES

Power comes from a variety of sources – some are provided by the organization; others have to be earned.

- O **Organizational position** – your title and the benefits it confers on you from the point of view of decision making.
- O **Resources** that you hold – money, time, access to people.
- O **Social** connections – your access to networks of people who can make things happen.
- O **Expertise** – in a particular field, a particular scientific discipline or a process expertise such as creative problem solving.
- O **Personal** charisma – the quality that makes people want to do things for you, for no other reason than it was you.
- O Access to **information** – either tacit or formal knowledge.

In flatter organizational structures, the use of power arising from social networks, expertise, charisma or information is likely to have the most value, as these are **earned** by the individual rather than **given** to the individual by the organization.

IDENTIFYING AND USING YOUR POWER SOURCES CREATIVELY (SEE FIGURE 7.12)

1. Describe a specific situation where you want to be more influential.
2. Identify your **major** power sources in this situation and mark them down with a tick in Column 2 of the grid.
3. Identify the **major** power sources of the key stakeholder(s) in the situation.
4. Identify a valid power transaction that will increase your influence in this situation, that is *What do they value that you can provide?* This is the creative step – Ashby's law of requisite variety provides us with the insight that the individual with the greatest flexibility of thought and behaviour can (and generally will) control the outcome of any interaction. Not all transactions are effective, for example charisma can be annoying for the other person or even dangerous for the user when used to influence someone who only has position power.
5. Develop a strategy to put this into action. Practise by acting it out with a trusted friend if it helps.
6. Reflect on how you could use your power sources more effectively in other 'difficult' situations.

Power source	Your main sources	Stakeholder A	Stakeholder B
Position 			
Resource ££			
Social 			
Expert			
Personal 			
Informational 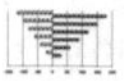			

FIGURE 7.12   Power transactions grid.

CREATIVE LEADERS DO IT DIFFERENTLY

> Whatever you do, do it with foresight; look to the end.
> (*Marcus Aurelius, Emperor of Rome AD 161–180*)
> (http://www.Roman.Empire.com)

Common attributes required for creative leadership include:

○   The ability to set a direction that excites others, rather than bland 'mission' statements. In practice this often involves the ability to be **specifically vague**.

○   Leaders as idea advocates, sensing and moving ideas around the organization so that they attract resources and gain acceptance.

○   Giving a tangible example to the concept that failure is a learning opportunity and encouraging risk-taking.

○   Building teams that have high levels of trust. This includes the ability to have conflicts and recover from them.

○   Giving freedom to 'bootleg' by providing encouragement, mental and physical resources to spend on speculative projects.

○   Enabling others to make meaning and sense out of their environment.

○   Leadership styles, ranging from coach through counsellor, conflict generator, comedian to hero. An ability to move rapidly from one role to another without losing credibility.

The following cameo illustrates the responsible use of leadership to influence the culture of a whole organization. The example is that of the National and Provincial Building Society (N&P), which faced the challenge of the changes created by the Financial Services Act which effectively exposed building societies to the commercial world. Under the leadership of David O'Brien, the organization realigned itself to meet the external challenges in a highly effective and efficient way. Part of this process was a creative communications approach to sense and respond to the issues that presented themselves as the organization embraced an environment of continuous change.

USING LEADERSHIP RESPONSIBLY AT THE NATIONAL & PROVINCIAL BUILDING SOCIETY

Under the leadership of David O'Brien an important part of the culture change was the 'Understanding Process'. This was initiated within a week of the latest Executive Management Direction event and was a very effective means of two-way understanding.

Each understanding 'event' would commence with the team leader/manager facilitating the team through four considerations:

1.   What has gone well that we can learn from since our last event?
2.   What has not gone well that we can improve?
3.   What ideas have we thought of?
4.   What concerns have arisen?

The considerations could be within the teams' direct area of influence or anything happening in the organization at that time.

The facilitator then updated the team on the output from the latest Executive Management Direction event. This would either cause more considerations or answer previous questions raised within the teams or by other teams.

The team then decided what actions it would take to resolve issues or improve results where the opportunity was within its area of responsibility. At the same time the team decided what output should be created to raise questions that other parts of the organization should consider, plus any positive feedback the team wished to give others in the organization. This action recognized the interdependencies within an organization and encouraged other teams to be pro-active and aware of the value of recognition.

The output was collated with that of all the other teams and captured in the organization's 'issueometer' and 'progressometer'. The content, patterns, dispersions and trends of these two qualitative measures were then used by the executive team to understand the dynamics of the members in the organization, how much people understood/misunderstood/welcomed/feared/developed and contributed to improvement and creativity.

The frequency of the 'understanding events' was geared to the management process cycle and occurred every two weeks. The frequency was geared to the degree to which an organization needs to be 'on the ball'; clearly, retailing needs a more frequent cycle than, say, engineering.

The N&P example is an illustration of how a large service-based organization can stimulate creativity and learning by designing and implementing an appropriate organization design and complementary leadership.

(*David O'Brien*)

CREATIVE LEADERSHIP ICONS

This exercise requires you to think of a creative leader and list the attributes that you believe the leader possesses as a means of identifying and adapting relevant leadership qualities within your organization (Table 7.2). Please complete the questions using as much detail as possible.

1.   Name your leader – s/he can be from a political, religious, business or any other background – it is important that you pick someone that you know something about.
      My chosen leader is:
2.   In Column 1, list the **attributes** that you believe this leader possesses.
3.   In Column 2, mark with an asterisk those attributes that you believe to be the factors that are **critical** to success as a leader in the particular context.
4.   In Column 3, tick those attributes that you believe will enhance creative leadership within your organization and give some explanation of the reasons why you believe this to be so in Column 4.
5.   Taking the attributes you listed in Column 3, now identify a number of initial practical steps that need to be taken in order to achieve the desired attributes.
6.   What have you learned in general about leadership from this?

CREATIVE LEADERSHIP AS METHOD

If you love somebody, set them free.
(*Sting*)

The discipline known as transactional analysis (TA) identifies a number of 'ego states' that people 'adopt' at various times:

O   The **controlling parent** – tells, lectures, disciplines.
O   The **nurturing parent** – encourages, protects, shows warmth.
O   The **adult** – encourages responsibility taking, rational, non-judgemental.
O   The **free child** – is spontaneous, fun-loving, uninhibited, thinks laterally.
O   The **adapted child** – is obedient, does what it is told, may be angry.

TABLE 7.2 Leadership attributes

Leadership attributes	Critical factors	Qualities relevant to my organization	Benefits/notes of explanation

Although it is dangerous to over-generalize, creative leadership requires the predominant use of the 'nurturing parent' 'free child' and 'adult' states. Many leaders see the process of leadership as drama – good acting skills are required. The degree of flexibility required to 'jump between states' can confuse followers who would like their leader to be the same at all times and the most effective leaders find ways of signalling state changes. I know one creative leader who regularly invited his team to his house where he would cook them a meal (nurturing parent), then organized games which involved fancy dress, the wearing of wigs and playing musical instruments (free child). These team events were clearly marked out as being separate from work, where his predominant style was that of adult for achieving goals and nurturing parent for solving problems.

People's reaction to creative leadership varies and leaders need a variety of responses to cope with differing reactions. One example of this in action comes from Stephen Rees, who is responsible for raising the level of productive action on environmental issues at Kent County Council (KCC) (Table 7.3).

TABLE 7.3 Leadership flexibility in action	
Reaction to creativity	*Strategy for individual reactions to creativity*
Cynical	Finding ways to break down barriers
Pragmatic	Giving people practical things (on a plate) that they can do which fit in with particular constraints, such as time, resource, work priorities
Idealistic	Enabling people to translate ideas into action by finding methods, catalysts and incentives

Points to ponder

O   Create micro-environments where new 'happenings' and new conversations can occur.

O   Concentrate on the future and act in ways that suggest that the future has already happened.

O   Lead by example. This may include being willing to admit that you are baffled from time to time (probably not at shareholder meetings!) Be clear on the goals (ends) but give people sufficient latitude over means of achieving them.

O   Develop your talent for acting. Stand in the mirror and act as though you are externally sober whilst feeling internally delirious and vice versa.

O   Go to the theatre to learn about the dramatic elements of leadership.

O   Put on a Christmas play in which staff can participate in a dramatic comedy. Ensure that you take part. Resist any attempts by staff to link the play back to the world of work.

ALIGNING VALUES

To use a Music Hall analogy, it is important for an organization to get the words (values), music (climate) and dance (behaviour) in harmony for maximum effectiveness.

One response to the need to align values is the articulation of expected behaviours through competency and other frameworks. There are two principal dangers associated with taking this approach too far:

O   **'Rules' for creativity** – competency frameworks often concern the 'here and now' and do not always accommodate breakthrough behaviours that take the organization beyond its current level of development. There is a danger that articulating some rules for creativity will prevent other approaches from developing because of the development of a paradigm.

O   **The crisis of red tape** – competency frameworks can become bureaucratic – this is out of harmony with the intention.

Some organizations have managed to engage their employees though simple yet timeless sets of values that are **specifically vague** in the sense that they are meaningful to the majority, yet they can be extrapolated to local contexts and particular situations. Far from being bland mission statements, these values set the organization apart from its competitors. One such example is that of Johnson & Johnson, who have a set of values called the *Credo*.

THE JOHNSON & JOHNSON CREDO

The culture, business philosophy and stakeholder priority for the Johnson & Johnson global business are outlined in the Credo, written in the mid-1940s by R. W. Johnson. Local subsidiaries are, therefore, in a position to base their own local mission statement in the context of both the Credo and local operating circumstances.

Our Credo

We believe our first responsibility is to the doctors, nurses and patients, to mothers and fathers and all others who use our products and services. In meeting their needs everything we do must be of high quality. We must constantly strive to reduce our costs in order to maintain reasonable prices. Customers' orders must be serviced promptly and accurately. Our suppliers and distributors must have an opportunity to make a fair profit.

We are responsible to our employees, the men and women who work with us throughout the world. Everyone must be considered as an individual.

We must respect their dignity and recognise their merit. They must have a sense of security in their jobs. Compensation must be fair and adequate, and working conditions clean, orderly and safe. We must be mindful of ways to help our employees fulfill their family responsibilities. Employees must feel free to make suggestions and complaints. There must be equal opportunity for employment, development and advancement for those qualified. We must provide competent management, and their actions must be just and ethical.

We are responsible to the communities in which we live and work and to the world community as well. We must be good citizens – support good works and charities and bear our fair share of taxes. We must encourage civic improvements and better health and education. We must maintain in good order the property we are privileged to use, protecting the environment and natural resources.

Our final responsibility is to our stockholders. Business must make a sound profit. We must experiment with new ideas. Research must be carried on, innovative programmes developed and mistakes paid for. New equipment must be purchased, new facilities provided and new products launched. Reserves must be created to provide for adverse times. When we operate according to these principles, the stockholders should realize a fair return.

An important test of a value statement is its use in critical moments in history. In Johnson & Johnson's case the Credo was a vital ethical reference point in the 1982 Tylenol crisis, when one of the company's products was tampered with. The company withdrew all supplies of the product and did not relaunch it until tamper evident packaging was available. This took the company a considerable length of time and it voluntarily incurred substantial financial losses in order to protect the public safety.

THE POWER OF POSSIBILITY THINKING

Possibility thinking is typified by the question:

> What would you attempt to do if you knew that you could
> not possibly fail?

Creative organizations espouse and live values that give permission for people to take risks. For example:

> With creativity and daring Matsushita will continue to fulfil
> its responsibilities as a corporation and citizen of the world.
> (*Matsushita Electric*)

> Whatever it takes.
> (*Digital Corporation*)

> We will encourage each other to question, create and
> innovate.
> (*Glaxo-Wellcome*)

In such organizations, excitement is a permissible behaviour.

Points to ponder

○   Is it necessary for personal values to align with expected behaviour in your organization? Can you cite any examples of where this has made a noticeable difference to the performance of an individual, group or the organization?

○   What might happen if you allowed your best personal values to 'interfere' with the normal processes of work? Imagine what the results might be two years down the line.

SUMMARY

We have considered the powerful effect that culture can have on the generation of the conditions necessary for creativity to flourish. It can take years to build a culture that inspires creativity – and five minutes to destroy it. Key points that arise from the chapter include:

○   There is no single preferred creative culture.
○   It is important to find ways of setting a culture without engendering too much permanence in a changing environment.
○   Strong cultures have certain weaknesses. Provided you are aware of the weaknesses, it is possible to minimize them.
○   There is a case for organizational re-invention to 'refresh' the paradigm. Processes such as the N&Ps 'Understanding' and David Bohm's 'Dialogue' can be of assistance here.
○   Conflict over ideas is a valuable resource provided it is harnessed and used.
○   Creativity is a relevant quality for dealing with emergence in strategic thinking. Emergent strategy requires a continuous ability to think outside the box.
○   The creative leader adopts many roles and is master or mistress of personal change which gives a positive example to others.
○   The creative leader's job is to align values, climate and behaviour in a way that delivers the goals of the organization whilst simultaneously encouraging dissonance with the paradigm.

You will find it useful to consolidate your reading by reviewing the following questions.

About what you have learned

O   What has reading this chapter confirmed in your mind?
O   What new curiosities has it raised about the role of creativity in culture change?

About putting the ideas to work

O   Where are there opportunities to introduce conflict in the pursuit of higher quality results?
O   How can you adapt the N&P case study to improve dialogue in your organization?
O   Where would 'not only but also thinking' be of use to your organization? Can you devise a way of introducing this so that it is not perceived as a 'fad'?

A final thought

Question: *Why did the creative leader cross the road?*

Answer: *To model the strategies of the visionary chicken.*

8

STRUCTURES AND SYSTEMS

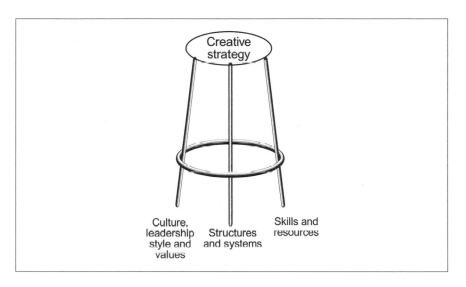

Getting employees to think like barbarians not bureaucrats.
(*Philippe Kahn, Software Chief, Borland*)

We now examine elements of structure and systems in generating a more creative organization. We include both formal and informal elements of structure, such as organization design, information structures and the 'shadow side' of the organization. 'Systems' will include rewards, recognition and career systems. Whilst it is not necessarily true that good structures and systems assist creativity, poor structures and systems do seriously hamper creativity. In process terms, structure should contribute to the conversion of inputs (ideas) into outputs (innovations) at lower cost, faster, to higher return. Our pipeline model (from Chapter 4) will be extended to accommodate the influence of structure on creativity and innovation.

PRINCIPLES OF STRUCTURE

All organizations have some form of structure. I currently work within several virtual organizations. Even in this type of organization it has been helpful to establish certain structural disciplines that enable the company to function effectively. Examples of the required structures include:

O   The need to support knowledge-sharing actively.
O   Defining the links required for the development of trust despite physical distance. I have worked for one virtual organization for three years and have not yet met any of their members face to face.
O   A project management approach to the relationship.

The need for and nature of the structure varies according to the virtual organization in which I am working. As mentioned in Chapter 7, it is fashionable to say that bureaucracies are bad for creativity. A counter-intuitive reality is that there is a need for some bureaucracy in a creative organization.

The traditional view of structure is that it makes possible the application of management and creates a framework for communication through which the activities of the organization can be planned, organized, directed and controlled. Thus an appropriate structure will facilitate the achievement of the aims of the organization and an inappropriate one will not. In reality, most formal structures involve some level of compromise, that is they are imperfect, due to the need to resolve a number of competing aims. This imperfection arises from the use of simple and rational devices, such as two-dimensional organization charts, for structuring complex and often irrational activities.

When we come to examine the role of structure in assisting creativity, we must understand the assumptions and design principles upon which structures exist.

ON WHAT ASSUMPTIONS ARE ORGANIZATIONAL STRUCTURES BUILT?

Some traditional assumptions about structure include the following.

Big is beautiful

Such an assumption permits the organization to generate economies through large-scale operations. The metaphor of the creative organization as an 'earthworm' was proposed by one group that I worked with, on the basis that it is possible to divide an earthworm (accidentally) and both halves live on and grow bigger. This trait also makes the earthworm less vulnerable to birds. Some innovative organizations set a lot of store by keeping things small, for example, by breaking up a unit as soon as it becomes a certain size. One company has a 'magic number' of 1200 that signals the need to subdivide a unit. In his book, *Maverick,* Semler (1993) suggests that people will only perform at their potential when they know everyone around them – usually approximately 150 individuals. (Incidentally, only the half of the earthworm with the 'saddle' survives when it is bisected, which serves to demonstrate the fact that metaphors are partial realities!)

Concentrate expertise

Advantage can be gained through specialization, since this allows units to gain experience more rapidly.

More resources make for faster innovations

The assumption here is that adding people to the process shortens the length of the process. Research in project-based engineering organizations indicates just the opposite. The probable explanation is that work expands to fill the time available at little or no greater quality.

In a rapidly changing environment, these assumptions need to be questioned. An important principle to use when designing a structure is the need to make these assumptions explicit as a good accountant would when drawing up a budget.

Formal structures are not the only ones. Perhaps more powerful are the informal structures, such as political, career and networking structures, that exist within most organizations. These are more relevant to a creative organization and will be explored later in this chapter.

DESIGN PRINCIPLES

Most organization structures can be defined by the following parameters.

What is the strategy?

The prime factor in designing a structure should be the extent to which it facilitates the delivery of the strategy. In a creative organization, this 'end game' must be balanced by a number of other factors that concern 'means' of achieving the strategy.

How many indians per chief?

The number of subordinates directly reporting to an individual will be affected by the degree to which the individual's work depends on others.

Tall or flat?

Levels of hierarchy. The present trend is to remove layers of management dramatically. Although I have met many people who have been traumatized by 'flatter' structures, a number of them have actually admitted that the flattening is good for creativity in the long run, in spite of the negative personal impact.

Where is the power concentrated?

The power that managers possess at each level reflects the degree to which power is centralized or decentralized. Both have their advantages and disadvantages. Paradoxically, some centralization is often helpful in creative organizations, especially concerning supporting resources and providing rapid response funding for promising projects.

Rigid or flexible?

The breadth of an employee's job, may be related to the degree of **expertise** needed to perform the job and the extent to which the job itself is **fragmented** into smaller tasks which are distributed between individuals. Experts are valuable when the organization needs to use new skills, techniques, experience and/or knowledge and cannot expect existing staff to acquire them whilst concentrating on their current jobs. Breaking the job into smaller elements can have the disadvantage of reducing motivation through an inability to see the 'big picture'.

Clear or fuzzy boundaries?

The extent to which people's jobs are precisely defined through 'devices' such as job descriptions, competency frameworks, key performance indicators etc. The advantages and disadvantages of high degree of definition are shown in Table 8.1.

TABLE 8.1   Advantages and disadvantages of job definition

Advantages	Disadvantages
Ambiguity removal for the individual; clarity about how roles inter-relate	Restricted flexibility where people are expected to 'muck-in'. Tendency to introduce dependency into the relationship
Clarity for performance assessment	Excessive paperwork. An impression that there is no room for individual flair
Improved co-ordination	Too rigid In times of change

On balance, I am not in favour of high levels of job definition. However, there can be exceptions to this rule, when the disadvantages are not significant in a particular organization.

The degree of definition can also be related to the 'fried egg' and 'four P' models we saw in Chapter 3. Definition over the demands provides a sense of positivity and can lead to persistence. High definition over constraints leads to a loss of passion and playfulness, and definition over choices leads to a loss of persistence and playfulness (see Figure 8.1).

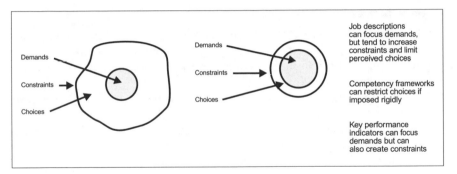

FIGURE 8.1   The impact of definition on opportunities for creativity.

How many chiefs does one indian serve?

Whilst it has been considered desirable for people to have only one manager, this may make the organization slow to adapt to new and changing circumstances. However, having more than one boss requires high levels of skill in contracting over goals and priorities. An alternative strategy is for the 'chiefs' to co-ordinate their demands, leaving the 'creatives' relatively unfettered by such distractions.

How does information flow?

Since organizational structure is intended to facilitate communication, it would make sense to group together people who communicate regularly. Where this is not possible or desirable, there are many other ways of facilitating good communications.

However, opinion is divided as to whether it is best to physically separate functions who have to work closely. Glaxo-Wellcome and Novartis currently separate responsibility for research and development on the basis that invention requires a creative spark, whereas getting the invention to market requires different qualities. On the other hand, Zeneca and SmithKline Beecham currently give joint responsibility for these functions. It is not possible to assess whether either arrangement provides particular advantages in performance terms. However, it is likely that the particular arrangements provide an internal context which leads to a higher probability and frequency of external success. (Source: *Financial Times.*)

Conclusions

In resolving the dilemmas of structure, it is wise to attempt to reach the 'best available outcome' rather than the 'lowest common denominator'. This involves finding and/also solutions to the conflicting elements rather than reaching decisions on an either/or basis.

Points to ponder

O   Beware the lure of the magic meeting in the corridor. Leading orga-
      nizations do not merely rely on serendipity to make creativity hap-
      pen. Collaboration should be assisted through both formal and
      informal structures.
O   Co-operation across organizations must be enabled. If power rests
      in particular areas or business units, special attention must be given
      to encouraging co-operation and influence of people outside a
      given unit. For example, senior people must have a cross-divisional
      focus to minimize the tendency for local optimization.
O   Recognize and encourage a nomadic element because people work-
      ing on the same project need to communicate.
O   The role of the future-oriented Human Resources function is not to
      create organization charts but to help the organization design tem-
      porary structures that enable the organization to achieve its outputs
      whilst holding the organization in tension to do new things.
O   Since big ideas come from small teams, a key role in large organiza-
      tions is that of designing the organization so that it feels small but
      benefits from the wider resources that are commonplace in larger
      organizations.

ORGANIZATIONAL STRUCTURES AND CREATIVITY

TRADITIONAL STRUCTURES

There have been a number of attempts to suggest that organizations do not
need a structure. This requires a utopian view of the relationship between
employer and employee, where the employee is self-directed and free from
wishes of personal career enhancement etc. I am not persuaded by the argument that structure is unnecessary for most organizations. Indeed, structure
can provide an important anchor point for many people. Lack of structure in
a traditional organization tends to lead to creative chaos, where individuals
pursue their own whims.

Bureaucracies

There is still a place for bureaucracy in creative organizations (see Figure
8.2). The challenge then becomes how to lead creative people in a structured environment. The case study of Kent County Council, in Chapter 6,
gives good examples of how creative enclaves can flourish in large bureaucracies. In particular, bureaucracies can encourage the persistence dimension of the four P framework. They are not so good at encouraging
passion. Sometimes an acceptable alternative way of saying passion in a
bureaucracy is 'interest' or 'drive'.

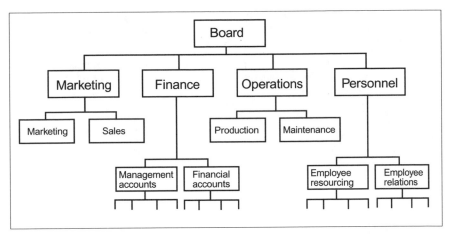

FIGURE 8.2   A bureaucratic structure.

The following case illustrates how creative projects can sit inside a bureaucratic 'container'.

LOVE IN AN ELEVATOR – CREATIVITY IN A BUREAUCRACY

This case illustrates a creative project within the Research and Development function of Kent Training and Enterprise Council. By its very nature, the organization has to respond to Government-led policy initiatives and this tends to result in standardized approaches. The organization has a predominantly bureaucratic structural design which makes the emergence of creativity more interesting than in a 'loose' structure.

The return to learn project

This project is concerned with getting adults to restart the process of learning, so that basic numeracy and literacy levels improve. Kent Training and Enterprise Council (TEC) decided to take a novel approach, which was ahead of its time with respect to prevailing thinking.

The basis of the project was a 'creative swipe' of the Ford EDAP programme, whereby employees are paid £100 to learn something of interest to them, as long as it is unrelated to work. In this case the TEC partnered with businesses, offering them £50 per employee which the employer was expected to match, with the same condition attached, that is learning unrelated to work.

The project had to overcome the following barriers:

○ Criticism concerning wasting public money.
○ Cynical reactions of some employees and unions, who believed that
    the scheme was a smokescreen to achieve other employee deals.

The project has changed the way that individuals see lifelong learning. In some cases this has led to increased willingness to undertake work-related learning. For example, at Royal Mail, Maidstone:

'We had a chap who did Maths and he wanted to progress to a higher grade postman. He had to pass a maths test for that and could never manage it. After taking a return to learn maths course, he has succeeded.'

The project was launched as a pilot scheme with eight companies and was delivered as a mainstream project within the bureaucratic structure. The success factors were:

○ It was explicitly agreed at the outset that it might fail.
○ It was not a 'scheme'. TECs get accused of devising complex schemes.

This project was unusual because the employers 'wrote the rules' and it did not become overcomplex.

Reflections

Creativity within Kent TEC benefits from the following factors:

○ Thinking end results, not structure.
○ Not being constrained by money. If the idea is good enough, money will arrive.
○ Using people that are practised in idea generation techniques and who have good modelling and conceptual thinking skills.
○ The need to be politically astute.

(Ian White, Business and Economic Development Manager, Kent TEC)

The matrix organization

Matrix structures are combination structures which are intended to allow enhanced product/service focus (see Figure 8.3). They are fashionable and tend to increase identification with end results, yet they are not without problems. These typically arise from:

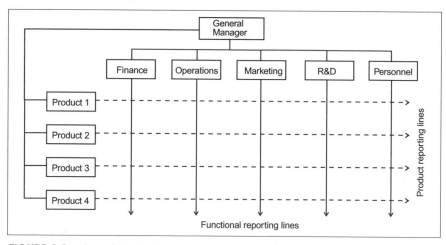

FIGURE 8.3   A matrix structure.

○   Lack of good informal contacts with functional managers.
○   Corrosive competition for resources which tends to be bad for the
       playfulness dimension of creativity.
○   Dissipation of passion through the reality of individuals reporting to
       more than one manager.

To make a matrix structure work well it needs support from good information systems. Individuals that work in the matrix must have a high tolerance
of ambiguity and be self-starters. Matrix managers must also learn to strike
contracts with employees that take account of multiple demands.

   A variant on the matrix form is a project-based organization (Figure 8.4).

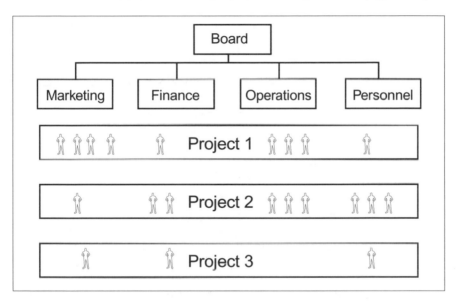

FIGURE 8.4   A project-based structure.

   Here, the difference is that people are organized around projects, creating
a greater sense of project 'ownership' for the individuals concerned. This
can improve the passion, persistence and playfulness dimensions of creativity. The same requirements concerning information and contracting apply to
project-based organizations, and there can be difficulty in switching
resources to different projects or killing unpromising projects in such structures.

Point to ponder

○   Can creativity be made a cross-disciplinary function in traditional
       organizational structures?

INFORMAL STRUCTURES ARE VITAL TO CREATIVITY

I heard it on the grapevine.
(*Marvin Gaye*)

Informal structures are generally more helpful in generating and sustaining organizational creativity. In particular the shadow side of the organization tends to be an important area where seeds of creativity germinate. If this is controlled formally, it tends to lose its effectiveness. Now that many organizations are becoming more rational through re-engineering, creativity can suffer due to the removal of apparently low value-adding structural elements, such as 'smoking rooms'.

To facilitate informality, some of the following formal structural elements are found in creative organizations:

O   Minimum hierarchy.
O   Organization based on organic networks rather than two-dimensional fixed structures.
O   Rotation of staff out of their primary professional role, for example moving production people into marketing and vice versa.
O   Use of venture groups and other 'micro-structures' to progress 'out of phase' organization goals.

A by-product (unintended or deliberate) of traditional organization structures is the segregation of different thinking styles by function, geography or both, thus the detail-conscious accounting department is kept away from research and development. There is underlying sense in this in so far as people know that these groups find it hard to understand one another. We have to start with a new set of assumptions about organizations to design the structure in a different way. The single most important assumption is that conflict over ideas is a necessary condition for creativity to flourish.

STRUCTURES THAT CAN PROMOTE CREATIVITY

In discussing structures that may promote creativity, it is useful to update the pipeline analogy developed in Chapter 4.

This version is closer to the reality of many organizations (Figure 8.5).

O   The pipeline is distorted in places. The variable **width** represents resource fluctuations caused by imperfect structural design.
O   The pipeline has **bends** and the liquid flowing through it may be **viscous**. This represents the culture.
O   There are **dead legs** and **mazes**. These represent committees and other structural barriers.
O   The speed through the pipeline can be increased in the following ways: (1) Increase the **pressure** on the liquid flowing into the pipe.

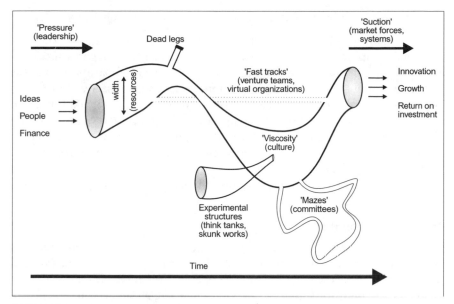

FIGURE 8.5   The ideas pipeline.

This is a function of creative leadership; (2) Increase the **suction** on the liquid flowing out of the pipe. This is a function of market forces and systems which encourage faster innovation; (3) Modify the structure to achieve more rapid results by building fast tracks and using experimental structures to **bypass** the restrictions; (4) Speed up the **flow** by lowering the viscosity of the liquid (by warming it up). This is a function of culture change and the use of integrating mechanisms such as employee involvement programmes, idea champions and boundary crossers.

Earlier chapters have examined leadership and cultural issues. Now, we shall concentrate on structural forms that can be of assistance.

Venture teams

Venture teams are used to promote entrepreneurial behaviour inside an organization. In some ways they can be seen as a variant of an independent project team. The following are their characteristic features:

- Relatively small.
- Full-time membership.
- Set up to take risks.
- Start with a poorly defined objective at first.
- Segregated from the formal organization.
- Greater freedom and fewer rules.

○   Responsible for successful development and exploitation of ideas.

Venture teams can be used for whole product/service innovations. The IBM personal computer was the product of a venture team. A smaller-scale example of venture teams in action is that of a social services department that was concerned about becoming more responsive to its clients. A venture team was set up to explore the problem. The team set its own agenda for action and visited a number of external organizations over a period of time, during which they learned from each visit and adapted what they had learned to their own situation. The team even visited hotels, since it was recognized that this was where customer service counted most. This radical step would have been considered counter-culture to many of the formal structures within the service.

The virtual organization

A current challenge to organizations concerns how to design organizations where there are few or no core elements. The advantage of such structures lies in their ability to allow different parts to operate in completely different structural (and cultural) ways. An example of such an organization would be a fashion house, operating with a core partnership of two people. It may hire design specialists on an *ad hoc* basis, contract with a flexible manufacturing firm who can rapidly adapt machinery and processes to produce the required garments, use a traditional accounting firm to manage its financial affairs, or hire a marketing agency for specific projects. Each separate organization has varying contractual and communications requirements with the core partnership (Figure 8.6).

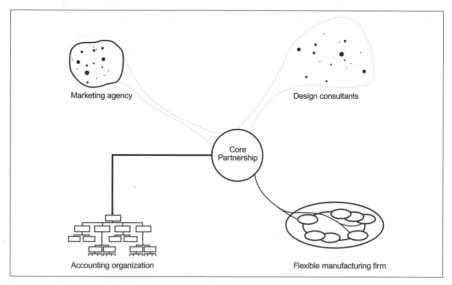

FIGURE 8.6   A virtual organization structure.

In structural terms, all that is required of each organization is the tacit agreement to work within a defined set of criteria that achieves the ultimate goals of the organization. Within these demands, each organization is free to structure its activities as it pleases. In some ways, this resembles a divisionalized organization, except there is no potential for direct control of the participating organizations. For such organizations to work effectively there needs to be a clear understanding of the nature of the contract and a bond of trust over issues which are critical to success. The relationship will vary between the different participating organizations. In the above example, a fairly bureaucratic relationship will be maintained with the head of the accounting firm. The relationship with the design specialists will be more about shared values and information exchange on an individual basis. Direct contacts will be established with key people in the manufacturing firm.

In the context of creativity, the virtual organization needs to be carefully arranged so as to preserve some **'rough edges'** and points of **'ideas fermentation'**. In the above example, there is theoretically no need for the separate organizations ever to meet, yet there may be some significant opportunity costs if they do not. There are several possible responses to this problem:

○   The core partnership decides what is relevant information and ensures it is conveyed to the places it is needed via the 'information conduit'.

○   The core partnership takes the lead in ensuring that the separate organizations come together on a regular basis with an explicit learning agenda that benefits all participants.

○   The separate organizations form local arrangements that suit their individual information and intelligence needs. For example, the design specialists may wish to network directly with the manufacturing firm to speed up the time to market.

Use of integrating mechanisms

In organizations that have separated functions, there can be many communication barriers to moving ideas into innovations. Responses to this problem include setting up employee involvement programmes to ensure that ideas are placed where they are visible on the organization's landscape, the use of 'idea champions' and 'boundary crossers'.

Employee involvement programmes   The IDEAs system of Post Office Counters Limited (POCL), mentioned in Chapter 6, is an example of an employee involvement system – as is the 'Office of Innovation' model used by more than 10 of Fortune's top 200 US companies. Eastman Kodak estimated that in one year alone, the harvest was $300 million (over the lifetime of the idea) from a network of offices whose cost was only 0.3 per cent of potential revenue.

Idea champions   Idea champions are mentioned in the Glaxo-Wellcome case study as being important to ensure that ideas are resourced, especially in larger organizations. Ideal candidates to act as idea champions are individuals who have some relevant understanding of the ideas, but who crucially have access to wide networks and who possess excellent advocacy skills.

Boundary crossers   Boundary crossers are individuals who move across organizational boundaries with the specific intention of integrating and networking the parts of the organization that need to co-operate together. They are needed in organizations that physically separate functions so that they can focus on their core expertise. The use of boundary crossers tends to contain conflict, since they act as 'translators' and 'mediators' between units that have diverse mind-sets.

Experimental structures

Change tends to start outside the formal structures of an organization, industry or country. Witness the rise of rock 'n' roll music in the 1950s and the punk movement in the 1970s. Punk arose as a 'shadow side' response to the lumbering activities of the progressive rock movement. Within a couple of years it had been absorbed into the mainstream activities of the music business and society in general. Thus, the 'shadow side' quickly became part of the formal structure. This then produced another 'alternative' view.

Attempts to organize the shadow side of organizations must be orchestrated carefully so as not to make it part of the mainstream. Some **think tanks** operate on this principle, one example is provided by an off licence chain that has a 'Shadow Cabinet'. This is composed of future directors of the company and is expected to formulate 'the alternative view' on specific issues of future importance to the company. It also acts as a development pathway for those who join.

Another approach, often called **skunkworks** operates on the principle of tolerating unofficial tinkering within the shadow structure. The 3M 15 per cent rule, mentioned in Chapter 3, is a form of legitimized skunkworking. The organization has to remain loose in order for people to be able to tinker effectively.

Knowledge- and skills-based structure

A knowledge- and skills-based structure enables resources to flow through the organization better. This structure is a way of formalizing and leveraging 'who knows what?' and 'who can do what?' in the organization and requires three components to work effectively:

O   **Individual clarity** Individuals have a clear sense of what it is that they contribute to the organization. This is not a curriculum vitae but a short statement of their personal contribution in the form of key knowledge and skills, as seen from the viewpoint of their major stakeholders. This statement will include other useful information that would potentially be of use to users, for example Myers Briggs Type Indicators, hobbies or star signs! One large pharmaceutical company has such a structure in place to help speed up its research and development process.

○ **Appropriate communication channels** There have to be a number of convenient communication channels that people are prepared to use. If information technology is used for this, it should provide significant advantages in terms of speed and precision of targeting compared with informal networking solutions.

○ **'Looseness' in the structure** The organization must be sufficiently loose to allow people to be able to resource other experts for periods of time. It is no good having a brilliant information system that lets you know who is good at what if you cannot get hold of them!

DEFINING YOUR KEY KNOWLEDGE AND SKILL ASSETS

This activity can be undertaken by yourself, yet it is far more useful when conducted as part of an organizational strategy to identify and enhance intellectual capital.

Find a colleague who you regard as a good 'coach'. Together, go for a walk outdoors to identify your key knowledge and skill assets using the following process:

1. Your goal is to talk about your key successes in an uninterrupted flow. You may recall all the successful milestones in your career and life to do this.
2. The coach listens for main themes and underlying knowledge and skills.
3. The coach then 'plays back' what he/she has heard you say in the form of a summary that identifies key knowledge and skills as they would benefit other stakeholders.
4. Spend some time in dialogue with your coach to clarify your top five unique qualities.
5. Commit the top five qualities to a 'personal value' statement of no more than 50 words.

Points to ponder

○ Set up the means for informal communications structures rather than trying to formalize these features. As soon as someone tries to standardize these, ensure that you reprimand them.

○ Ensure all your employees have a clear sense of what it is that they

contribute to the success of the organization. Develop personal contribution statements and ensure that they are updated regularly.
O   Replace your organization charts with knowledge, skill and networking maps.

SYSTEMS THAT ENCOURAGE CREATIVITY

Systems must either support creativity or, as a minimum, not get in its way. As with structure, poorly designed systems can impede creativity, but good ones may not necessarily enhance it. Amongst the systems that were mentioned in the research for this book as being helpful in maintaining creativity were:

O   Individualizing role specifications.
O   Simplified grading structures.
O   Career systems based on individual choice.
O   Moving from financial rewards to individualized reward and recognition systems.
O   Customer involvement in new product/service design.
O   Self-set goals and pay.
O   Continuous learning policy.
O   Project grant schemes.
O   Worker–Directors and children on the Board.

The question of rewarding creativity is worthy of further discussion.

FROM REWARDS TO RECOGNITION

> One person's reward is another person's demotivator.
> (*Roy Yates, Head of Research Human Resources,*
> *Zeneca Pharmaceuticals*)

Reward systems can become a hindrance to creativity, especially if they are unsympathetic to the expected behaviours. One company is presently experimenting with creative recognition strategies offering a more flexible menu of rewards (financial and non-financial) that are more closely aligned with individual motivators.

Some organizations have experimented with 'dual ladder' reward systems to recognize different career paths as specialists and managers. Such systems have to be operated very effectively if they, the dual ladders, are perceived to be of equal value.

There were differences in opinion as to whether effort was as valuable as results in terms of reward. One major pharmaceutical company rewards results (**ends**), that is drugs on the market rather than the process (**means**) of getting there. The advantage to them is that it allows considerable latitude of approach (how-to). It also assists in dropping research projects that are not delivering real benefits since people want to be associated with winning projects. It is also very difficult to measure 'means', although some organizations have used competency profiling successfully to do this.

The example of Zeneca Pharmaceuticals shows how rewards need to be shaped to the individual and the results of their work.

> At Zeneca Pharmaceuticals care is taken in staff selection and recruitment and the company has an innovative approach to career management. Dr Barry Furr leads the Therapeutic Research Department comprising over 600 people. He looks for individuals who possess the following attributes:
>
> ○ Problem-solving capacity.
> ○ Lateral thinking ability.
> ○ Real enthusiasm for science.
> ○ People of high intellectual ability who actually want to find drugs. This is a different viewpoint from wanting to understand disease as an end in itself.
>
> Zeneca recognizes success through both financial and non-financial rewards. In addition to the more traditional approaches of annual salary reviews, bonuses and non-monetary rewards are options open to managers who are given a review budget specifically for this purpose. Other examples of non-financial recognition in action include using the company's quarterly briefing meetings to give praise and recognition and progress up the scientific ladder as a status reward for those that wish to progress in this way.
>
> There are extensive opportunities to develop staff outside their speciality through project management, and by cross-departmental secondments and retraining. Zeneca has retrained 12 pharmacologists over the last four years as molecular biologists at Manchester University doing a M. Res.
>
> Furr distinguishes between 'failure', 'success' and 'triumph'. Failure involves incompetence (omitting key experiments, for example) and should be dealt with based on the fact that Zeneca expects its scientists to be working at the highest levels of professionalism. Success and triumph give meaningful answers to the hypotheses and questions asked.
>
> Success arises when an experimental result leads to a decision to abandon a project and stop investment. Given that Zeneca needs to fill the R&D pipeline with only the most promising compounds, this is an important result for the scientist and the company, even though the scientist may regard the result with some disappointment.
>
> On the other hand, triumph is an outcome that leads to further investment in the target approach. Both success and triumph are rewarded, if not in identical ways.

Points to ponder

○   How do you reward creative individuals in ways that are appropriate to their motivational strategies?

○   What opportunities are there for allowing individuals to develop outside their specialism?

○   What attempts do you make to benefit from the clashing of ideas from different professional disciplines?

○   What formal or informal structures exist to sense and respond to new ideas?

○   How much time is set aside for speculative projects with no obvious immediate payback?

UNCONVENTIONAL REWARDS MAY WORK BETTER (AND COST LESS)

Rewards must be relevant to the recipient's desired motivational strategy for maximum effect. For example:

○   Offering someone the opportunity to go out for dinner with their partner, to recognize work that has involved them being abroad or working long hours.

○   'Red letter days' – this is where an individual receives a voucher which can be exchanged for a wide range of benefits. These have included rides in hot air balloons.

Needs hierarchy		Creative applications
Self-actualization		Sabbaticals, 'dream jobs', 'trust time'
Ego		Awards, status symbols, autonomous working
Belonging and love		Cross-functional social systems, 'Elvis' days, works parties
Safety		Employability schemes, health care, counselling
Physiological	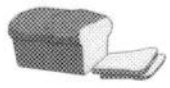	Financial rewards, good working environment

FIGURE 8.7   Creative applications of Maslow's needs hierarchy.

Although Maslow has been criticized for his assertion that his hierarchy of needs is sequential, that is one must have satisfied the lower-order needs before gaining access to the higher-order ones, the creative use of his model is the basis for a useful way of thinking about rewards and recognition (Figure 8.7).

One large distribution company has a 'Big Breakfast' reward ritual where the company gives its employees breakfast as a reward for special achievements. These types of rituals are changed regularly so that they do not become stale.

Another has a 'quality day'. This is a reward for something outstanding. The individual may decide to do anything they like within the organization for a day.

Other systems seek to reinforce the culture, such as the use of 'trust time', where people come and go as they please to model personal responsibility at work, the opportunity to attend a limited specialist symposium or present a paper, or a sabbatical to enhance expertise.

Some organizations separate **extrinsic** rewards (visible rewards that are 'outside' the person) from **intrinsic** rewards such as a sense of achievement, additional responsibility, autonomy, enhancement of skills and knowledge. Roy Yates, Head of the Research Human Resources Group at Zeneca Pharmaceuticals, says that he encourages the use of both extrinsic and intrinsic rewards. He states that extrinsic rewards should have the following characteristics if they are to operate as effective motivators:

O   Importance.
O   Flexibility.
O   Timeliness.
O   Visibility.

SUMMARY

This chapter has examined the various paradoxes of structure as an enabler of creativity. Whilst it would be easy to suggest that **no structure** is the answer to the question 'How do I best structure my organization to encourage creativity?', there is evidence to suggest that some structure is helpful in moving ideas into innovations. The key conclusions that may be drawn are:

O   Structures must be **designed** rather than seen as a chore of the Human Resources function.
O   Assumptions inherent in what the structure is trying to achieve must be made explicit and examined in context with the intended strategy.
O   Attempts to over-structure the organization must be resisted and punished.
O   The pipeline model helps identify where there are opportunities for

improving the speed, number and quality of ideas that are converted into productive action.

O　　Structures should have redesign capability built in, much as some computer systems have certain upgrade capabilities.

O　　Integrators and champions are necessary to make some of the more modern structural archetypes work in practice.

You will find it useful to consolidate your reading by reviewing the following questions:

About what you have learned

O　　What has reading this chapter confirmed in your mind about the role of structure as an asset or liability for creativity?

O　　What new curiosities has it raised?

About putting the ideas to work

O　　What opportunities are there to unhook the organization from over-bureaucratic structures?

O　　How can you adapt your own ideas 'pipeline' to increase the speed, number and quality of the innovations that emerge?

O　　How can you widen the choices available to people in terms of career development and reward/recognition strategies?

A final thought

Nothing is impossible until it is sent to a committee.

9

SKILLS AND RESOURCES

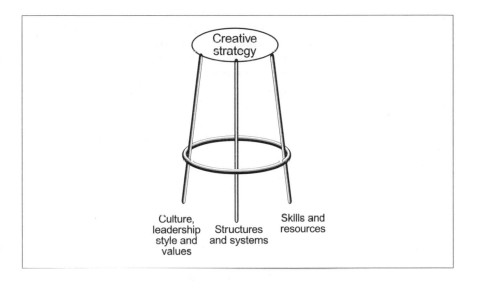

We cannot solve our problems with the same level of
thinking that created them.
(*Einstein*)

For maximum value, creativity requires an appropriate **context**. Context equates with culture, leadership style and values, and is supported by appropriate structures and systems. The next question to be raised is the **level** of creative activity, which relates to the degree to which an organization utilizes its skills and resources for creative advantage.

We look here at skills and resources and divide them into the following areas:

O   Resourcing creative people.
O   Developing creativity within the organization.

O   Setting an appropriate climate.
O   The application of resources, such as people management, finance and information, to draw the most out of creative people.

GETTING CREATIVE PEOPLE INTO THE ORGANIZATION

ATTRACTING CREATIVE PEOPLE AND CREATING ATTRACTIVE PEOPLE

There is a place for subscribing to the notion that the only way to build a creative organization is by ensuring that the raw materials are of the highest quality. Some companies 'codify' selection processes to identify and attract these people to their organizations. This is fine as far as it goes, yet in many cases the assumptions on which the selection procedures are built are shaky. A classic mistake is to assume that the most intelligent people are likely to be the most creative. Organizations that hold this view will typically search universities for new people, concentrating only on academic achievements as a measure of potential for creativity.

Increasingly, however, we are aware of a range of intelligences that are valuable for creativity, most of which are not deliberately enhanced during education – and some of which our education system attempts to extinguish. These have been described by Dryden and Vos (1994) as shown in Table 9.1.

TABLE 9.1 The seven intelligences	
Intelligence type	Typical traits exhibited by someone with this intelligence
Linguistic intelligence	Active listening skills, good writing and reasoning, public speaking capability
Logical–mathematical intelligence	Computing skills, problem-solving, structured approach, precision, abstract thinking
Visual–spatial intelligence	Uses images to think, has sense of the big picture, uses metaphor
Musical intelligence	Sensitive to pitch, rhythm, emotions
Bodily–kinaesthetic intelligence	Good timing, learns by tactile experience, mechanically minded, skilled at crafts
Interpersonal or social intelligence	Negotiates well, good communicator, relates well
Intrapersonal or intuitive intelligence	Sensitive to own values, intuitive skills, needs to be different, self-motivated

(Source: Dryden and Vos (1994) The Learning Revolution, Accelerated Learning Systems.)

Selection processes must model the qualities that they are seeking and look more widely than just technical intelligence. One example of this selection philosophy may be found at Drusillas Zoo, which includes non-conventional exercises (such as drawing) during its interviewing process as an indicator of risk-taking.

As well as attracting creative people, there is a case for creating attractive people, that is fostering talent to its maximum capacity and utilization. This can be achieved by mixing people who possess different 'natural intelligences', so that they question areas that are less developed in each other, or by providing the necessary support. For example, a high-technology organization that I once worked for wanted to be more creative and asked for some help with techniques. The organization had an 'introverted' culture and logical–mathematical intelligence was prized. Rewards were mostly based on individual achievement. As a result, not many people shared ideas. In this case, it was appropriate to employ some catalysts and provide some help with assertiveness so that people would put their ideas forward, rather than developing their creativity *per se*.

DIVERSITY IS THE KEY – TOO MANY CHIEFS AND NOT ENOUGH IDIOTS

Diversity is not just an idea – men and women bring different things to the workplace. Recent research indicates that there may be a genetic component to the popular notion that women are more intuitive than men. However, here we will widen 'diversity' to include all forms of difference. Tom Peters (1994) suggested that business would be better if we surrounded ourselves with disagreeing (and even possibly disagreeable) people. I would go further. There is enormous value in selecting people who import tension, unusual ideas and questions. I give these people the title '**idiots**' (in the best possible sense) since they will not be locked into accepted ideas about the nature of problems within the organization.

A story that illustrates the value of diversity is the one about Alfred P Sloan, of General Motors, who is reputed to have said to his board of directors:

> *'Gentlemen, I take it that we have complete agreement on the decision here.'* When everyone round the table nodded in assent he continued ... *'then I propose we postpone further discussion of this matter until our next meeting to give ourselves time to develop disagreement and perhaps gain some understanding of what the discussion is all about.'*

In the context of organizations, 'idiots' include the following.

Naïve contributors

A naïve contributor is not hampered by pre-existing norms, rituals and mindsets that exist within the main group. They could be the 'new boy/girl' who is initially untainted by the culture of the organization.

An example of the naïve contributor concept may be found at Drusillas Zoo, where a Junior Board (comprised of children) advises on a range of matters related to business development. This has resulted in a number of specific strategies and actions that have contributed to the Zoo's attractiveness to its targeted market segments.

A related example is the use of worker–directors who bring important questions into the boardroom. This approach has been a legal requirement in certain European countries for many years. Any good non-executive director can also add value by operating in this mode.

Outsiders

Outsider commentary can be **systematic** or **accidental**. An example of the systematic use of outsiders may be found in our case study of Kent County Council (seen in Chapter 6), which makes use of external consultants to import difference to the organization, especially where attitudes need to be altered, for example concerning environmental matters. Another way of using outsiders is to invite stakeholder groups to important meetings, specifically to give an external view.

As well as the Junior Board, Drusillas Zoo has a high natural turnover of talent through its policy of deliberately employing a number of students every year for seasonal work. This provides a constant source of new perspectives and ideas.

Finally, some comments from a research and development team leader on the need for diversity as an input to creativity:

> The organization is divided between people who always go
> to lunch with the same people and people who 'flit around
> a bit' – the second group are often ideas people or idea
> sensors/advocates. There needs to be a balance between
> creative people and people who can put ideas into action.
> On occasion, these talents reside within the same person,
> but more often they are present in different people.

CREATIVITY AS A LATENT TALENT

Some psychologists are fond of categorizing people into certain styles and roles. Over a number of years I have noticed that this can produce a limited set of behaviours. For example, it is increasingly common to find people on team development programmes saying things such as, *'Well, I'm not the creative one in the team – I scored zero on this factor in my test.'* Of course, they are right – if you believe you aren't creative, it becomes true. When this is confirmed by 'men and women in white coats' it becomes more than a rumour.

It is more helpful to make the positive assumption that creativity resides within everybody – but the right circumstances have not yet materialized for this latent creativity to emerge. As discussed in the earlier chapters on blockages, this could be for a variety of reasons.

In such circumstances, the job of leaders is to change the meaning of creativity, so that individuals can feel included in the definition, and to alter the climate to enable small increments of creative behaviour to be rewarded appropriately. Sometimes this involves sensitizing individuals to the notion that minor improvements are just as creative as 'big ideas', and ensuring that their contributions are taken seriously.

Points to ponder

O   Put fuzzy thinkers alongside detailed people, making sure that they recognize and get a positive value from the potential conflict.

O   Find ways of systematically or accidentally introducing 'idiots' into your organization.

O   Use absurdity wisely.

O   Employ a small number of 'creativity catalysers' and ensure that they are required to roam around the organization to the places they are needed.

DEVELOPING CREATIVE POTENTIAL

CREATIVITY 'IMPLANTS' NOT EASY

> Creative minds have always been known to survive any
> kind of bad training.
> (*Anna Freud*)

Most of the organizations I have worked with hold opposing opinions on the subject of developing creativity. On one hand, they feel that it is more important to select people who would bring creativity to the organization rather than try to 'implant' creativity into individuals whilst they are there. On the other, they have invested considerable resources in trying to develop individuals and processes that encourage creative activity. Bad training is indeed dangerous and there is a lot of it about. Good training works when training is the answer and the context is suitable for progress.

To draw more creative behaviours from people who believe themselves to be naturally uncreative, several approaches (which do work) may be utilized.

Firstly, individuals should be helped to recognize situations where creativity will be of value. This awareness-raising is performed through a variety of means, for example psychometric inventories, focus groups or critical incident reviews.

If raised awareness is insufficient then exposure to a number of creativity techniques can widen the repertoire of resources available to fit to particular situations. Pick a learning method that suits the individual or groups involved. More will be said about this in Chapter 10.

Thirdly, ask people to work in groups where creativity is the norm, and support them appropriately. In this way, individuals themselves adapt to the new work demands rather than trying to 'implant' creativity.

Finally, it is possible to introduce creativity through a metaphor such as art or music workshops. These introduce beliefs and confidence in creativity without launching straight into techniques. Thus, creativity is 'crept up on' from a tangent rather than by use of a high-profile creativity initiative (which often results in people reading the 'sub-text' – that the organization lacks creativity).

CREATIVITY TOOLKITS – THE ADULT EQUIVALENT OF THE SANDPIT

The right context

There are differences of opinion about the value of developing the creative thinking capacity of individuals and organizations via the use of creative thinking techniques. These differences are present both between and within organizations. Essentially, techniques can be valuable if they fit the context. This also means that different parts of the same organization may use different techniques. No technique can overcome poor context, that is one where the leadership is inappropriate or the skill levels of people unsatisfactory to use the technique well. This explains the bad press that brainstorming receives. Once the context is right, there can be great value in providing techniques to enhance creativity.

In most organizations I have found that a limited number of techniques were generally used and this would necessitate individuals and groups force-fitting the available techniques to the problems/opportunities under consideration. If techniques are to have a role there must be many more of them from which to draw, and an understanding of the type most appropriate for specific problems/opportunities.

> An example where creativity has been important is that of a
> business process re-engineering project. The challenge was
> to get people to change their mindset from local

optimization towards global solutions. This was done through a variety of people who were exposed to a wide menu of techniques for change from which they were able to pick combinations of techniques that were appropriate to particular situations. Many of these were drawn from the sphere of neuro-linguistic programming (NLP) and related psychological disciplines.

(Senior Executive, large pharmaceutical company)

Principles behind creativity techniques

Most creativity techniques work on a number of principles:

O   **Climate** – developing the conditions where 'playful' thinking is allowed and allowing space and time – thinking in different ways takes some time to get started.

O   **Problem/opportunity definition** – understanding the real problem/opportunity(s) and the context or frame before moving into options or solutions.

O   **Separation** – of key phases of the process.

O   **Detachment** – from the problem/opportunity.

O   **Flexibility**   viewing the problem/opportunity from different angles and use of all thinking styles, for example logic and intuition.

O   **Encouraging idiots** – involving non-experts (or novices) and people with different specialisms in the process.

O   **Connecting ideas** – being prepared to add on to ideas and listening intently to meanings.

O   **Iteration** – the practice of recycling through the process to improve the quality of ideas before deciding on a course of action.

A clear understanding of the principles enables organizations to invent their own techniques. These are often much more powerful than proprietary techniques which have to be adapted to fit the context. The do-it-yourself (DIY) approach does require good design skills for the highest quality results, and we will explore this in greater detail in Chapter 11.

GENERATING A CLIMATE WHERE CREATIVITY IS A WAY OF LIFE

Although **culture** is often persistent in the amount of effort that it requires to change it, the **climate** of an organization is something that can be changed quite quickly with dramatic results. A creative climate can help significantly, in both good and bad times: making people feel better about being at work; easing communication between those who are there; and allowing firefighting to happen more effectively.

Climate differs from culture in the sense that climate concerns how the organization feels at a particular time, whereas culture is about the way things are habitually done. A metaphor for climate is that of the 'weather conditions' of an organization. We think of geographical areas (and organizations) as having a characteristic type of climate which allows us to develop certain expectations about the scenery, the clothes the inhabitants might wear, how comfortable we will feel there, how predictable the weather might be and how strange it might feel for someone who is used to another sort of climate. The climate in the UK is temperate; however, it is possible to create different environments within this. For example, at Kew Gardens the environment can be forced to allow different plants to grow. Beneath the 'industry climate' umbrella, organizations and parts of them can create 'micro-climates' that differ from the overall environment, in order to suit their own internal goals.

Climate also defines the level at which one needs to pitch creative behaviour. If the creative climate is already 'wild' then the effort required to go beyond that would be greater than if the climate were 'flat'. In this sense, climate may be seen as a thermometer to let you know how far to go to 'think and act outside the box'.

Majaro (1988) illustrates the contribution of climate in his book, *The Creative Gap* (Longman). He states the main prerequisites for developing a dynamic spirit of creativity:

O   A suitable climate for creative thinking must be created.
O   An effective system of communicating ideas must exist at all levels.
O   Procedures for managing innovation must be in place.

Ekvall (1991, 'The organizational culture of idea management' in Henry J, Walker D (eds), *Managing Innovation*. London: Sage Publications, reprinted by permission) devised a model of climate as an intervening variable which affects the results of the organization. He identified 10 dimensions of climate:

O   Challenge
O   Freedom
O   Idea support
O   Trust
O   Dynamism
O   Playfulness
O   Debates
O   Conflicts
O   Risk-taking
O   Idea-time.

By use of this model, Ekvall was able to identify 'innovative' departments and separate them from 'stagnated' ones. He drew the following conclusions:

○   No idea-handling system can work successfully without a supportive climate.
○   An idea-handling system can make a good climate better.
○   An idea-handling system which is set up in an organization with a bad climate tends to make the climate even worse.

ASSESSING THE CLIMATE FOR CREATIVITY IN YOUR ORGANIZATION

Please rate your own unit and your organization or a relevant part of it (1 = low, 10 = high) on the following dimensions that encourage a creative climate. Make some notes that explain your ratings and your particular interpretation of the dimensions.

Dimension	Own unit	Organization	Notes
Challenge			
Freedom			
Idea support			
Trust			
Dynamism			
Playfulness			
Debates			
Conflicts			
Risk-taking			
Idea-time			
Total scores			

1.   Mark the total score in each case on the climate thermometers (Figure 9.1).
2.   Mark two more points on the climate thermometers that represent where you desire to be by a given time.
3.   Examine each dimension to determine which are the most important differences required to transform the climate towards the desired state of affairs?
4.   Which single factor would make the most difference to improving the climate? What is the first step towards making this happen?
5.   What would be the likely effects of making these changes?

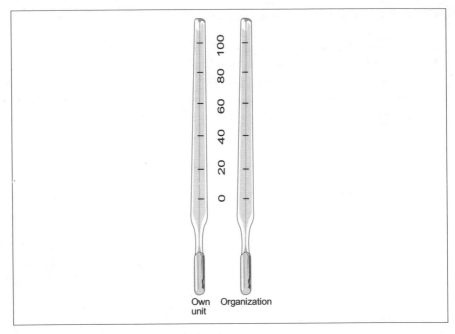

FIGURE 9.1   Climate thermometers.

An example of how a creative climate has been set up is that of a high-technology computer software company, where the Managing Director is known to arrive at work dressed as Elvis Presley or other famous characters from time to time. The impact of this 'extreme' dressing up policy is a climate where almost anything is tolerable. 'Dressing up' is a metaphor for a whole range of other ideas which would work in different contexts. In other words, it is not absolutely necessary to arrive in the office singing 'Hound Dog' to promote a creative climate.

RESOURCES THAT SUPPORT CREATIVITY

> For the creator to create suffering is needed.
> (*Nietzsche*)

THE ROLE OF HUMAN RESOURCES

> Quality without creativity is a dead end. You may get better
> and better at doing something which doesn't need doing …
> (*Edward de Bono*)

Some Human Resources departments disable their organization from creativity. Paradoxically, they are often uniquely positioned to have sufficient detachment that provides a much-needed quality to their organizations, but they often become engrossed in trying to systematize and constrain the organization. Increasingly, pro-active Human Resouces departments see their role as enabling the organization to move further and faster.

Ways in which Human Resources may become a key enabler of a more creative climate include:

O   Designing and administering flexible reward and recognition schemes based on individual passion rather than wants and needs.

O   Unwinding complex policies and procedures to give leaders and managers more latitude in decision making. Practically, this can mean setting a target to re-engineer the rule book to 50 per cent of its previous size. (Without using the photocopier set to 'reduce'.)

O   Taking up the role of company 'idiot' (remember the context of our use of the word) in problem-solving workshops. Flag occasions when this role has been taken up, so that it is not confused with habitual stupidity!

O   Training employees not to accept the first and most obvious solution to a problem/opportunity. This may mean insisting that no idea is put into action until at least 20 alternatives have been developed and evaluated.

O   Coaching individuals to work with high levels of ambiguity so that they will relish new challenges.

O   Creating 'stability zones' during continuous change as 'oasis' points for employees to refresh and reskill themselves, so that they maintain and enhance their confidence and commitment to change. Training and development and career coaching are examples of stability zones in action. These can also act as opportunities for employees to 'download' ideas to change the climate.

O   Using benchmarking to import difference and helping people to adapt ideas from outside the organization.

O   Removing every other page in the rule book. A more radical version of this idea involves translating the rule book into a foreign language and seeing if anyone notices, or even abolishing it.

O   Managing paradoxes rather than trying to equalize terms and conditions so that everyone is treated equally (badly).

O   Encouraging people to use informal networking, for example encouraging meetings in cafés and bars and organizing 'daydreaming' workshops and think tanks.

O   Acting as the 'creative inquisition' by questioning 'anti-creative' people about their behaviour and its effect on others.

O   Recruiting people into Human Resources with relevant business experience in a creative environment.

THE COMPETENCY TRAP – CREATIVITY IN A CAGE

The pitfalls of institutionalizing creativity through the use of bureaucratic competency frameworks has been mentioned in Chapter 7. However, in some circumstances there is a case for articulating competencies for the outputs of creativity, that is innovation. An example of innovation competencies comes from Post Office Counters Limited, which avoids the traps associated with them (Table 9.2).

TABLE 9.2   Innovation competencies

Value and constructs	Action	Measure
Innovation, valuing ideas	Encourage individuals to record ideas formally through the IDEAS scheme	Maintain tick list of number of times encouraged use of IDEAS and number of IDEAS team has put in
Innovation, valuing ideas	Plan opportunities to obtain ideas outside the team's everyday environment (for example, counter clerks to spend an hour evaluating local retail offers/standards of service)	Diarize time for activity by … /date (one month); team member to feedback learning points at subsequent team meeting; record number of ideas generated and number of ideas implemented
Innovation, sensible risk-taking	Before implementing new working practices, identify potential risks using appropriate tools and techniques (such as balance sheets, SWOT analysis); develop contingency plans	Keep records of tools and techniques used; risks identified – contingency plans; review effectiveness of implementation with team and customers and record learning points
Innovation, sensible risk-taking	Clearly identify and set up measures of success before change is implemented	Maintain log of review data with comparison to success criteria
Innovation, embracing change	Use new business developments or ideas as a stimulus to local quality improvement	Register quality improvements activity and complete progress forms; target – x (number) quality improve-

TABLE 9.2   concluded

Value and constructs	Action	Measure
	activity (for example, new product roll outs)	ment projects completed within .../date (six months)
Innovation, embracing change	Always be positive when communicating new ideas and changes to business policy by understanding reasons behind them and promoting the benefits	Test other's understanding by informal questioning; feedback from others, such as score chart completed by team (monthly); ask for feedback from line manager to check understanding of business policy

POCL's innovation competencies illustrate the positive use of a potentially bureaucratic system to enhance creativity in an organization where structure is valued.

FINANCIAL RESOURCES

A key question to be answered is whether more investment equates to more creativity.

In the 1997 DTI survey of spending on research and development, the UK was shown with the lowest ratio of R&D spending of any large industrialized country. This was seen as a criticism of the UK's potential for innovation.

On the other hand, our example of Dyson suggests that lack of financial resources does not necessarily preclude creativity. However, it does point to the need for persistence to secure them.

Although ideas cost very little, successful innovations often cost a lot. The entrepreneur needs to be capable of securing sufficient money at the right time. The onus is partly on the individual both to understand the networks within their own organization and to be able to package ideas in ways that are appealing to those who have access to funds. It is also incumbent on those who control financial resources to have a better understanding of the creative process so that they can make better decisions in this area.

Funds must be able to flow to the places where they are needed in organizations. More money then becomes replaced by 'better use of the financial resources available'. Creative organizations find ways of subsidizing projects that are promising through mechanisms such as project grants and project reviews where speculative resources can be allocated. An overly constrained financial budgeting system leaves little room for choice in this matter.

INFORMATION MANAGEMENT AND CREATIVITY

Information explosion may hinder serendipitous creativity

Creating, disseminating and embodying knowledge, both tacit and explicit, is a key strategic resource; it enables the organization to learn faster than its competitors.

We have joined the information revolution – it has been estimated that 80 per cent of all currently available information has only been in existence since 1964. Faced with this huge expansion, the possibility for serendipity in putting diverse pieces of information together will be reduced using existing technologies if their focus is on purely linear relationships. Increasingly, we need to manage information effectively.

March and Simon (1958) foresaw the problems associated with information overload in their book, *Organizations*. They proposed that people in organizations would make rational choices if all the relevant information were available to them, but …

> 'If the rational man lacked information, he might have
> chosen differently "if he had only known". At best, he is
> "subjectively" rational, not "objectively" rational. But the
> notion of objective rationality assumes there is some
> objective reality in which the "real" alternatives, the "real"
> consequences, and the "real" utilities exist.'

March and Simon (1958) proposed the concept of 'bounded rationality', where people consciously or otherwise made decisions based on the frame of available knowledge at a given time. This leads to the idea that optimizing is replaced by 'satisficing' – a good-enough solution. Whilst over-engineering is expensive and wasteful (providing customers with Rolls Royces when they wanted Minis) 'good-enough' product developments rarely produce extended competitive advantage.

In the context of looking for information to make breakthrough decisions or have new ideas bounded rationality presents a problem for creativity. Since there is more information available than most people can reasonably use, a key role of information management is the selection of facts that will guide and inform decision making. If this search concentrates in the 'expected' places where 'answers' are to be found, it is likely that 'unremarkable' decisions will be produced, yet it is clearly not (to date) possible to synthesize information from all sources. In short:

> One definition of insanity is doing the same things and
> expecting a different result.

Technology may be used to scan and order the vast amount of information resources available on both the Internet and the Intranet. For example, the use of unmoderated Intranet sites where people can drop in ideas can be said to amount to 'electronic serendipity'. Although some developers would argue that criticism stifles creativity, the psychological distance available through electronic communications makes it more possible to have robust conversations and recover from them. Some comments from leaders involved in the research for this book give graphic illustrations of this:

> We have developed the understanding that you expect
> your own ideas to be challenged.

> If someone comes up with a crap idea, we tell them so.

To deal with the problem of information overload, one organization involved in my research study was experimenting with news groups as a means of recording learning for ideas transfer and adaptation.

Creativity will suffer if information equals power

One challenge in managing information and ideas is that in many organizations information is power. Many individuals choose to keep information to themselves (metaphor – information stored in a 'battery'). Other organizations choose to distribute it through a network (metaphor – information distributed through a 'National Grid'). Rover Group operates an ideas transfer network that works on the 'National Grid' model, from which people are encouraged to 'swipe' ideas so that they can be successfully transferred from location to location (see Chapter 10).

In the battery metaphor, as batteries lose their power if they are not used so it is that outdated information loses its value. Indeed, much business information depreciates more rapidly than a battery, since it often has zero value if it is not timely (see Figure 9.2).

Another challenge for the future is that of creating environments where information and ideas will flow more freely without overloading recipients.

The *Financial Times* 'Mastering Management' series identifies four levels of information culture:

1. **Functional culture** – managers see information as a means of exercising influence or power over others.
2. **Sharing culture** – managers and employees trust each other to use information (especially about problems and failures) to improve their performance.
3. **Enquiring culture** – managers and employees search for information better to understand the future and ways of changing what they do to align themselves with future trends/directions.

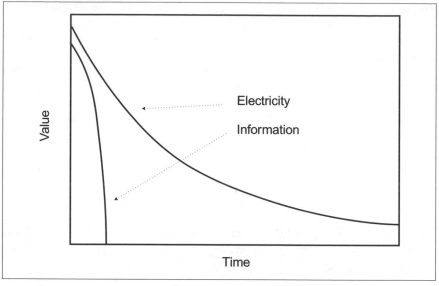

FIGURE 9.2   **Comparative depreciation curves – information versus electricity stored in a battery.**

4.   **Discovery culture** – managers and employees are open to new insights about crisis and radical changes and seek ways to create competitive discontinuities.

A creative organization needs to operate at Level 2 as a bare minimum and more likely at Level 4 and beyond. A range of options for improving idea transfer and learning across organizations is shown in Figure 9.3.

Points to ponder

O   Invest in information processing systems that enable you to cope with high volumes of information from diverse sources rather than ignoring peripheral information that may contain the seeds of future success.

DESIGNING YOUR OWN IDEAS TRANSFER STRATEGY

1.   Examine each option on the idea transfer tree diagram in Figure 9.3 and adapt them to your own organization.
2.   Devise your own idea transfer tree diagram using the blank model in Figure 9.4.
3.   Look for links between the options on your diagram so that you may begin to integrate approaches and consolidate an action plan.

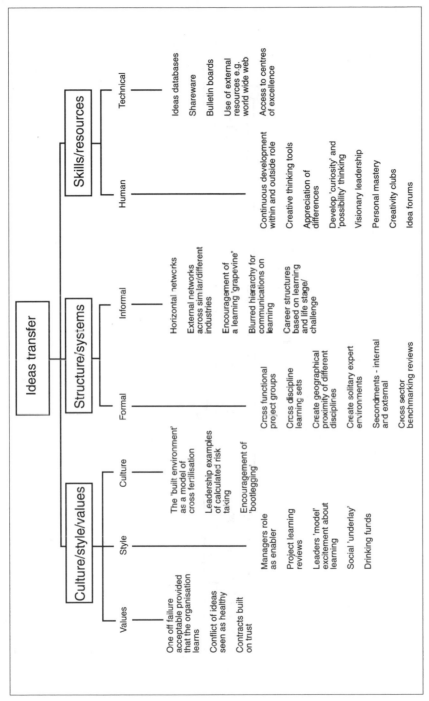

FIGURE 9.3   Generic idea transfer strategies.

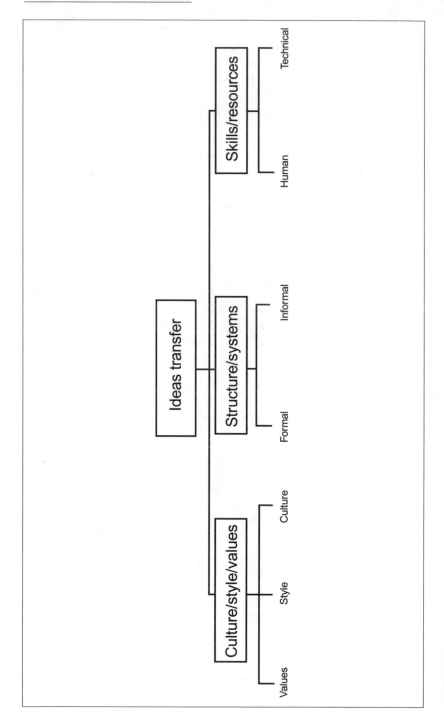

FIGURE 9.4   Idea transfer strategy.

O   Encourage people to ask radical questions for which there are no immediate answers.

O   Browse in unfamiliar places for information rather than using a few regular sources.

SUMMARY

This chapter has explored creativity and skills and resources from a wide perspective. Whilst the raw materials must be right for creativity to emerge, there is an important contribution to be made from developing talent and providing the right resources, such as information, to act as the basis for creative thinking and action. The main points that arise from this chapter are:

O   Developing people to be creative may not always involve training in creative problem-solving techniques.

O   The climate for creativity is more important than most organizations realize.

O   Unlike culture, climate may readily be changed and this is a function of leadership.

O   Future information management systems need to cope with combining ideas from different disciplines.

O   There is a need to ensure that 'thinking spaces' are maintained in organizations as technology impacts on the frequency of informal conversations.

You will find it useful to consolidate your reading by reviewing the following questions:

About what you have learned

O   What has reading this chapter confirmed in your mind?

O   What new curiosities has it raised?

O   From what personal skills and resources will your organization gain the most long-term benefit?

About putting the ideas to work

O   Where are there opportunities for free transfer and trading of information in your organization?

O   How can you update or modify your selection procedures to attract and retain a specified quota of creative people?

O   What rituals can you create to enhance the climate for ideas?

O   Where would techniques enhance the level of creativity and what prerequisites are necessary to ensure that they will work?

A final thought

> The artist finds a greater pleasure in painting than having
> completed the picture.
> (*Seneca*)

10

LEARNING AND CHANGE

The only thing certain about the future is that the future is
uncertain.
(Charles Handy)

In most organizations today, change is becoming a continuous and more
rapid process rather than a project. A quick review of any quality newspaper will reveal the vast numbers and types of changes that are taking
place in the world. For example:

O   Communications technology allows even the smallest business to
       act in partnership with others to form a critical mass that can deliver
       projects across the world.
O   The currency of learning is being devalued. It is estimated that the
       'half-life' of an MBA is approximately three–four years. As a conse-
       quence, there is a need for lifelong learning.
O   An increasing number of people are seeking a 'portfolio' career,
       requiring lifelong learning and continuous change.
O   We have moved from the agrarian age through the Industrial
       Revolution and post-modernist era to the learning society.

The business of change has changed fundamentally and therefore our
responses to change must change as well. People exhibit the following
responses to change.

Four responses to change

1.   Freeze
       Faced with change some people decide to stop in their tracks. This
       is similar to the situation of a rabbit caught in a car's headlights –
       with similar consequences.
2.   Fight

When life becomes complex, some people pretend that life is simpler than it really is and continue to do the same things. This is fighting with change. At best this is dangerous, at worst suicidal.

3.   Flight

This is the equivalent of deciding not to participate in change mentally, physically or both, by withdrawing from it.

4.   Flexibility

This is the creative response, requiring tolerance of uncertainty and a willingness to take calculated risks to provide a superior payoff.

To respond to change in organizations, we need to adopt the flexible response more often. This involves adopting new beliefs, giving new performances and sometimes destroying the past. Change is a creative act.

Here, we shall explore the linkages between change, learning and creativity. In the context of organizations, we shall consider how this relates to the development of a learning organization, leading to a number of ideas for leading change.

LINKING LEARNING AND CHANGE

THE HUMAN DYNAMICS OF LEARNING AND CHANGE

Revans (1982) pinpointed the relationship between learning and change in his 'formula for change'. For sustainable growth, organizations and the individuals within them must learn at a rate that is faster than the pace of change. In short:

$$L > C$$

where L = the rate of learning and C = the rate of change

Since the types of change we are experiencing are discontinuous, our approaches to learning must also be discontinuous. This is when 'thinking and acting outside the box', that is creativity, is of value.

WHAT IS LEARNING?

'... here is Edward Bear, coming downstairs now, bump, bump, bump on the back of his head behind Christopher Robin. It is, as far as he knows, the only way of coming downstairs, but sometimes he feels that there really is another way, if only he could stop bumping for a moment and think of it ...'

(*AA Milne*)

Learning and training are often used as equivalent terms. However, there are important distinctions between them in the context of organizational change.

Training is a **process** that **may** lead to learning.

Learning is the **outcome** or **result** of a learning process.

Learning processes at work are diverse. The following integrated model of learning links learning needs with the various learning methods and the blockages to learning (Figure 10.1).

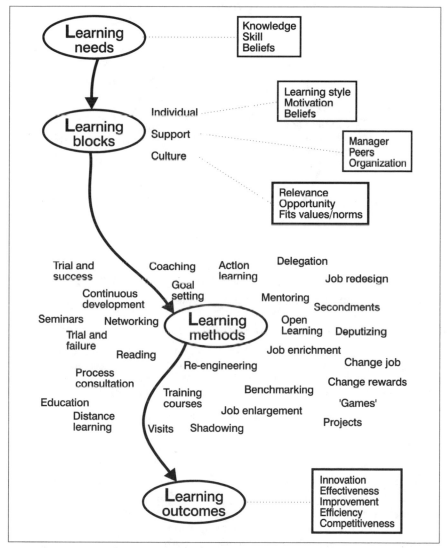

FIGURE 10.1   Integrated learning model.

Training is just one of a huge variety of methods that may be more or less effective learning vehicles in a given situation. When deciding whether training is the best way to learn, we must decide whether it can fulfil the identified learning need and to what extent it removes blockages to learning. One of the important factors to take into account is learning style.

At an **individual** level, Honey and Mumford (1986) described four 'learning styles' that align loosely with the Kolb 'learning cycle' (Figure 10.2).

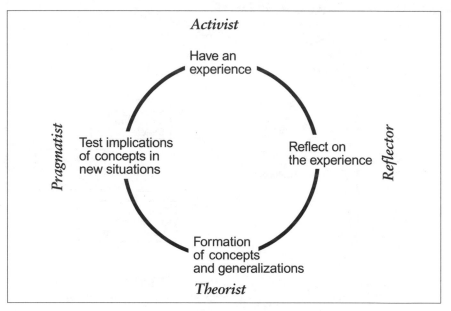

FIGURE 10.2   The adapted Kolb learning cycle.

AN EXAMPLE OF THE LEARNING CYCLE IN ACTION

Immediate experience (**Activist**) of an unsatisfactory sales visit, leads to observation and review of what happened (**Reflector**). This is followed by generalizing and theorizing (**Theorist**) about the possible implications for future interactions, which are subsequently tested (**Pragmatist**) in new situations.

In this example, all stages of the learning cycle are attended to. Some individuals possess a learning cycle that emphasizes some learning styles over others. Thus, a salesperson with a strong activist tendency may rush between sales visits, never stopping to reflect on why none of them has produced results. There is a consequent loss of learning from such an unbalanced approach, leading to a lack of change, with serious consequences for the employability of the salesperson if he or she continues to operate in this fashion.

Just as individuals have preferred learning styles and 'blind spots', so organizations have preferred ways of learning (with consequent 'blind spots'). Two such stereotypes are shown below.

○   An organization involved in manufacturing activities with a strong preference for activist and pragmatist styles. The typical response to problems and crises will often involve taking more action (**fight with change**). If the action is the source of the problem, this will lead to a larger problem rather than its resolution. In this type of organization, there is advantage in balancing action with some reflection and conceptualization of why the problem occurred.

○   An academic organization with a strong preference for reflector and theorist styles. This organization will be less prone to using action as a means of learning new things, preferring to reflect endlessly (**freeze in the face of change**) on the current situation, generate theories and propose research to explain the change. Whilst this may be acceptable in steady state conditions, it is unhelpful when a more rapid response is required.

Thus organizational learning is affected by the predominant culture(s) within the organization. In times of significant external change, the 'blind', 'deaf' and 'numb' spots of an organization may lead it to make assumptions that are no longer valid in the wider environment. At best, this can result in poor performance, at worst insolvency.

LEVELS OF LEARNING

Much learning is concerned with acquiring and patterning of information, so that we can adapt this to deal with specific situations. This type of learning is called **adaptive** learning and is concerned with the 'what' of learning.

A second level of learning is concerned with challenging assumptions and attitudes in order to change our behaviour. This type of learning is called **generative** learning and is concerned with the 'how' of learning.

The third level is called **transformative** learning and is concerned with the 'why' of learning, that is a fundamental change in mindset or paradigm to create new meanings.

Creativity is increasingly involved as we move up the levels. Fundamental organizational change is mostly concerned with generative and transformative learning.

Points to ponder

○   Know your own learning style and challenge it.
○   Know your organization's predominant learning style and what is missing so that you can make up for the deficiencies.
○   Keep your eyes and ears outside the organization to scan for early signs of change that will affect you.

LET US NOT FORGET UNLEARNING

> We must learn to unlearn.
> *(Benjamin Disraeli)*

> There's always something there to remind me.
> *(Sandie Shaw)*

Unlearning is the process of letting go, adapting or forgetting past beliefs and behaviours that have somehow become inconsistent with current and future needs. Anyone who has tried to give up a habit such as smoking will have an idea of what unlearning is all about. An immense amount of energy is invested in persuading us that we need to learn and change. Just think of the number of seminars, events and programmes that feature learning in their main title. Rather less time is spent requiring us to forget or adapt outdated habits. Consider the following examples.

O   It is very difficult to attend an 'Unlearning' seminar, where success is measured by the knowledge, skills and attitudes that attendees are prepared to remove from their curricula vitae.

O   Many performance appraisal systems tend still to concentrate on 'industrial archaeology', reviewing past performance rather than future challenges.

O   Very few organizations have rituals and systems that ask employees questions such as 'What did you forget today?' or 'What norm did you successfully challenge today?'

A lack of unlearning is responsible for lack of fundamental change in the way we do things. Consider the following example.

> The US standard railway gauge is four feet eight and a half inches. It was built to this gauge because that was the standard in Great Britain, which adopted the standard tram gauge. This, in turn, was influenced by the tools used to make wagons which used the same wheel spacing, which was determined by the existing ruts in the road. The initial ruts were made by Roman war chariots that were built to accommodate the width of two horses, which equated to four feet eight and a half inches. It may therefore be argued that the railway gauge was determined by the Roman Empire.

Successful change management has more to do with **unlearning** than learning. Unlearning is considerably harder to achieve, since much learning has been internalized as an unconscious mindset. As mentioned in Chapter 7, the collective mindset of an organization is usually called a paradigm. Johnson and Scholes' (1989) model of the components of the organizational paradigm illustrates the self-reinforcing nature of these systems (Figure 10.3).

Change must address all elements of the paradigm for optimum results. A

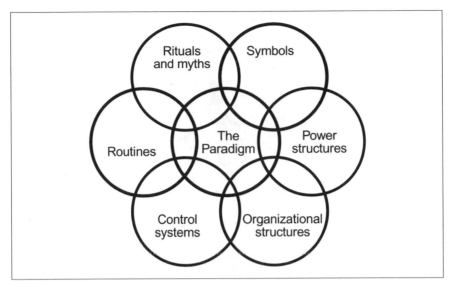

FIGURE 10.3 The paradigm. (Adapted from Johnson G, Scholes K (1989) *Exploring Corporate Strategy*. London: Prentice Hall, p. 41.)

key blockage in achieving organizational change is the old paradigm. When challenged, I often hear people in organizations defending the paradigm. This typically emerges in phrases having structures such as:

○   We have never done it before.
○   We have never known anyone else who has done it before.
○   Everyone else who has tried this has failed.
○   We cannot admit our mistakes.
○   We don't have the know-how.

AN INTEGRATED MODEL OF LEARNING, UNLEARNING AND CHANGE

It's OK to stay where you are ... as long as you change it.

In his book, *The Fifth Discipline* (published by Hutchinson), Senge (1990) develops Robert Fritz's concept of 'creative tension'. Creative tension occurs as a result of the juxtaposition of future vision with a clear picture of the present (where we are relative to what we want). The tendency is to attempt to achieve a resolution of the tension.

At an individual level, people involved in change are often 'pulled' in two directions simultaneously by different 'parts' of themselves. They are pulled forward towards their future vision and held back by beliefs of powerlessness (the inability to act in a situation) or unworthiness (the belief that we do not deserve what we want). Fritz envisioned this process as if the person is being pulled forward and back by rubber bands (Figure 10.4).

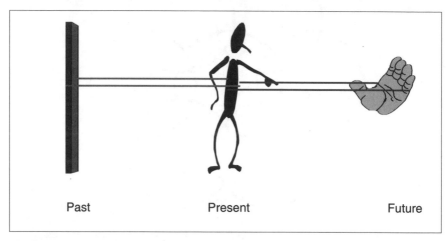

Past   Present   Future

FIGURE 10.4   Creative tension.

Any attempt to move towards the future will be balanced by a pull towards the past and vice versa.

This model can be extended in the context of learning and unlearning. The removal of tension from the past requires **unlearning** and the creation of movement towards the future requires **learning** (Figure 10.5).

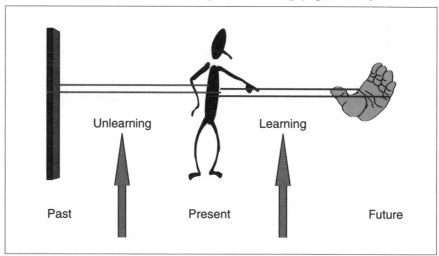

Unlearning   Learning

Past   Present   Future

FIGURE 10.5   Learning and unlearning in organizations.

A creative response at an individual level requires that the individual challenges, reframes or lets go of the past, whilst developing greater potency of vision and the willpower to move forward. This requires self-leadership, a clear sense of purpose and a positive attitude towards learning from the past on the part of a given individual. Senge (1990) points out that these qualities are not widely distributed. They can, however, be learned.

If the organization is substituted for the individual, a number of strategies can be identified that create unlearning and learning (Figure 10.6).

Many of the above strategies can assist both learning and unlearning. Thus coaching can be used constructively to challenge outdated practices as much as it is more typically used to promote totally new behaviours.

Figure 10.6 also gives an explanation as to why structural change processes such as business process re-engineering (BPR) often fail to work when used alone. By use of the rubber band analogy, BPR equates to someone 'cutting all connections with the past' by reorganizing processes so that they cannot revert to their previous arrangements. The strong task emphasis, often driven by information technology, tends to ignore cultural change and other systemic changes needed, such as changing the reward systems to encourage new performance. The result is that culture becomes a significant impediment to change later on, since the hearts and minds of the organization have not learned new beliefs to support the required new ways of working. The consequence is that many BPR projects return to the *status quo* some time after the change has been completed at the structural level.

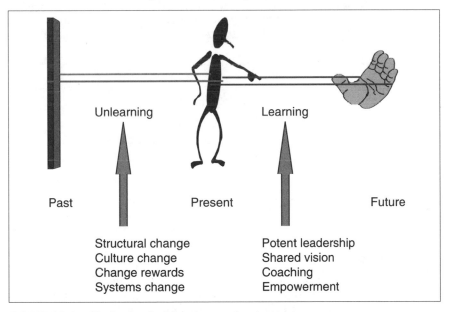

FIGURE 10.6   Strategies for learning and unlearning.

A number of processes that can be used to aid unlearning and learning are described in Chapter 12. The College of Guidance Studies case study below is illustrative of some of them.

CASE STUDY UNLEARNING AT THE COLLEGE OF GUIDANCE STUDIES

Faced with the need to let go of a number of past beliefs that were inconsistent with developing a strategy for growth, the College of Guidance Studies used a number of approaches to unlearning in order to clear the past and refocus on the future:

1. As part of the strategic review process, a beliefs-surfacing exercise had been conducted, to reveal hidden constructs that the College held about itself and its environment.

2. A second set of beliefs were then prepared. These included: new beliefs that were based on work previously done on future visions – these were likely to drive more positive performances in the future and would ensure survival and growth; reframes of limiting beliefs from the past, where appropriate.

3. The strategy group then devised and enacted a ritual that enabled the College to let go of the previous beliefs. This involved a ceremonial 'burial' of the 'baggage' from the past, the College being satisfied that all useful elements were present in the new beliefs.

4. Once this process was complete, the strategy group was able to develop objectives arising from the new beliefs. An adaptation of the familiar SMART criteria that fitted the need of the College to emphasize creativity and focus were used to bulletproof the objectives, known as the SMARTIE criteria:

S   =   Specific

M   =   Measurable and Meaningful

A   =   Action-focused

R   =   Relevant (that they fitted in with each other)

T   =   Time dependent

I   =   Innovative

E   =   Exciting at a personal level.

(Alaine Sommerville, Chief Executive, The College of Guidance Studies)

Points to ponder

O   Convene 'unlearning workshops' in your organization, to concentrate on the creative reinterpretation of past assumptions and behaviours so that they fit in with the present and future environment.

○   Reinforce unlearning through 'symbolic interventions' such as the creative destruction of artefacts and symbols that represent out-dated thinking. For example, a large bakery replaced all petrol cars with diesel ones as a sign of cost consciousness. Although this change increased costs in the immediate term, it served as a power-ful example of the death of old thinking.

○   Accept that unlearning is likely to be painful for some people and manage the process using a variety of approaches.

○   Structural change on its own is rarely sufficient to achieve a lasting transformation. Work on all the components of the paradigm to gain the greatest leverage and momentum.

WHAT IS A LEARNING ORGANIZATION?

The concept of a learning organization has been around for at least 20 years, yet there is considerable variation in what is meant by the term. The learn-ing organization can be considered both as an **organization** which learns continuously and as an organization which encourages **individual** learning in all of its people. There are vast differences in the reality, dependent on which philosophy is adopted. Some observers argue that the very existence of an organization does not permit learning, since there are competitive and political factors that mitigate against the conditions required for learning. On the other hand, a number of organizations have overcome barriers to implementing a learning culture – with consequent outstanding perfor-mance. It is just such organizations that have been creative in managing the inevitable tensions between apparently conflicting strategies.

There are many definitions of a learning organization and this creates the situation where it is almost possible for any organization to say it is one, just by picking an appropriate definition. Here are some of the best known.

> Learning organizations are organizations where people continually expand their capacity to create the results they truly desire, where new and expansive patterns of thinking are nurtured, where collective aspirations are set free and where people are continually learning how to learn together.
> (*Senge, 1990*)

> A learning organization harnesses the full brainpower, knowledge and experience available to it, in order to evolve continually for the benefit of all its stakeholders.
> (*Mayo and Lank, 1994*)*

* This material is taken from *The Power of Learning* by Andrew Mayo and Elizabeth Lank (1994) and reproduced with the permission of the publisher, the Institute of Personnel and Development.

An organization which facilitates the learning of all its
members and continuously transforms itself.
(Pedler, Boydell and Burgoyne, 1991)

Learning organizations experiment more, encourage more
tries, permit small failures, encourage internal competition,
maintain a rich formal environment, heavily laden with
information which spurs diffusion of ideas that work.
(Peters, 1994)

Is a lot of people learning.
(Gaines)

Within these definitions, there exists considerable variation as to what con-
stitutes a learning organization, ranging along a continuum from the conceptual to the pragmatic. It is this variation in definition that gives rise to the
difficulty in identification of a learning organization in practice.

LEARNING ORGANIZATIONS – TWO VIEWPOINTS

At the conceptual end of the continuum, Senge (1990) describes five interconnected 'disciplines' that are necessary for the generation of a learning
organization.

Personal mastery

Learning to expand our personal capacity to create the
results we most desire, and creating an organizational
environment which encourages all its members to develop
themselves towards the goals and purposes they choose.
(Senge, 1990)

This is 'beyond personal development' and involves becoming outcome-
focused and aware of personal needs as they fit those of the organization.
Mastery is often connected with an unconscious competence in a given
field. Excellent performers in the field of music and the arts are often 'magical' in their approach and, in many cases, they are not able to articulate how
they create this state and thus make poor teachers of their subjects.

Mental models

Reflecting upon, continually clarifying and improving our
internal pictures of the world, and seeing how they shape
our actions and decisions.
(Senge, 1990)

In other words, becoming more aware of the unconscious assumptions that support the behaviour of the organization. Being able to explain and compare our 'maps of the world'. Part of the problem associated with this is that language is a fairly imperfect medium for communication, with only 7 per cent of interpersonal communications being attributed to the actual words being used.

Shared vision

> Building a sense of commitment in a group, by developing
> shared images of the future we seek to create, and the
> principles and guiding practices by which we hope to get
> there.
> (*Senge, 1990*)

This discipline requires the alignment of goals beyond mere compliance, such as may occur when the 'mission statement' is imposed on the organization, towards the commitment that arises from a vision which is built in a participative manner.

Team learning

> Transforming conversational and collective thinking skills,
> so that groups of people can reliably develop intelligence
> and ability greater than the sum of the individual
> member's talents.
> (*Senge, 1990*)

This discipline moves 'beyond team building' and involves processes where the collective wisdom of teams can be tapped and used. Senge points out that team learning is common in sports but rare in organizations. Teams need to ask continually 'what have I learned?'. Defensive routines avoid verbalizing issues and prevent us learning from what causes the pain in the first place. To achieve this state we need to challenge existing mindsets by giving and receiving honest feedback and using a disciplined approach to our own learning. None of this is easy.

Systems thinking

> A way of thinking about, and a language for describing and
> understanding, the forces and interrelationships that shape
> the behaviour of systems. This discipline helps us see how to
> change systems more effectively, and to act more in tune
> with the larger processes of the natural and economic world.
> (*Senge, 1990*)

Systems thinking involves the ability to think across and beyond the boundary of the organization as a system of interconnected components.

Senge points out that it is the fifth discipline, that is systems thinking, that makes the important difference compared with piecemeal approaches. This requires a thorough understanding of the systemic relationships within and outside a given organization to ensure that change genuinely adds value to the organization in its wider system.

CASE STUDY – 'REPETITIVE STRAIN INJURY OF THE COLLECTIVE ORGANIZATION MIND'

Figure 10.7 illustrates a simple use of systems thinking, where a customer-focused organization found itself losing satisfied customers since it was responding to minority complaints by continuously changing the nature of its products and services.

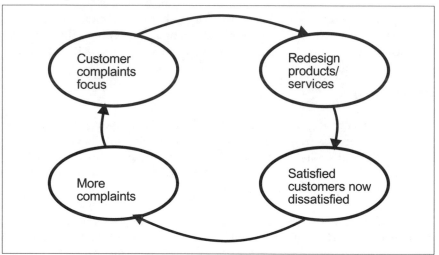

FIGURE 10.7   Repetitive strain injury in action.

When such cycles become embedded into the unconscious practices of the organization, they can become self-perpetuating systems of failure, or 'repetitive strain injuries' of the collective organizational mind. A learning organization will identify these limiting systems and break the pattern in ways that lead to a successful system. In this example, better understanding of customer satisfaction and dissatisfaction and an improved inquiry method yielded better information on which to act.

A more positive approach is given by the example of Boeing, which was concerned to transfer learning achieved into more effective organizational practices. This meant learning from their most successfully launched planes by setting up teams to analyse the learning in great detail and transfer it into future practices.

The approach to learning organizations taken by Mayo and Lank (1994) is more pragmatic than Senge (1990) in so far as they examine practices and link them to an overall model of the learning organization which is based on the European Quality model (Figure 10.8).

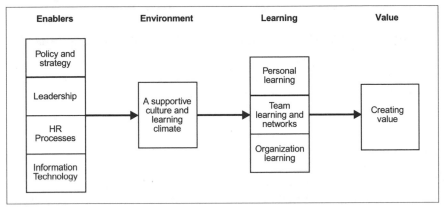

FIGURE 10.8   European Quality model.

Enablers and environment represent the 'context' necessary for success, whereas learning and value represent the 'results' available from a learning organization. Mayo and Lank have developed their approach so that it is possible to benchmark the learning organization by use of a weighted questionnaire. Whilst this is a helpful comparative tool, it should not be taken to imply that it is possible to find a single 'success recipe' for becoming a learning organization by slavishly following any one 'fashionable' approach.

Mayo and Lank concur with Senge by their insistence that individual learning is not sufficient to become a learning organization. Other outcomes, such as achieving team learning, organization learning and placing a value on learning, are also considered necessary. Another key area where Mayo and Lank and Senge are in agreement is that learning is intentional rather than reactive. This separates learning organizations from others which do learn, but only as a response to crises.

Organizations also exhibit a number of levels of learning:

O   Acquiring new ideas, knowledge, skills and beliefs.
O   Converting ideas, knowledge, skills and beliefs into action (innovation).
O   Moving ideas, knowledge, skills, beliefs and innovations around the organization.

Different organizational cultures find different levels of ease or difficulty in achieving these levels which are not a hierarchy. For example, it is common to find very internally focused organizations that do not take in many new ideas but make the most of their existing resources and vice versa. For long-term survival, a balanced approach is needed.

There are no easy **prescriptions** to facilitate becoming a learning organization. However, a number of common factors required to begin the journey may be identified. These do not constitute the necessary and sufficient conditions for a learning organization, but they do ensure that any strategy has a chance of survival.

COMMON FACTORS REQUIRED TO BEGIN THE LEARNING ORGANIZATION JOURNEY

My research on what separates learning organizations from the rest has identified a number of factors that are important prerequisites to becoming a learning organization:

O   An increase in vision and communication of the vision to align individuals and organization.

O   Active support and commitment from the top with bottom-up strategy implementation.

O   Working on change quickly at all organizational levels.

O   Ensuring that organizational systems support the desired changes, such as creative reward strategies.

O   Leadership reinforcement of new behaviours through modelling.

O   Devolving responsibility for performance outcomes and careers.

Rover Group provides a graphic example of learning organization strategies in action.

> CREATIVE THEFT IS OK – IDEA TRANSFER AT ROVER GROUP
>
> At Rover Group, the business of learning across business units is taken very seriously.
>
> Electronic networking is used to ensure that a communication channel for ideas exists across geographical and functional boundaries.
>
> They link this to a scheme based on Tom Peters' notion of 'Creative Swiping', which rewards innovation through copying ideas – both the originator of an idea and the 'thief' are rewarded for demonstrating the adaptation and application of ideas in different settings. This is also used at group level.
>
> The company also makes extensive use of 'best practice' information to constantly challenge acceptance of the *status quo*.
>
> All the above has been pursued within the business as a whole rather than as a pilot process in a single part.
>
> (Bernard Sullivan, former General Manager, Rover Learning Business)

LEARNING ASSETS AND LIABILITIES ASSESSMENT

1.   Table 10.1 lists a number of elements that will affect the learning capability of your organization. Identify specific examples of your own organization's assets and liabilities and make an assessment of these using the scoring system below:

1 = very weak asset or liability
2 = mediocre asset or liability
3 = moderate asset or liability
4 = very strong asset or liability

2. Add any other elements that contribute to or prevent learning in your organization.

3. **Critical reflections** What does this tell me and what do I need to do about it? This could include better use of assets, removal of liabilities etc.

TABLE 10.1 Learning assets and liabilities

Elements	Description of specific learning assets and score (1–4)	Description of specific learning liabilities and score (1–4)
Culture, for example rituals, routines, 'myths', high- and low-profile communications		
Values the things that are at the heart of the organization		
Leadership style, for example autocratic, benevolent, participative		
Structures both formal and informal such as career and political structures		
Systems, for example reward and recognition systems, information systems		
Skills both technical and human		
Resources people, information and financial		
Sum of scores		

HOW DOES CREATIVITY FIT IN WITH LEARNING AND CHANGE?

> One doesn't discover new lands without consenting to lose
> sight of the shore for a very long time.
> (*Goethe*)

A 'FORMULA' FOR LEADING CHANGE

It is helpful to return to the model of change in order that it may be developed in a practical way (Figure 10.9).

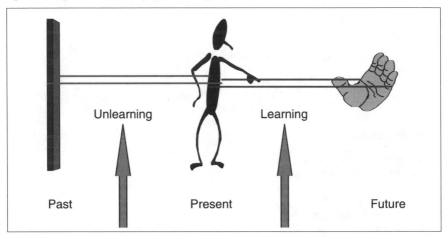

Unlearning

Learning

Past

Present

Future

FIGURE 10.9   Linking change to learning and unlearning.

Another way to look at the model is to link it to the 'Gleicher formula' for managing change.

> For change to occur, the drive for change must be more
> potent than the 'costs' of change. This is represented by
> the 'formula' below:

$$D + V + F > C$$

where
D = the level of **dissatisfaction** with the present situation;
V = a shared potent and desirable **vision** of the future
situation;
F = the awareness of some actionable **first steps**;
C = the 'cost' of change, emotionally as well as practically.

Elements D, V and F are essentially concerned with learning, whereas C is mostly concerned with unlearning.

If the formula is adapted to read D x V x F > C, it becomes clear that change will not occur at all if any of the elements in the left-hand side of the equation has a value of zero. In other words, it is insufficient to use the formula as an accountant's balance sheet. It is equally important that each element has a sufficient potency for change to proceed. Many organizations I have consulted with have had elements missing. Typically, the vision and practical cost–benefit analysis have been taken good care of but the other elements have been overlooked.

It is possible to make a number of deductions from this formula:

○   Creatively increase the level of dissatisfaction associated with the present situation. This is a function of creative leadership.

○   Make the vision a shared one and make it more potent and desirable. This requires the use of creativity in strategic thinking.

○   Increase the awareness of actionable first steps in change. This requires the use of empowerment strategies that are aligned with the vision. Many empowerment strategies are not strategically focused and it is important to separate these approaches.

○   Lower the threshold 'cost' of changing. This is creative transition and typically involves coaching, facilitation and other approaches that allow people to make sense of change so that they may let go without significant losses.

If any of the elements are missing, change will be difficult or even fail. Many change strategies use 'pain' as the primary lever, with long-term consequences for employee motivation and commitment. An alternative strategy is to use 'gain' as a lever for change. Using both 'pain' and 'gain' provides the greatest **leverage** for change. Practical strategies for gaining maximum leverage for change are described later in this chapter.

ASSESSING CHANGE READINESS BY USE OF THE 'GLEICHER FORMULA'

1.   Identify a change that you are making or one that you wish to make.
2.   Identify the meaning of each specific element of the formula in this change. Give each element a rating from 1 to 10, where 1 = low and 10 = high.

$$D + V + F > C$$

where
D = the level of *dissatisfaction* with the present situation;
V = a shared potent and desirable *vision* of the future situation;
F = the awareness of some actionable *first steps*;
C = the 'cost' of change, emotionally as well as practically.

3.   Add up the numbers you have ascribed to elements D, V and F and divide the total by three to get an overall impression of the degree of leverage for change by comparison with the value of C.

4.   Note down strategies for increasing the leverage for change: Are any elements missing? Are there untapped sources of energy that need to be mobilized?

CONVENTIONAL WISDOM ON CHANGE

Whilst the conditions where change are possible are easy to articulate, change is often difficult to produce. The following is a summary of the conventional wisdom on the management of change in organizations, described under three headings: understanding change; designing strategy for change; and implementing change.

Understanding change

During this stage, it is important to get beyond the **symptoms** to the **causes** of the need for change. Our iceberg metaphor is helpful here where symptoms are visible, but these represent only the tip of a much deeper issue (Figure 10.10).

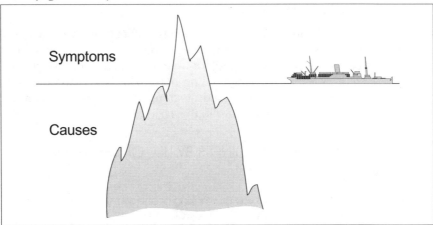

FIGURE 10.10   The iceberg metaphor.

Research shows that people in organizations spend little time understanding the need for change. The consequence of this is that the wrong things get 'fixed', leading to poor performance and cynicism of future change initiatives. The following processes help:

○   Identify key stakeholders and understand their multiple viewpoints, that is anyone who has a significant part to play in the change is likely to be viewing the change from different positions. What are these perspectives and how can you converge them creatively?

O   'Measure' the current situation so that you will be able to track progress later on. Choose measures which are meaningful rather than those which are convenient or easy.

O   Set clear outcomes for change, even if it is of an emergent nature. In these cases, specify intermediate outcomes. Major change is often an untidy process and it is not possible to know at the start how it will turn out. In such circumstances it is essential to establish means by which the top team can learn continuously.

O   Identify, mobilize and support champions of change. These are the people who will make things happen later on.

O   Create the conditions where change is possible. This may mean building an understanding of a desirable future before trying to dismantle what is currently in place. Change also requires people to feel that old ways are out of date. Leaders must create tension to increase perceived dissatisfaction with the *status quo*.

O   Reveal assumptions – both your own and those of others whose support is needed later on in the process.

O   Reduce or eliminate resistance to change using a variety of strategies ranging from consultation to coercion, dependent on the circumstances and the stakes involved. Paradoxically, this often means getting those who are actively blocking change to join the 'supporters club'. Anyone who has an opinion, whether positive or negative, is worth motivating. By far the hardest group of people to move is the indifferent majority. Often these people make their decision when they see how the other groups react.

O   Maintain constant communications using a variety of appropriate media, both formal and informal.

Designing strategy for change

O   Identify a timescale – it is inappropriate to have a full employee involvement programme in a business that is failing. Conversely, it is often inappropriate to introduce change faster than it needs to be done in a 'steady state' operation.

O   Consider the impact of the change on the total system. Changes in one unit will usually affect other parts of the organization.

O   Setting milestones for change will assist in monitoring implementation and provide visibility of progress.

O   Set up processes to assist with the management of ambiguity. These may include forums to enable people to make sense of chaos and paradoxes as 'the new' contrasts with 'the old'.

O   To involve or to steamroller employees? A steamroller approach to introducing change may well work in the short term, but can leave people feeling demotivated and manipulated. On the other hand, an empowering approach often needs strong leadership.

O   Top-down, Bottom-up or Sideways? Many changes use elements of all three designs. The strategic vision of change may be created high up in the organization, with some involvement from key personnel, with a bottom-up approach to deciding exactly how the strategy will be implemented.

O   Maintain constant communications – often this will be the time when nothing is heard about change, which can allow for cynicism to creep in.

Implementing change

Until this point, nothing has changed in the organization, and nothing will unless this phase is given due attention. The creation of plans effectively gives you a 'map' of the territory to be covered on the 'journey'. Key points to be addressed are:

O   Find ways of loosening up the organization for change. These can often be small symbolic gestures that affect every employee, yet convey a powerful message about change.

O   Work hard at it! The people who have carefully designed the change process may not always be the best individuals to generate the energy required to implement the change. Mobilize your change champions and provide forums for keeping their motivation and commitment.

O   Solve new problems as they occur – new issues will probably arise as the change comes to the implementation stage. It is important to build the capability of reacting to these issues into any plans. A process for listening to the organization's concerns and responding positively to them should be explicitly established (such as O'Brien's 'Understanding' process, mentioned in the N&P case study in Chapter 7).

O   'Measure' the changed situation to determine the degree to which you have been successful in institutionalizing the change. Changes which are 'grafted' on to the organization rarely last a long time and do long-term damage to the possibility of introducing further changes in the future.

O   Reward positive examples of change in action. Change inevitably means that old reward and recognition systems need to be changed as these reinforce the past.

O   Provide appropriate learning opportunities. It is important to win the hearts and minds of those involved in change. Persuasive communication is essential, but it should be reinforced by pro-

viding opportunities for learning new knowledge, skills and
beliefs.

O   Communicate – identify 'quick wins' that are consistent with longer-
term goals and reward and recognize them. In any change, there are
usually individuals who adopt the change rather more quickly than
others. Let people see, hear and feel that the change has occurred
using a variety of appropriate media, both formal and informal.

LEARNING FROM RADICAL CHANGES IN OTHER DOMAINS – THE ART OF REVOLUTIONS

A number of writers have drawn parallels between the ways in which revolutions have arisen and change programmes in organizations. They are of
interest since most revolutions are creative in the sense that they are radical
transformations that overturn established orders on a large scale.

Revolutions are often accompanied by the convergence of a number of
potent forces for change, which arise from a number of areas. For example,
the American, Russian and French revolutions originated from political and
social forces. They may be due to changes in technology, such as the information and green revolutions. They may also be intellectual, for example in
paradigm shifts, such as those caused by Copernicus and Newton.

A revolution attempts to achieve fundamental change. However, some
successful revolutions degenerate into tyranny not greatly different from
that which preceded them. In this respect organizations share this difficulty
when undertaking change.

In the case of the Russian Revolution of 1917 a number of factors combined to create the conditions where revolution was possible: massive discontent, the revolutionary movement and World War One. These factors
were operating in the context of a rigid, absolutist state. Lenin was able to
mobilize for power and used 'specifically vague' but appealing generalizations such as 'Peace, Land and Bread' to capture the popular imagination.

Setting aside political and moral aspects of this and other revolutions,
note that all aspects of the 'change formula' are present in this example.

Dissatisfaction = Massive discontent

A shared potent and desirable vision = Lenin's use of
appealing generalizations

Actionable first steps = Mobilization of the revolutionary
movement

Low cost of change = Presence of a rigid, absolutist state,
that is, 'the only way is up'

Points to ponder

O   Balance creative destruction with appropriate levels of supportive facilitation to enable people to let go of the past in ways that enable them to move forward positively.

O   Make ambiguity tolerance a key organizational competence and encourage others to be curious in the face of change rather than to need an instant answer.

SUMMARY

In this chapter, we have explored the relationships between learning, creativity and change. In a turbulent environment, the organization that has the most flexibility stands to move fastest. This requires that its people are creative and rapid learners. More importantly it requires the organization to devise methods of forgetting worn out 'success recipes'. Creativity is at the heart of unlearning which is predominantly an emotional process.

In keeping with this theme, ask yourself some simple but important questions:

O   What have I learned from this?
O   What existing assumptions have I challenged?
O   What questions do I have for further learning?
O   What first steps will I take to acquire this learning?
O   What could stop me from acquiring this learning?
O   How will I circumvent obstacles to learning?

A final thought

It's the end of the world as we know it (and I feel fine).
(REM)

PART FOUR
RESOURCES

❖

11

A CREATIVITY TOOLKIT

If you only have nails in your toolkit, you will tend to use a hammer.

A practical set of techniques and processes is offered here that can be used or modified to encourage greater levels of creative thought and action in your organization – assuming that the context is suitable for their use. Some advice is also given about the need for preparation if you are to make the most of creativity techniques.

CREATIVE PROBLEM SOLVING – AN OVERVIEW

There are many descriptions of the creative problem-solving process. One of the most robust involves successive phases of divergent and convergent thinking (Figure 11.1).

Its various stages may be further defined as follows:

○ Problem/opportunity definition – the scope is defined, a number of alternative problem/opportunity statements are devised and one or more of these is chosen.
○ Generating ideas – many possibilities are generated without regard for their practical value.
○ Choosing ideas – ideas that are most promising are developed before final choices are made.
○ Solution implementation – potential blockages are considered and strategies devised to overcome or minimize them. A detailed plan of action is produced.

It is worth repeating the conventional wisdom on structuring a creative problem-solving process here, since people still ignore it:

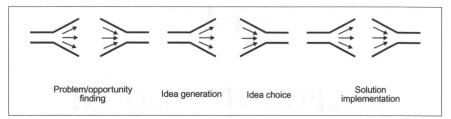

FIGURE 11.1   The creative problem-solving process.

○   Clearly separate the phases of creative problem solving, emotionally and physically.

○   Ensure that the group adopts the appropriate mindset for the particular phase, for example if the group is concentrating on divergent thinking, the ground rules and practices should encourage this and discourage convergence.

○   Use a variety of techniques rather than sticking to a single favourite one. Practice, and a wide repertoire, will provide the flexibility to pick the right tool for the job rather than having to force-fit the problem/opportunity into the only available technique.

○   Resource the process adequately. It is no good having a two-hour meeting and expecting to have resolved the problems of world peace. People need time to build confidence in creativity and gain experience in using techniques.

SETTING THE CLIMATE

Techniques are useful 'coat hangers' for groups of ideas, so that they can be seen by the organization. However, they can only work adequately when the climate supports their use. There are key elements that can help to set the climate.

LEADERSHIP MODELLING

If leaders (formal or informal) model the belief that creative problem solving is a useful organizational practice, it quickly becomes a positive hallucination for others who may initially feel less confident about creativity. Leaders must live and breathe the ground rules for creative problem-solving sessions. These are described later on.

CREATIVE ENVIRONMENT

Environment plays an important part in setting the creative climate. If creative sessions are held in places where more formal meetings are held, the environment should be modified to symbolize the different sort of meeting that is about to take place there. Highly effective creativity facilitators encourage climate change by:

○   Using music appropriately. This can range from certain types of classical music, to encourage reflection and conceptualization, to disco, rock etc., to alter the mood of participants.

○   Feeding the participants' minds and bodies. Some of the most effective sessions I have witnessed have included personal touches such as the host bringing in some food that he/she has prepared. Whilst it is certain that this fulfils certain biological needs, the real value is more symbolic.

○   Altering the furniture. Dispense with traditional furniture arrangements and bring in other 'creative artefacts'.

○   Changing the location. Creativity sessions do not have to be held in remote locations, but it is sometimes helpful to hold them in someone else's environment.

ENCOURAGING CREATIVE CONTRIBUTION

> I'm going to give you some rules on how to be creative.
> (*Creativity consultants' 'joke'*)

'Rules' are helpful only in so far as they provide some fairly common guidelines that are generally helpful. In some organization cultures, certain 'rules' are far more important than others. For example, a colleague who works in a large accounting firm says that the culture tends to support instant judgements and is quick to blame 'failure'. In this situation, the typical 'no criticism' brainstorming rule is needed to have any chance of open-ended thinking. In this example, it is unlikely that this would be sufficient to open up the climate.

Conversely, one social service agency that I worked in was good at contemplation but not so good at evaluation and action. It was quite unnecessary to have a 'no criticism' rule here, indeed, a 'criticism' rule was necessary to stimulate this type of thinking.

The point about ground rules is that they must be created for every group. They are not a standard and, as shown by the examples mentioned, inappropriate ones are bad for creative problem solving. Some typical ground rules are shown in Table 11.1.

Points to ponder

○   Can you identify an environment that is 'uncontaminated' by

TABLE 11.1   Divergent and convergent thinking

Divergent thinking	Convergent thinking
No judgement – remain open to all ideas even if the first suggestion is a real winner	Act purposefully – be systematic and structured
Quantity breeds quality – aim to obtain many ideas without regard for their practicality at this stage	Act with integrity – ensure that 'hidden agendas' are revealed
Build on ideas rather than criticizing them – includes saying 'yes, *and*' rather than 'yes, *but*' which usually means 'no'	Look for the best solution rather than knocking down other options – all options have some merit. See yourself as an optimizer rather than taking a reductionist approach
Incubate ideas – leave space to reflect and develop them	Take final decisions as late as possible – the best-quality decisions are ones that have synthesized earlier partial solutions
Get off 'planet earth' – find ways of leaving your own comfort zone to explore initially 'far out' ideas	Use valid criteria for making decisions – stay focused on the goals of the process
Open all the senses – if what you are doing isn't working, do something different	Ask difficult questions – creative problem solving is **not** about making sloppy decisions that ignore account of company politics etc.

unhelpful processes that could be used for creative problem-solving sessions?

O   What can you do to 'clean up' unsatisfactory environments at work so that they can become a creative climate when needed?

O   Which of the above ground rules are essential for creative problem-solving in your environment?

SELECTING THE PEOPLE

One reason why creative problem-solving workshops fail to deliver optimum outcomes is that the right people do not attend them. This does not mean selecting a group of people who all think the same way. It does mean that choices need to be made about individuals who may need to be excluded from certain phases of the process, or who must be carefully managed if they attend them.

It is common to ascribe the following roles at workshops:

O   **Problem/opportunity owner** – either an individual or the group itself. If an individual, there can be occasions when it is best that he/she does not directly participate in the process.

O   **Process facilitator** – will attend to ensuring that the group moves through the process and will monitor/adjust conditions so that they are conducive to creative thinking.

O   **Scribe** – does not formally participate or influence the process, but has the essential skill of being able to summarize complex ideas in a lucid and readable manner.

The other participants should include individuals who have relevant contributions to make, and others, who have seemingly irrelevant contributions to make, but who have a reputation for being able to contribute an above-average number of ideas and who are comfortable with the ambiguity involved in working 'blind'. Sometimes an organization has a supply of 'wild men' and 'wild women' who fulfil this role. Occasionally, 'out of role artists' and other specialists who think differently may be needed if the organization does not have these people within its ranks.

DESIGNING YOUR OWN TECHNIQUES

THE STRUCTURE OF CREATIVITY TECHNIQUES

As mentioned in Chapter 9, many creativity techniques are based on a number of key parameters:

O   **Climate (CLIM)** – developing the conditions where 'playful' thinking is allowed and allowing space and time – thinking in different ways takes some time to get started.

O   **Problem/opportunity definition (POD)** – understanding the real problem/opportunity and the context or frame before moving into options or solutions.

O   **Separation (SEP)** of key phases of the process.

O   **Detachment (DET)** from the problem/opportunity.

O   **Flexibility (FLEX)** – viewing the problem/opportunity from different angles and use of all thinking styles, such as logic **and** intuition.

O   **Encouraging idiots (ID)** – involving non-experts (or novices) and people with different specialisms in the process.

O   **Connecting ideas (CON)** – being prepared to add on to ideas and listening intently to meanings.

○   **Iteration (ITER)** – the practice of recycling through the process to improve the quality of ideas before deciding on a course of action.

An example illustrates how these criteria may be designed into a bespoke process for divergent thinking where there is particular need to think radically. The abbreviated design criteria are shown at the stages where they are most relevant.

CASE EXAMPLE – DESIGNING YOUR OWN CREATIVE PROBLEM-SOLVING TECHNIQUES
DOCTORS AND NURSES – A TECHNIQUE FOR RADICAL IDEA GENERATION

This technique requires group members to assume the identity of various stereotypical medical characters and then to use these characters as springboards for idea generation. The process is as follows:

○ A problem definition phase (**POD**), using conventional techniques. The group is built during this phase by ensuring that all members contribute and are rewarded for their inputs. This leads to a climate of safety and trust (**CLIM**).

○ Descriptions of the various roles (**FLEX**) are then given. Some common ones are: Surgeons (fix problems by attending to the offending organ); Homeopaths (may look at the problem from the whole system viewpoint and devise a low-level intervention that has impact on the specific problem); Witch doctors (devise rituals and spells that are magical); Nurses (provide appropriate nurturing and administer appropriate medication to control the condition).

○ Group members select one of the characters and assume its identity. Costumes can be provided to heighten the sense of engagement (**DET**). Each member then personalizes his or her character by describing specific strengths and weaknesses.

○ The various characters then produce ideas from their own roles (**ID**) and suggest/build on ideas from the other characters.

○ The process will then be halted for incubation of ideas (**ITER**), (**SEP**).

○ A further meeting is convened for the adaptation of ideas and their selection and implementation. This meeting is typically run conventionally.

One example of the technique in action concerned a problem with a university that claimed that it had too many committees which led to a loss of momentum on strategic projects. Amongst the ideas that came from the surgeon was a need for a full diagnosis (evaluate the purpose of the meeting) before leaping to the prescription (attending). These ideas prompted a number of strategies for deciding who should attend. From the ideas that came from the witch doctor was one about changing the committee environment. Having identified the fact that the environment was a limitation (large committee tables meant that all meetings were habitually attended by a minimum of 20 people) the witch doctor offered a solution involving the use of a chainsaw to cut the tables into four or five pieces. This led to solutions involving holding the meetings in small rooms or changing the dynamics of the meetings through breaking larger groups into smaller sets.

CHOOSING AND ADAPTING PROPRIETARY TECHNIQUES

> It ain't what you do, it's the way that you do it (That's what
> gets results).
> (*Bananarama*)

Rather than designing techniques from scratch, another choice is to adopt or adapt existing techniques. The major criteria for making choices between techniques are summarized in the matrix below (Figure 11.2).

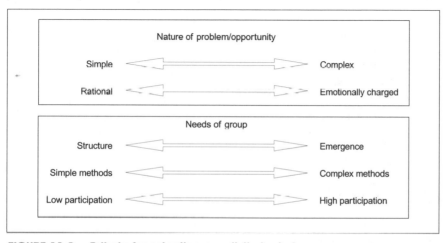

FIGURE 11.2   Criteria for selecting creativity techniques.

Each of the techniques in the following section can be assessed by use of these criteria. This matrix can be used to pick the best-fitting techniques for a particular problem/opportunity by finding a match between the needs of the situation and a given technique.

A CREATIVITY TECHNIQUES MENU

Many books outline a wide variety of creativity techniques. The Open University Business School MBA course 'Creative Management' provides a rich source of techniques which have helped inspire this book and from which may of the techniques given below are derived. (See in particular Henry and Martin (1993) *Creative Problem Solving Guide*, and Martin (1991) *Creative Management Techniques*, both Milton Keynes: Open

University Press.) Some techniques are provided here that may encourage the development of your own techniques to widen the repertoire. A menu of techniques, broken down by their primary applications within the creative problem-solving process, is given below.

PROBLEM/OPPORTUNITY DEFINITION

O Complexity mapping
O Progressive abstractions
O Reframing
O Bitching with attitude
O Why? technique
O 5W's & H
O Multiple redefinitions
O Mind mapping
O Synectics
O Fishbone diagrams
O Bug listing
O Wishing
O Failure prevention analysis
O Systems thinking approaches: relevance trees; cognitive mapping
O Outcome elicitation
O Rich picturing

GENERATING IDEAS

O Classical brainstorming
O Nominal group technique
O Provocations
O Forced relationships
O Reversals
O Two words
O Collective notebook
O Metaphors
O Brainwriting
O Synectics
O Bionics
O Lateral thinking
O Paradoxical thinking
O Relaxed attention and hypnotic methods
O Value analysis
O Creative visualization
O Laddering

O   Bunches of bananas
O   Doctors and nurses
O   KJ technique using 'Post-it' notes
O   Disney creativity strategy
O   Attribute listing
O   Reframing
O   Morphological analysis
O   Theme analysis
O   Mind mapping
O   Checklists: SCAMPER; CREATIVITY; 5 W's & H; Product improve-
       ment checklist.

CHOOSING IDEAS

O   Sorting
O   Critical success factors
O   Stakeholder analysis
O   Impact–acceptability analysis
O   Top five
O   Q-sort
O   The snowball method
O   Star rating
O   Advantage–disadvantage matrices
O   Paired comparison analysis
O   The balance sheet method
O   Matrices
O   Disney creativity strategy
O   Reverse brainstorming

SOLUTION IMPLEMENTATION

O   Bullet proofing
O   Stakeholder analysis
O   Commitment charting
O   Implementation checklist
O   Potential problem analysis
O   Force field analysis
O   Acceptance finding
O   Balance sheet
O   Bitching with attitude
O   Help/hinder matrices
O   Disney creativity strategy
O   Critical path analysis

A small selection of techniques is described in the following sections.

PROBLEM/OPPORTUNITY DEFINITION

Redefinition using the 'Why?' technique

Small children are fond of asking 'Why?' The 'Why?' technique capitalizes on this to reveal a number of levels of problem/opportunity abstraction. It is good at probing beneath the surface of multifaceted problems. The process may be summarized as follows:

1.   State the problem/opportunity as initially defined.
2.   Ask why you want to do whatever is stated in the problem/opportunity.
3.   Answer the question in Step 2.
4.   Redefine the answer as a new problem/opportunity question.
5.   Repeat steps 2 and 3 until you have a number of redefinitions.
6.   Pick the problem/opportunity statement that is most appropriate.

In answering the 'Why?' question there are two likely answers:

'Because … ' – this tends to dig into the structure of the problem.

'In order to …' – this goes up the ladder of inference to recover a higher purpose.

Dependent on which answer is encouraged, the technique can be used to analyse a problem/opportunity or capture the bigger outcome. For example:

Q   Why did the chicken cross the road?
A   In order to get to the other side.
Q   Why did the chicken want to get to the other side?
A   In order to eat the cat.
Q   Why did the chicken eat the cat?
A   In order to satisfy its fundamental life needs etc. …

In this case you may then wish to explore alternatives to the dangerous practice of crossing busy roads with the chicken, in order to satisfy life needs etc!

Comment   The technique can deal with moderately complex problems, although it is likely that this will lead to a series of topics for idea generation. When used with emotionally charged problems, people can become defensive when asked 'Why?' continuously. It also tackles the need of the group for structure, is simple to use and can be used in one-on-one situations or group environments where high participation is required.

Outcome checklist

Where the need is not so much to explore the origins of a problem but to concentrate on an outcome this checklist may be used to sharpen the emphasis on the outcome. It also allows you to discover any weak criteria in the chain. The process is as follows:

1. Think of the outcome that you would like to have. Write it down in the form, *'I really want to x ...'*

2. Run through the checklist below and observe how the outcome changes. When you have completed the exercise, re-write the outcome in the form, *'I really really want to y ...'*

Stated positively, that is what I really really want rather than what I do not want. For example, if someone states, *'I want less machine defects'* ask them, *'What would you rather have?'*

Owned, that is what part does the individual play in achieving this outcome? For example, if someone states, *'We have to improve the department's performance'*, ask them, *'What part will you play in this?'*

As specific as possible, that is how exactly am I to achieve this? For example, if someone states, *'I need an improvement'*, ask them, *'Who, where, when, what and how specifically?'*

Assessable, that is how will I know when I have succeeded? This requires the development of some measurable and meaningful criteria for success. For example, if someone states, *'I want a successful production line'* ask them, *'What will you see, hear or feel when you have success?'*

Achievable, that is do I have all the resources at my disposal to achieve a result? For example, if someone states, *'We'll start the project tomorrow'* ask them, 'What resources do you need to achieve this outcome?' These may be personal or physical resources.

Sized right, that is is the outcome too big to manage or too small to bother with? If it is too large, for example if someone states, *'I want to change the organization but I can't'* ask them, *'What part of the organization could you change?'* If it is too small to be motivating ask them, *'If you got this outcome, what would it do for you?'* Move up until you relate to an outcome that is sufficiently motivating to drive passion.

Fitting, that is how does this outcome integrate with other things in my world? For example, if someone states, *'I think that I want to do this'* ask them, *'What would happen if I got it?'* or *'If you could have this right now, would you really really want it?'* and listen for a definite 'YES' reply. If there is any doubt in the response, such as *'Yes, but ...'* this may signal a need to re-check other elements of the framework, or it indicates that the outcome is inappropriate in some way.

Each of these factors must be checked – and we must be prepared to check them several times. Often we are not passionate about outcomes because one of these essential ingredients is missing, for example we do not really want a change because the outcome is too small to invest the time in (size) or that it would not integrate with our other outcomes (fit).

Comment The checklist can be applied to a wide variety of problems/opportunities. By defining the outcome precisely it is common to find some solutions along the way. The checklist may also be used with emotionally charged problems, as it reveals the blockages to change. It tackles group needs for structure, but can be moderately complex to use. The key to using the checklist is to maintain **flexibility**. For example, some people manage to achieve outcomes which are poorly specified or even woolly. In other situations, some iteration is needed to clarify the real problem/opportunity. It can be used in one-on-one situations or group environments where high participation is required.

5Ws & H – the six questions technique

A structured method that examines a problem/opportunity from multiple viewpoints. The process may be summarized as follows:

1.   State the problem/opportunity using the format 'In what ways might … ?'
2.   Write down separate lists of who?, what?, when?, where?, why? and how? questions that are relevant to the problem/opportunity.
3.   Examine the response to each question and use them to stimulate new problem/opportunity redefinitions.
4.   Write down any redefinitions suggested.
5.   Select one redefinition that best captures the problem/opportunity you are trying to resolve.

Comment The technique can deal with quite complex problems, as it covers a variety of angles on the problem/opportunity, although it is likely that this will require a separation and prioritization of issues for idea generation. It is best used with rational problems/opportunities due to its complexity. Because it is structured, some fuzzy thinkers find the approach too rigorous. It is relatively simple to use and can be used in one-on-one situations or group environments.

Cognitive mapping

Mapping techniques are especially useful for handling complexity. A technique that uses 'Post-it' notes is given here.

1. Collect relevant information relating to the problem/opportunity definition by writing each separate piece of information on a 'Post-it' note.
2. Spread all the 'Post-it' notes out and group those that seem to belong to each other.
3. Label the groups with a 'theme'. Form any remaining 'Post-it' notes into a group called 'lost sheep'.
4. Examine the themes. Look for linkages between them and represent these linkages by arrows and other symbols. Look also for importance and hierarchy of problem/opportunity definitions, so that you may make a choice of entry point for the idea generation phase.

Comment   Cognitive mapping can be used for both problem/opportunity definition and solution finding. Often the process of becoming clear about the complexity leads to some new ideas. There are many variations on this theme. Some are more structured, such as the fishbone diagram, and others more emergent, such as rich picturing. The example of storyboards in Chapter 12 uses rich picturing as a subsidiary method.

The technique is well-suited to complex problems/opportunities and it can handle both rational and emotionally charged issues. It promotes emergence and can become quite complex to administer, but can be very participative. People often feel a real sense of ownership of their 'map' which makes it useful in situations where this is required.

GENERATING IDEAS

Classical brainstorming

Alex Osborn developed brainstorming as a technique for finding a solution for a specific problem/opportunity by amassing all the ideas spontaneously contributed by its members. It has origins in India and the original name carries the meaning of 'outside yourself' and 'question'.

Most effective brainstorming occurs when the group is in a playful state. Some brainstorming groups do not produce novel ideas. Over the years I have observed that people may well have knowledge about how to conduct an effective brainstorming session, yet they do not act in accordance with this knowledge. In many cases a skilled facilitator is needed to conduct an effective brainstorming session, viz:

1. Develop a problem/opportunity statement.
2. Select a group of between six and 12 participants.
3. Brief them on the nature of the problem/opportunity.
4. Conduct a 'warming up activity', such as 'how to get more angels to dance on the head of a pin' and reinforce the rules for divergent

thinking (see Table 11.1 earlier in this chapter). These are often summarized as follows: record all ideas; no criticism; freewheel and build on ideas; if you think it say it; everyone participates.

5.   Write the problem/opportunity on a chart visible to the group.
6.   Request ideas by asking people to raise hands whenever they wish to make a suggestion.
7.   Write down all ideas.
8.   After 30 minutes of activity, terminate the session.
9.   Select an evaluation group, present the ideas to it and instruct the group members to pick the best ideas.
10.   Present the selected ideas to the person responsible for the implementation of solutions.

Comment   Brainstorming can provide a large number of ideas in a short space of time and it is easy to use. It can also act as a climate booster in its own right. On the negative side, the 'no criticism' rule can be hard to realize in practice and it can emphasize contributions from extroverts. Brainwriting is a variant that addresses this problem by gaining contributions from each individual in the group on cards which are exchanged in an ideas 'pool'. Brainstorming is a very powerful tool when implemented properly but it has come to be misused and this has led to a decline in its image.

The technique works best with relatively simple non-emotional problems/opportunities. It can be given a relatively tight structure or allow for emergence, and is best used in participative group situations.

SCAMPER

SCAMPER is one of a range of creativity checklists that are used to stimulate thinking through making forced relationships between the problem/opportunity and one of the checklist words. The process is as follows:

1.   Develop a problem/opportunity statement.
2.   Ask 'In what ways could we resolve the problem/opportunity by applying one of the options from the SCAMPER list?' The mnemonic stands for:
      Substitute
      Combine
      Adapt
      Magnify or **M**inify
      Put to other uses
      Eliminate or **E**laborate
      Rearrange or **R**everse.
      For example, if the opportunity was concerned with increasing market share of baked beans, a magnification of the issue would lead to ideas about larger cans and multiple packs. Ideas from 'substitute'

could lead to novel packaging solutions such as see-through packaging, re-sealable lids and packaging that can be microwaved directly and so on.

3.   Generate a list of ideas.
4.   Evaluate the ideas.

Comment   The checklist is rigorous and works best with simple problems/opportunities that require a lot of ideas, although it can be adapted for more complex situations. It is not particularly good with emotionally charged problems, since it tends to be quite mechanistic. It is highly structured, relatively simple to use and can be used in one-on-one situations or participative group environments. Because it requires a force-fit of the issue to the checklist words, some participants have difficulty in making the mental leaps required to get ideas from some of the categories. The checklist needs to be used flexibly for best results.

Reversal

In situations where people find it hard to produce ideas, the reversal technique may be used to overcome the blockage. Typically, reversal produces wilder ideas than conventional brainstorming. It is good for encouraging the playfulness dimension of creativity. The process is as follows:

1.   Develop a problem/opportunity statement.
2.   Reverse the direction of the problem/opportunity in any way possible. For example, if the opportunity statement were 'In how many ways may we improve the image of the department in the eyes of key stakeholders?', one reversal would be 'In how many ways might we seriously damage our reputation with stakeholders that would lead to a long-term memory of the department as worst in class?'
3.   Take any of the ideas developed in Step 2 and see if they can be re-reversed to produce new ideas for the original problem/opportunity. This does not mean adding the word 'not' to the ideas, but a creative reversal of the idea.
4.   If practical solutions are not feasible, reverse the problem/opportunity in a new direction.
5.   Continue reversing the problem/opportunity until a satisfactory solution is produced.

Comment   Reversal is a simple technique which is useful for unblocking complex and emotionally charged problems and opportunities, since the act of reversal tends to make the issue amusing. This seduces participants into productive conversation. It is also good in situations where the group is only offering 'planet earth' type ideas, since it tends to place distance between the issue and reality.

People can find reversal ridiculous, since it produces emergent solutions, and they detach from the session as a result. Minimize this tendency by managing expectations over the reasons for use of the technique and making it acceptable to generate frivolous ideas. It can be used in one-on-one or group situations.

CHOOSING IDEAS

Stars method

A very straightforward method for the evaluation of ideas. The process is as follows:

1. Display ideas prominently.
2. Agree ground rules for choosing ideas.
3. Give each voter three stars and let them stick their stars one at a time on their favourite ideas. Depending on the nature of the group, the facilitator may allow individuals to place all three stars on one idea or insist that a maximum of one star per person is placed on a given idea.

Comment   The technique is simple, structured, participative, fast and can give a rapid evaluation of many ideas. Although simple, groups have a habit of making this process more complicated. If openness is a problem, a 'closed ballot' may need to be arranged. This allows the technique to accommodate both rational and emotionally charged problems/opportunities.

The process does tend to concentrate on 'here and now' ideas rather than more radical thoughts and this can be accommodated by building in a recycling phase.

Sorting categories

Another easy method that builds on the three stars approach but adds in a further level of discrimination. The process is as follows:

1. Display ideas prominently.
2. Agree ground rules.
3. Agree a mark for each idea, as follows:
    ✓ = possibly a good idea
    ? = not applicable
    W = 'weird idea'.

Any 'W' ideas should be reprocessed to see whether they can be made more acceptable.

Comment   The process is simple, structured, participative and fast. The addition of a recycling phase ensures that 'ideas from outer space' are not instantly discarded. The method needs to be modified where large groups or large numbers of ideas are involved. The comments regarding openness for the stars method also apply to this technique.

Two-dimensional grids

For more complex idea evaluations, a number of two-dimensional grids can be set up to screen ideas so that the best possible solution emerges. The exact criteria to be chosen will vary according to the issue under consideration, but the outline process is the same:

1.   Identify a number of valid criteria for judging the value of the ideas generated.
2.   Pick pairs of criteria that may be usefully combined into a two-dimensional grid and produce a series of idea screens. For example, a set of screens for the assessment of new product ideas could be as shown in Figure 11.3.
3.   Run the ideas through the screens until a clear winner emerges. In some cases a fine filtration screen may be needed (using numbers rather than high or low).

Comment   The technique can address complex problems/opportunities, provided that the screens are chosen appropriately and sequenced correctly. It is not good for emotionally charged problems, although it can be used to narrow the possibilities where widely divergent views are involved. It is structured and can cope with group needs for an intellectually challenging method to solve a problem. There is a limit to the degree of open participation as this tends to lead to lobbying, especially if there are power differences within the group. Ballot boxes can be used to minimize this situation. Of course, there are situations where lobbying can be used deliberately as part of the convergence process.

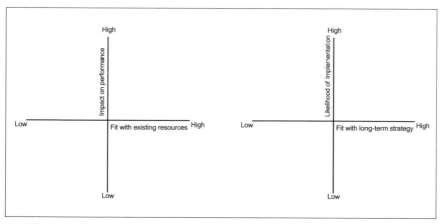

FIGURE 11.3   Idea screens.

SOLUTION IMPLEMENTATION

'Bitching' with attitude

Since many ideas are not implemented, barriers to implementation must be identified and eliminated or planned for. This technique legitimizes initial dissent and conflict as a means of predicting all the possible problems associated with implementation of a new idea. The process is as follows:

1.   Define the intended action plan.
2.   Generate all possible problems. The 'bitching' process can be enhanced by permitting people to stand on soapboxes if appropriate to legitimize dissent.
3.   Evaluate each problem from the perspectives of possible causes, potential impact and likelihood of occurrence.
4.   Change the group's state from convergent to divergent thinking.
5.   Generate ideas to prevent the cause or minimize the effects. This is the 'with attitude' part of the technique.
6.   Develop contingency plans for addressing the problems with the highest impact and probability of occurrence.

Comment   Bitching with attitude legitimizes dissent in a positive way. One of the essential ground rules is, 'if you bitch in the first phase, you must suggest a way forward in the "attitude" phase'. It is mostly applicable to simple problems that are rational in nature. It is simple to use and highly participative. The main disadvantages concern a lack of vision of possible pitfalls and some groups find it hard to be overtly critical.

Balance sheet

A balance sheet is a valuable way of assessing the likelihood of successful implementation. The essential dynamic for change is that the assets must outweigh the liabilities. This technique may be summarized as shown in Figure 11.4.

The process is as follows:

1.   List all the assets for implementing the solution.
2.   List all the liabilities that will hinder the implementation process.
3.   Examine both lists. Find ways of leveraging the assets so that they have more effect whilst finding ways to remove, reduce or reframe the liabilities so that they cease to be a hindrance or become assets.

Comment   This approach is simple to use, participative and puts a rational face on creativity. It is favoured by people who think in very logical ways. In some cases it is helpful to supplement the approach with weightings and real figures if this is practical. It can accommodate relatively complex problems/opportunities and either rational or emotionally

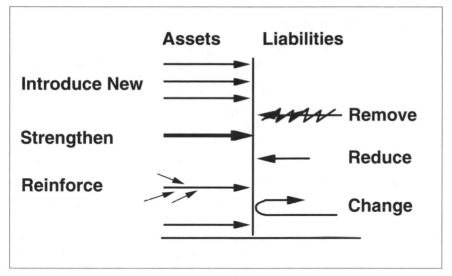

FIGURE 11.4   The dynamics of change.

charged issues. The technique can be used to understand problem/opportunity definition, to check out the dynamics of the situation and it can be adapted to use the dynamics of change diagram as the main output for 'softer' issues. It is often called 'force field analysis' when used in this way.

Commitment charting

Where implementation requires the commitment of multiple stakeholders, it is wise to understand the power dynamics of the key personnel, so that a variety of strategies may be put in place to deal with them. The process is as follows:

1.   Define the intended action plan.
2.   Identify the stakeholders and categorize them on the grid as shown in Table 11.2, according to whether they will make implementation happen, let it happen or stop it happening.
3.   Agree a position where you need to move each stakeholder to by marking a second spot on the grid.
4.   Identify strategies and tactics to enable this to happen.

Comment   Commitment charting is good for implementation issues where there are emotional barriers to change; it can deal with average levels of complexity. Since it is relatively structured and simple to use commitment charting can provide a focal point for participation.

TABLE 11.2   Commitment chart

	Enthusiasm 'Make it happen'	Indifference 'Let it happen'	Blockage 'Stop it happening'
Stakeholder A			
Stakeholder B			
Stakeholder C			

CREATIVE PROBLEM SOLVING IN ACTION

Table 11.3 lists the outcomes of a workshop that used a number of techniques to identify options for improving communications across a sales team. In this case the group had been asked specifically to suggest options without knowing the exact nature of the problem. Thus, a list of possible problem definitions were produced and a number of options identified. The most promising of these have been summarized below:

TABLE 11.3   Creative problem solving in action
Problem as given: Poor communications across a sales team

Level	Problem definition	Some possible options
Environment	People who need to communicate are geographically remote	Improve horizontal communications by use of IT; change geography/structure
Behaviour	Poor-quality listening resulting in missed opportunities to pass on work	Survey feedback to raise sensitivity to the issue; improve active listening through coaching; review appraisal/reward systems to encourage referral
Capabilities	People lack skills in information management and use of IT to network customer intelligence	Provide skills training in information gathering and transmission using IT; devise systems to facilitate knowledge sharing
Beliefs	People holding on to particular clients, since	Change reward system; change the culture;

TABLE 11.3   *concluded*

Level	Problem definition	Some possible options
Identity	they believe that they will erode their client base by referring	restructure the job/role; change leadership practices
	Poor match of person–role	Personnel changes; improve selection process

In this case the problem owner was able to reflect on and pinpoint the main sources of the problem **after** the options had been produced.

SUMMARY

By far the most important part of any creative problem-solving process is the preparation phase. This includes the setting of an appropriate climate, the acquisition and alignment of the right people and gaining access to a menu of techniques so that it is possible to be flexible. Once these conditions are established, technique becomes a ritual to move from the current reality towards a desired future situation.

Although proprietary techniques provide a useful set of coat hangers, the real organizational payoff arises with the design of organization-specific thinking rituals that fit the desired culture. Although the design criteria are spelt out in this chapter, with practice, design becomes an unconscious practice.

The menu presented here is not sufficiently wide to give true flexibility. However, it will provide some ideas about the design of your own techniques. You are encouraged to read and practise widely if you wish to acquire a wider repertoire.

A final thought

It is fairly certain that you will not find the solution to a problem if you don't understand where the problem is.
(*The 'Heisenberg certainty principle' – adapted by the author*)

12

CREATIVE LEARNING AND CHANGE

❖

This chapter contains a number of processes that may be used to induce learning and change within organizations. Unlike the techniques discussed previously, they are whole processes, that is not only do they cover one phase of the creative problem-solving process but are directed towards particular organizational problems and opportunities. With practice, these processes may also be adapted to other contexts.

A MENU OF CREATIVE PROCESSES FOR LEARNING AND CHANGE

A menu of processes for learning and change appears below. Some are concerned predominantly with learning and others with unlearning.

O   Corporate jesting
O   Corporate jousting
O   Corporate boxing
O   Human dynamics
O   Rock 'n' roll management
O   Storyboarding
O   Post-modernist theatre of change
O   Scenario planning
O   Deconstructionist cinema of learning
O   Assumption surfacing
O   Audiovisioning.

A number of these are described further.

CORPORATE JESTING

> We all know that there is only one step from the sublime to
> the ridiculous; the more surprising that psychology has not
> considered the possible gains which could result from the
> reversal of that step.
> (*Arthur Koestler*)

The word 'witticism' is derived from its original sense of ingenuity and inventiveness. Koestler (1964) points out that the jester's riddles provide a useful back door into the inner workshop of creative originality. This idea can be adapted into the world of organizations, where humour is an effective way to explore ideas outside conventional wisdom. This is because the structure of humour relies on seeing something different in 'ordinary' situations. In ancient times, the court jester was the only person in the court who was 'allowed' to challenge the paradigm. More recently, British Airways has used a corporate jester to provoke learning and change. Corporate jesting capitalizes on the powerful value of humour in revealing 'undiscussable' issues.

What is required?

In the corporate version, humour may bypass or overcome conventional blocks to addressing organizational problems/opportunities; for relatively 'difficult' or intractable problems of an organizational nature where there are no obvious solutions. Since it requires an external facilitator, corporate jesting may also be helpful in politically charged problems, provided that some basic ground rules are agreed about staying at the problem level and keeping away from personalities unless they are the agreed source of problems.

To be effective, the facilitator needs several qualities:

O   The ability to reframe organizational problems/opportunities from a ridiculous perspective.

O   The ability to model the corporate jesting approach so that others will move into a playful state, balanced by a mature 'adult' phase for defining the real problem and evaluating the ideas.

O   Excellent logical and creative problem-solving skills through access to a wide repertoire of techniques in order to achieve worthwhile results.

Process description

Corporate jesting is flexible as it relies heavily on a skilled facilitator who knows how to stay on the edge of acceptability in an organization. Typical processes to be employed include:

O   An **opening up** phase, where people are gradually encouraged to become playful about the nature of problems in general. This is facilitated by getting into the role of a jester and will often include wearing of appropriate costumes and hats.

O   A **problem escalation** phase, where the chosen problem is examined from a number of ridiculous perspectives, including ways to make the organization significantly worse and/or a laughing stock as a result of amplification of the original problem.

O   This leads to a **consolidation** phase which will produce a 'real problem definition'.

O   A further **opening up** phase is then used to generate ideas to solve the problem. This often uses aspects of the previous phases, suitably reframed into potential solutions.

O   The process will then be halted for **incubation** of ideas.

O   A further meeting is convened for the **selection** of ideas and their **implementation**. This meeting is typically run in a more conventional manner. If further ideas are needed for implementation a second round of corporate jesting can be used.

Advantages/disadvantages

The process is rapid and reaches the heart of the problem very quickly. One disadvantage is that of potential for detachment from the solution, since it was developed in a light-hearted fashion. Some organizations (hierarchical and with a strong sense of ego) do not value humour as a means of overcoming problems and this can be a limitation.

HUMAN DYNAMICS

This process uses human models to act out complex situations so that the dynamic consequences of changes in one part of the system can be seen in others. Human dynamics is effective for examining complex interpersonal group situations involving conflict resolution and change and can be adapted for whole-organization strategic simulations.

What is required?

The benefits of the process are:

O   **Involvement** through the participation of staff in the human modelling process.

O   **Projection** which enables people to describe emotionally charged issues in ways that do not point fingers at individuals.

To be effective, the facilitator needs three qualities:

O   Sensitivity when dealing with 'difficult' interpersonal problems.

O   A good understanding of systems thinking.

O   The ability to open up the group to suggest new options, even if these involve changing the behaviour of the problem owner in the system.

Process description

O   A description of the problem is outlined by its owner. This will include the essence of the problem, pen pictures of the key personnel involved and any necessary 'history'. Having described the situation, the problem owner then becomes a detached observer.

O   Participants are asked to take the roles of the key players, modelling elements of psychological distance through physical separation and 'attitude' through the pen pictures, plus any other relevant dimensions that relate to the particular problem.

O   The problem owner is asked to direct a short sequence of typical activity between the actors. This then becomes a description of the current situation. At this point feedback is sought from each participant and any observers.

O   In a second phase, the problem owner is asked how s/he would like the situation to be different. The actors are then asked to improvise new behaviours that are more likely to achieve this outcome. Observers are also asked to offer guidance and ask questions. The objective of the process is to identify the most elegant sequence of changes that will break the present system and produce the desired result.

O   If success is not achieved at the first pass, observers may 'tag' themselves into the situation if they can offer new strategies.

The problem owner is asked to evaluate the best strategy and is then asked how s/he will put it into action.

Advantages/disadvantages

The process is rapid and enables people to see the big picture easily. Compared with systems diagramming methods, it is relatively easy to try out options and see the effect on the whole system quickly. This gives groups the power to learn from the future in a realistic way. A disadvantage is an unwillingness to act out the process by some people. This can be overcome by selecting the actors carefully and by building a supportive environment in the initial phases. Because the process can reveal personal weaknesses, it is best conducted by mature teams or in nominal groups.

SCENARIO PLANNING

A scenario is a way of describing a possible future. Scenarios may be produced for the organization or its environment and may be seen as a means of 'purposeful daydreaming'. They are very good for planning in uncertain environments since they will picture a number of probable futures against which a strategy can be planned. A good scenario will generate tension for change by challenging assumptions about the future.

What is required?

The learning value of scenario planning may be placed above traditional strategic thinking processes because it offers:

○   **Ambiguity tolerance** through accommodating multiple uncertainties.

○   **Involvement** through participation in the 'futurology' process.

To be effective, scenario planning requires that the daydreaming process is supported by good analysis. Participants should be asked to scan the media for trends and '**messages from the future**' for some time before the scenario process begins. The facilitator must ensure that the scenario is correctly 'positioned' so as to drive purposeful action.

Process description

The process may be summarized as follows (see also Figure 12.1):

○   The time frame and objectives for the scenario modelling process are set. Each scenario should have a title, giving a sense of its content, for example an off-licence chain developed scenarios called 'Decade of drinking' and 'Home shopping revolution'.

○   The organization then sets out to learn about the environment in which it lives, by gathering information from a variety of sources on social, technological, economic and political changes that may affect it.

○   The information is then assembled into a likely series of events, with likely dates for them attached. This forms the basis for the scenarios.

○   Scenarios are produced rather like constructing a retrospective newspaper article reviewing significant events through time.

○   Analyse the scenarios, paying special attention to key discontinuities and decision points.

○   Derive a set of policies and strategies that will accommodate the various scenarios and assess them for their robustness.

Advantages/disadvantages

The main attraction with scenario writing is that it can accommodate multiple futures. It has been referred to as a 'history of the future'.

The purpose of scenarios is to create momentum for change. If they are to do this, they must not be outlandish, since the organization will reject them as being 'science fiction'. Neither should the scenarios be very similar

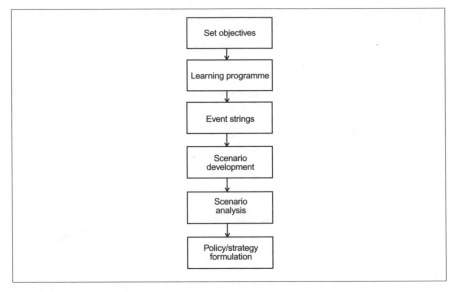

FIGURE 12.1   The scenario planning process.

to the current situation, since they will be ignored as 'boring'. The ideal scenario is believable but challenging in such a way that it drives action. A facilitator is needed to ensure that the group does not end up with either extreme, and to make sure that the scenarios are grounded in good quality information rather than being the product of a think tank.

ASSUMPTION SURFACING

Organizations commonly expect the future to be like the past, yet this is rarely so. Assumption surfacing enables the organization to make explicit the beliefs and values that support its strategy, so that these can be challenged. Chris Argyris refers to this as 'double loop learning'.

What is required?

Any assumption surfacing exercise is likely to lead to some surprises, so expectations must be managed before, during and after the process. A skilled facilitator is normally needed to ensure that the group confronts the assumptions rather than artfully dodges them if they are unpalatable or fearful.

Process description

1.   Identify a number of strategies in the organization that are critical to success.

2. Examine each strategy and ask the question 'What assumptions are implicit in this strategy?' Classify answers under themed groups such as customers, market, competition, pressures for change etc.
3. Challenge the assumptions according to their impact on the organization if they were untrue.
4. Identify specific actions to minimize the impact of the assumption on the organization's strategy.

Advantages/disadvantages

Assumption surfacing puts an organization in the mode of 'being prepared' for anything. Given the number of organizations that go out of business by not being prepared, this would seem to be a sufficient reason to invest in this approach.

The assumptions that underpin an organization's strategy can be irrational and this can raise concerns within groups that undertake this work. Sensitivity is needed on the part of the person who convenes such groups, to ensure that emotional distance is maintained, or that conflicts are properly managed. Projective methods may be used as a way of entering the relevant territory if direct challenges to strategy are skilfully avoided.

STORYBOARDING

Because our intuitive consciousness communicates more easily in impressions and symbols than in words, drawing is a marvellous way to bring out group insight and vision. Storyboards are used regularly in advertising and marketing, but have only recently been applied to strategic thinking and change management.

What is required?

One member of the group is elected as the 'artist'. Under guidance from the group, the artist produces a number of pictures, sequenced by time, that build into a storyboard. The structure of a storyboard shows where the organization is now (in the first box) and where it desires to be (in the final box) with a number of intermediate turning points in the remaining boxes (usually four to six frames). The structure is depicted in Figure 12.2.

In each frame, there is the possibility of contemplating the assumptions inherent in the drawing, with any blockages or decisions that are implied by the pictures.

An example of a storyboard used to design a strategy for making virtual teams work is shown in Figure 12.3.

Some practical considerations

To obtain the maximum benefit from storyboarding, the facilitator usually offers some guidelines and support:

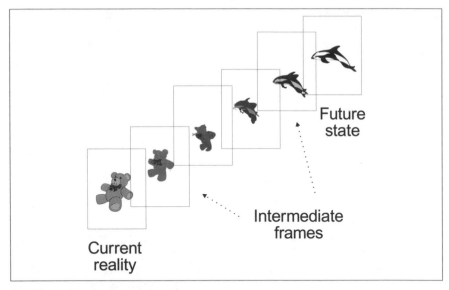

FIGURE 12.2   Storyboarding process.

O   A perceived lack of ability to draw is no barrier to use of the tech-
      nique. It is better to produce a picture using 'stick' people than no
      picture at all.
O   Encourage participants to use colours throughout.
O   Use words as well as drawings if explanations are needed, for exam-
      ple 'speech bubbles'. Magazine cut-outs and other resources may
      also be used as necessary.
O   Storyboards may contain many disjointed elements. This is the
      nature of the process and it does not all have to 'make sense'.

Advantages/disadvantages

Storyboards tend to direct the organization towards the future, with little or
no regard for the past. This can be a release for organizations that would
otherwise tend to spend strategic thinking sessions doing 'industrial archaeology'. Although they are simple, the story can become a powerful symbol
and plan for change.

Since storyboards use the principle of projection, some people 'detach'
themselves from the story and this needs careful management.

SUMMARY

The processes we have just described are the tip of a much larger iceberg.

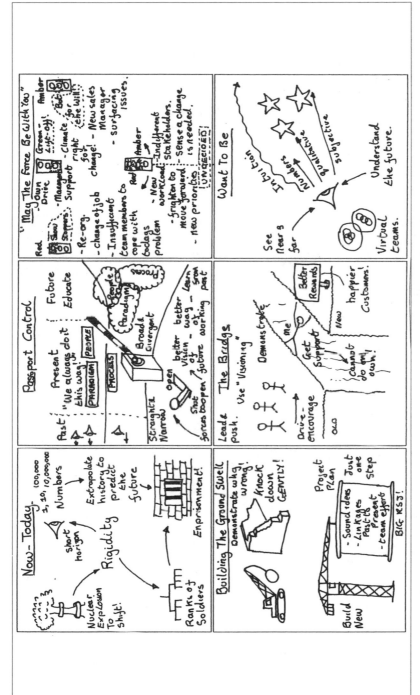

FIGURE 12.3   Storyboarding in action – the example of moving towards virtual teams. (Courtesy of Ian Groves, British Telecom)

The creative leader needs an array of these processes, enabling a choice to be made based on the needs of the situation. The menu of processes presented here is intended to promote thinking and the design of original processes that will work for specific situations within your organization.

A final thought

> If you love what you do, you will never work another day in
> your life.
> (*Confucius*)

101 IDEAS FOR INCREASING ORGANIZATIONAL CREATIVITY

The ideas that follow are intended to help readers determine what might work in their organizations. Some would be inappropriate or even counter-productive in some environments. A number of them are framed in a deliberately radical way in order to stimulate further thinking.

Bear in mind that ideas taken from one location must be adapted or radically altered if they are to fit a different environment. A set of questions designed to drive this 'creative swiping' process is given at the end of the ideas list.

1.   Hire people who challenge the *status quo*.

2.   Invite people in off the street to comment on your organization.

3.   Create groups of people who would radically disagree with your own views.

4.   Use 'corporate jesting' sessions to examine 'undiscussable' problems using the power of humour, in order to convert problems into opportunities.

5.   If you are using techniques to encourage creativity, make sure that sessions are managed properly using people who know how to select suitable techniques and get the best out of them.

6.   Model aberrant behaviour, for example sit in cupboards to think.

7.   Move people out of role on a consistent basis.

8.   Persuade people to move themselves into unfamiliar roles.

9.   Develop people in a wide range of creativity techniques so that they are in a position to fit a technique to the prevailing issue rather than having to force-fit the issue to the technique.

10.   Remove job descriptions.

11.   Remove symbols of status, such as job titles, car parking restrictions, executive dining rooms etc.

12.   Use outsiders more.

13.   Set up multidisciplinary think tanks and ideas 'fairs'.

14.   Use processes for strategic planning that can accommodate chaotic and emergent activity, such as visioning and scenario development.

15.   Evaluate the success of meetings by the level of purposeful conflict that has occurred.

16.   Find ways of letting the shadow side of the organization ferment and grow **without** adding elements of formal structure.

17.   Remove some low value-adding elements of formal structure, for example committees.

18.   Reshape ineffective rituals.

19.   Make fun a cultural imperative.

20.   Set up forums to encourage peers to share ideas and practices.

21.   Recycle ideas that are not ready to be launched.

22.   Encourage a rapid turnover of staff and continue to use them for their ideas after they have left.

23.   Reframe rewards systems to encourage persistence as well as results.

24.   Use unrelated stimuli, such as music, theatre or dance, to help solve problems.

25.   Create micro-environments where people of dissimilar backgrounds can listen to one another and question.

26.   Devise informal and formal systems for the capture, fermentation and distillation of ideas.

27.   Always carry a pack of 'Post-it' notes or a tape recorder with you to capture random thoughts.

28.   Introduce 'corporate daydreaming' sessions into the fabric of the organization.

29.   Build a 'corporate talent' database, to enable people to access specific qualities outside their awareness.

30.   Use notice boards and water fountains as nominal idea generation environments.

31.   Introduce fancy dress days.

32.   Use alternative forms of communication, for example make contributions at a meeting using only a musical instrument, or use silence.

33.   Use flexible strategic processes, such as scenarios or creative visualization, supported by hard thinking skills to 'make the strategy happen'.

34.   Make 'valuing differences' a cultural imperative.

35.   Keep an ideas diary.

36.   Telephone 10 people who do different jobs in the same industry sector. Ask them what was the best idea they have ever had and what circumstances caused the idea to be recognized.

37.   Telephone 10 people who do similar jobs in different industry sectors. Ask them what was the best idea they have ever had and what circumstances caused the idea to be recognized.

38.   Use music at work.

39.   Accept that different people need different motivational styles and adjust your own behaviour.

40.   Develop a creative structure.

41.   Ask children to comment on the organization.

42.   Use worker–directors to advise on strategy.

43.   Make enthusiasm and passion selection criteria.

44.   Find ways of changing leadership of a creative project as it changes status from 'discovery' through 'development' to 'routine operation'.

45.   Set aside separate funding for venture activity.

46.   Reward adaptive as well as radical creativity.

47.   Encourage corridor chat and informal networking.

48.   Send groups to see/work in the customer's environment.

49.   Organize customer involvement in product/service design.

50.   Introduce learning outside the professional discipline as a means of generating a thirst for enquiry/tolerance of ambiguity.

51.   Mix idea generators with idea sensors and advocates.

52.   Reposition the manager's role as a resource and enabler.

53.   Encourage people to walk the job regularly.

54.   Encourage people to take frequent short breaks from work.

55.   Develop stability zones as resources during rapid change.

56.   Encourage people to tell stories and metaphors as a way of using unrelated stimuli.

57.   Encourage people to believe that they can achieve the impossible and convince them to commit to stretch targets – 'if you play at being a genius, you become one'.

58.   Develop the organization's ability to forget (unlearn) limitations and past ceilings of achievement.

59.   Create thinking space as an organizational 'ritual' and give it high-profile acceptance through formal and informal communications systems.

60.   Make notes and review your level of creativity; learn from your mistakes and successes.

61.   Challenge assumptions on a regular basis.

62.   Do not tolerate complacency, indifference and a lack of questioning.

63.   Use humour to overcome thinking and judgement blocks.

64.   Build psychological safety into creativity processes.

65.   Introduce 'anti-status' symbols, for example executive donkey jackets.

66.   Send people to the nearest park to think.

67.   Demand reports on the numbers and quality of ideas successfully implemented.

68.   Reward idea 'theft' and adaptation to different environments.

69.   Encourage the use of a 'too difficult' pile for ideas that cannot be implemented immediately and ensure that these ideas are recycled into the organization periodically.

70.   Mix 'small and big chunk' thinkers together.

71.   Set up conference phone calls or e-mail conferencing on specific issues of importance to the organization.

72.   Develop an 'Intrapreneur of the year' award.

73.   Develop conferencing across and outside your organization on non-intellectual property issues.

74.   Send people to conferences on subjects outside their professional interest.

75.   Place 'Post-it' notes by the water fountain.

76.   Set up action-centred opportunity finding groups.

77.   Set up creativity focus groups.

78.   Devise informal and formal systems for the capture, fermentation and distillation of ideas.

79.   Use collective notebooks to stimulate thinking.

80.   Introduce problem notice boards where people can post problems and opportunities without being named for comment by others.

81.   Set up electronic and manual graffiti boards for new product/service idea generation and unrelated thinking.

82.   Send your business plans to your competitors (so you'll really need to become creatively competitive!).

83.   Randomly pick several words from the daily newspaper. Force-fit the words into a current business problem/opportunity and identify 10 new options for improvement that are suggested by them.

84.   Insist that each of your employees goes for a walk once a month with someone they don't know from the organization to discuss cross-organizational problems/opportunities.

85.   Change the pondwater – have your backroom people spend some time with your toughest customers and then ask them what they would change within your organization to gain more business.

86.   Have people research, prepare and give a 10-minute talk on subjects that are alien to them but not to their audience.

87.   E-mail 25 people requesting 20 ideas from each of them for stimulating creativity in organizations.

88.   Encourage the use of transcendental meditation.

89.   Issue pocket-type tape recorders, exchanging and circulating tapes every week.

90.   Change the written reporting norms – on fancy dress days all reports have to be written in verse.

91.   Eliminate all negative words (for example, no, never, cannot, impossible etc.) for the day and 'fine' anyone who uses them.

92.   Eliminate all industry jargon for the day and 'fine' anyone who uses it.

93.   Invite people back to school for a day – hire local junior school teachers to re-teach your people the skills and fun of learning. Start at the top.

94.   Encourage personalization of the workplace.

95.   Have 'F 'n F' days where family and friends are invited to work alongside your people helping to solve their work problems (and being suitably rewarded too).

96.   Turn your people into Martians. The man or woman from Mars approach says that your people know everything there is to know about life on Earth except for the problem at hand.

97.   Use only animal/baby/cartoon character sounds to communicate at a meeting.

98.   Communicate in sign language or drawing only.

99.   Undertake research by encapsulating the organization's problems/opportunities in art form and displaying in galleries with comment/suggestion forms for members of the public to fill in. Ditto using the World Wide Web.

100.   Encourage your people to write articles for the industry press. Reward those that attract the greatest number of responses or any that provoke competitor comment resulting in worthwhile creative ideas.

101.   Produce your own list of 101 ideas.

Questions for applying the ideas

Questions for 'adaptive' individuals	Questions for 'innovative' individuals
What is your experience and how could this be used to alter the basic idea presented into one that would work in your organization?	How can you make the idea wilder?
If the actual idea presented is not suitable, what is the principle behind the idea? Can you adapt the principle into a more suitable idea?	What is a stranger way of fitting the idea to the organization?
How could this idea work in the culture?	Is there a more radical way of making this work?
What are the barriers and how might these be removed?	In how many ways could you radically alter this idea so that it would be acceptable?
What is the most sensible way to move forward?	

REFERENCES

Adair J (1990) *The Art of Creative Thinking*. London: The Talbot Adair Press.

Corporate Research Foundation (1995) *Corporate Strategies of the Top 100 UK Companies of the Future*. Maidenhead: McGraw Hill.

de Bono E (1984) *Lateral Thinking for Management*. Harmondsworth: Penguin.

Dryden G, Vos J (1994) *The Learning Revolution*. Aylesbury: Accelerated Learning Systems.

Ekvall G (1991) 'The organizational culture of idea management' in: J Henry, D Walker (eds), *Managing Innovation*. London: Sage Publications.

Ghiselin B (1985) *The Creative Process*. Berkeley, CA: University of California Press.

Handy C (1985) *Understanding Organizations*. Harmondsworth: Penguin.

Handy C (1989) *The Age of Unreason*. London: Hutchinson.

Handy C (1994) *The Empty Raincoat*. London: Hutchinson.

Henry J (1991) *Perspective*. Milton Keynes: Open University Press.

Henry J, Martin J (1991) *Creative Management* Milton Keynes: Open University Press.

Henry J, Martin J (1993) *Creative Problem Solving Guide*. Milton Keynes: Open University Press.

Henry J, Walker D (1991) *Managing Innovation*. London, Sage Publications.

Honey P, Mumford A (1986) *Using Your Learning Styles*. Maidenhead: Peter Honey.

Johnson G, Scholes K (1989) *Exploring Corporate Strategy – Text and Cases*. London: Prentice Hall.

Kirton M (1989) *Adaptors and Innovators*. London: Routledge.

Koestler A (1964) *The Act of Creation*. London: Hutchinson.

Majaro S (1988) *The Creative Gap*. London: Longman.

Makridrakis S (1989) *Long Range Planning*. London: Pergamon Press.

March J, Simon H (1958) *Organizations*. New York: John Wiley & Sons, Inc.

Martin J (1991) *Creative Management Techniques*. Milton Keynes: Open University Press.

Mayo A, Lank E (1994) *The Power of Learning – A Guide to Competitive Advantage*. London: Institute of Personnel and Development.

Pascale R (1990) *Managing on the Edge*. Harmondsworth: Penguin.

Pedler, Boydell and Burgoyne (1991) *The Learning Company – A Strategy for Sustainable Development*. Maidenhead: McGraw Hill.

Peters T (1994) *The Tom Peters Seminar*. London: Macmillan.

Philips K, Shaw P (1989) *A Consultancy Approach for Trainers*. Gower: London.

Revans R (1982) *The Origin of Action Learning*. Charkwell-Bratt.

Schein E (1988) *Process Consultation*. New York: Addison-Wesley.

Senge P (1990) *The Fifth Discipline*. London: Hutchinson.

Stewart R (1982) *Choices for the Manager*. Maidenhead: McGraw Hill.

Twiss B (1974) *Managing Technological Innovation*. London: Longman.

Wallas G (1926) *The Art of Thought*. New York: Franklin-Watts.

RECOMMENDED READING

Adams JL (1987) *Conceptual Blockbusting*. Harmondsworth: Penguin.

O   An excellent book, mainly useful for personal creativity, but many of the ideas may be adapted to organizations. Especially good on blocks to creativity.

Adams S (1996) *The Dilbert Principle*. London: Boxtree.

O   A witty and cynical view of organizational 'illnesses'. A good platform for thinking positively about improvements.

Allen R (1995) *Winnie the Pooh on Management*. London: Methuen.

O   An amusing metaphor that works! Cuts through the jargon and makes good creative sense. An excellent alternative to a Certificate in Management for the aspiring creative manager.

Blanchard K, Johnson S (1983) *The One Minute Manager*. London: Fontana.

O   Although the title suggests that this parable is about management, much of what is discussed concerns creative leadership. Written in the form of a short story, it summarizes mainly what we would call 'good practice'.

Brown M (1988) *The Dinosaur Strain*. Shaftesbury: Element Books.

O   An amusing yet serious look at personal creativity. Many original ideas.

Carter R, Martin J, Mayblin B, Munday M (1984) *Systems, Management and Change – A Graphic Guide*. London: Paul Chapman.

O   A light-hearted book about a difficult subject. The reader is seduced into becoming a systems thinker due to the highly interactive style.

de Bono E (1971) *The Use of Lateral Thinking*. Harmondsworth: Penguin.

O   A classic short text on the basis of all good divergent thinking. de Bono has a way of getting his ideas across simply and effectively.

de Bono E (1991) *Handbook for the Positive Revolution*. Harmondsworth: Penguin.

O   Not so much a book on creativity as an outline of the mindset required for transforming individuals and organizations.

de Bono E (1993) *Serious Creativity*. London: HarperCollins.

O   A good review of much of his earlier work.

Drucker P (1985) *Innovation and Entrepreneurship*. London: Heinemann.

O   Peter Drucker explores the role of the entrepreneur in achieving innovation in this book. Good on the need for organizational creativity.

Fritz R (1994) *Corporate Tides*. Oxford: Butterworth–Heinemann.

O   Fritz is a leading influence on many of the writers on learning organizations. This book gives a good insight into systems thinking and the need to break repetitive cycles of stagnation.

Garratt R (1990) *Creating a Learning Organization*. London: Institute of Directors.

O   A pragmatic look at the learning organization.

Gleick J (1987) *Chaos*. London: Abacus.

O   A very good introduction to the subject from a scientific point of view. This is not a management text.

Ground I (1989) *Art or Bunk?* Bristol: Classical Press.

O   A short book about the philosophy of art. Excellent as a stimulant to thinking about organizational creativity.

Hanfling O (1992) *Philosophical Aesthetics – An Introduction*. Oxford: Blackwell.

O   A much deeper treatment of aesthetics. Useful from the point of view of strategic thinking and marketing, although one needs to make certain mental leaps of faith to achieve this.

Leboeuf M (1990) *How to Develop and Profit from your Creative Powers*. London: Piatkus.

O   A good book covering personal creativity.

McKenna P (1993) *The Hypnotic World of Paul McKenna*. London: Faber & Faber.

O   Useful as an insight into flexibility of thought and deed, but relatively unrelated to organizational creativity.

Morgan G (1986) *Images of Organisations*. London: Sage Publications.

O   Very strong on metaphors and organization strategy. Contains a number of important insights into organizational design that have consequences for creativity.

Morgan G (1993) *Imagination – The Art of Creative Management*. London: Sage Publications.

O   Builds on the 'Images' book. Delves into organizational creativity from a conceptual and practical level. Thought provoking.

Peters T (1994) *The Tom Peters Seminar – Crazy Times Call for Crazy Organizations*. London: Macmillan.

O   Summarizes most of Peters's famous books. Excellent on 'out of box' thinking and packed with examples.

Porter M (1985) *Competitive Advantage*. New York: The Free Press.

O   Although not directly related to creativity, Porter's text is a standard in terms of strategic thinking and positioning. A very important contribution.

Redfield J (1994) *The Celestine Prophecy – An Adventure*. London: Bantam Books.

O   A novel with a message about the future. If read at a structural level, there are important lessons here about seeing the future and detecting weak signals of change on the horizon. It emphasizes the need for use of intuition as a key competence for decision making.

Redfield J, Adrienne C (1995) *The Celestine Prophecy – An Experiential Guide*. New York: Warner Books.

O   The companion volume, offers lots of practical exercises and tips to implement the principles of the Celestine Prophecy.

Redfield J (1996) *The Tenth Insight – Holding the Vision – Further Adventures of the Celestine Prophecy*. London: Bantam Books.

O   A follow-up to the Celestine prophecy.

Richer J (1996) *The Richer Way*. London: Emap Business Communications.

O   A down-to-earth book that describes the application of creative management in the retailing sector. Refreshingly honest.

Rose C (1985) *Accelerated Learning*. Aylesbury: Accelerated Learning Systems

O   Particularly good at expanding personal creativity through a number of practical techniques. It is the standard as far as accelerated learning books go.

Rosen S (1982) *My Voice Will Go With You – The Teaching Tales of Milton H. Erickson*. London: Norton.

O   Of tangential interest. This book documents a number of stories used by the famous therapist, Milton Erickson. Illustrates flexible thinking and use of metaphor in healing situations. Parallels may be drawn with organizational change.

Semler R (1993) *Maverick*. London: Arrow Books.

O   A highly readable book that describes 'upside down' thinking in action. Relevant given the difficult conditions faced by the organization, which Semler has revitalized.

Senge P, Kleiner A, Roberts C, Smith B, Ross R (1994) *The Fifth Discipline Handbook*. London: Nicholas Brealey.

O   The practical text associated wtih Senge's *Fifth Discipline* book. Practical exercises, stories and case studies in abundance that bring the learning organization to life.

Seymour J, O'Connor J (1990) *Introduction to Neuro-Linguistic Programming*. London: Mandela.

O   Neurolinguistic programming is the art of flexibility in thought and deed. This is the most readable and detailed introduction to the subject available.

Shone R (1990) *Creative Visualization*. London: Thorsons.

O   A good practical book that gives insight into processes for visualization. Although aimed at the individual much of what it contains translates to organizations.

Sim S (1992) *Art, Context and Value*. Milton Keynes: Open University Press.

O   A philosophy text that addresses the question of evlauating art. Many of the lessons are relevant to the evaluation of creativity in organizations, especially concerning meaningful measurement.

Stevens M (1988) *Practical Problem Solving for Managers*. London: Kogan Page.

O   A good basic techniques book.

Tushman M, Moore W (1988) *Readings in the Management of Innovation*. USA: Ballinger.

O   A number of key readings about organizational creativity and innovation.

Van Grundy Jr, AB (1988) *Techniques of Structured Problem Solving*. New York: Van Nostrand Reinhold.

O   The 'gold standard' text for techniques and their application. It has been described as 'mechanistic', yet the techniques may be adapted to different contexts with skill.

Watzlawick P (1993) *The Language of Change*. New York: Norton.

O   Excellent book on how language affects change. Many indirect lessons for creative organizations.

Watzlawick P (1993) *The Situation is Hopeless but Not Serious (The Pursuit of Unhappiness)*. New York: Norton.

O   A highly amusing book about how individuals (and organizations) arrive in places they would rather not remain in.

West MA (1997) *Developing Creativity in Organizations*. Leicester: BPS Books.

O   Good overview of the subject from a psychologist's perspective.

INDEX